POSTCARD HISTORY SERIES

Abington

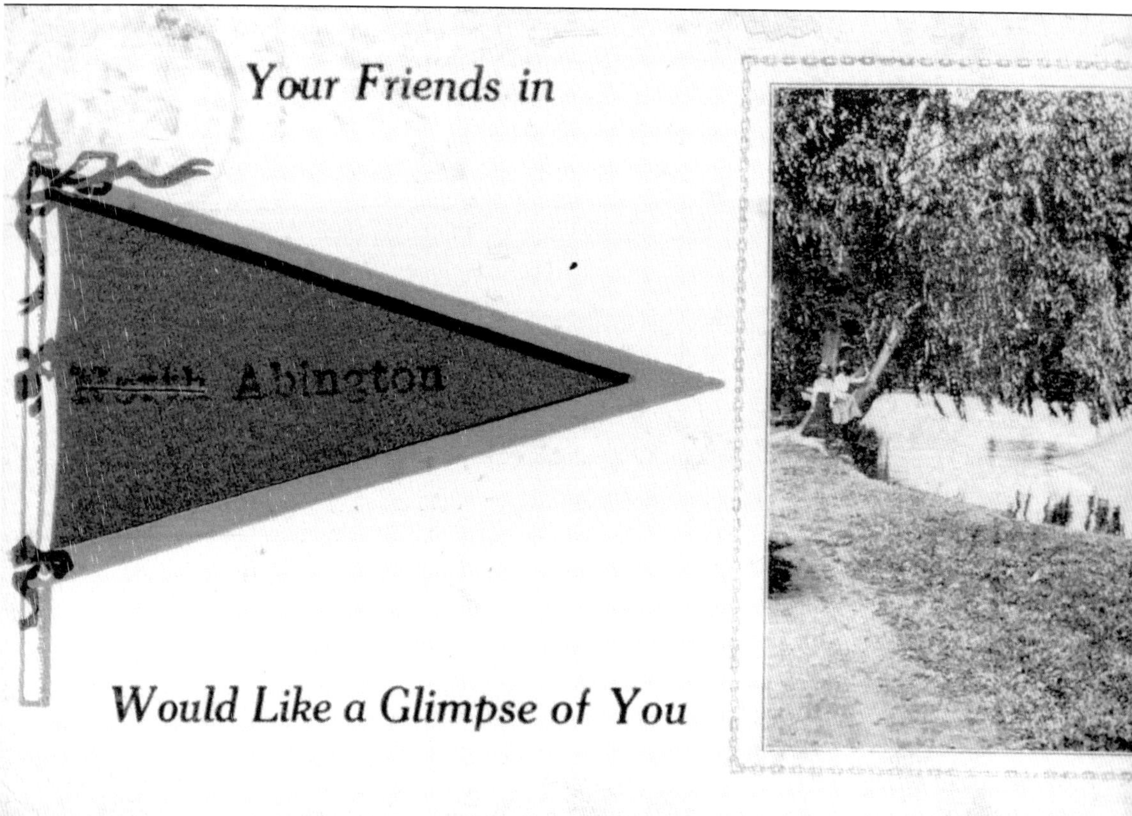

Postcards came in all styles, including those bearing generic banners that could be changed from community to community.

POSTCARD HISTORY SERIES

Abington

Donald Cann and John Galluzzo

ARCADIA
PUBLISHING

ISBN 978-0-7385-3607-1

Published by Arcadia Publishing,
Charleston, South Carolina

Printed in the United States of America

Library of Congress Catalog Card Number: 2004103630

For all general information, contact Arcadia Publishing:
Telephone 843-853-2070
Fax 843-853-0044
E-mail sales@arcadiapublishing.com
For customer service and orders:
Toll-free 1-888-313-2665

Visit us on the Internet at www.arcadiapublishing.com

To Abington's postcard photographers, publishers, and collectors.

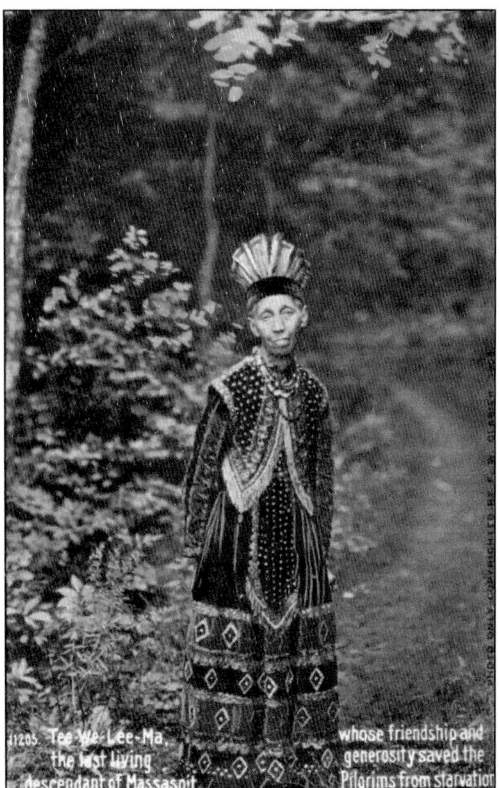

Some postcard publishers sought to print the exotic or unique.

Contents

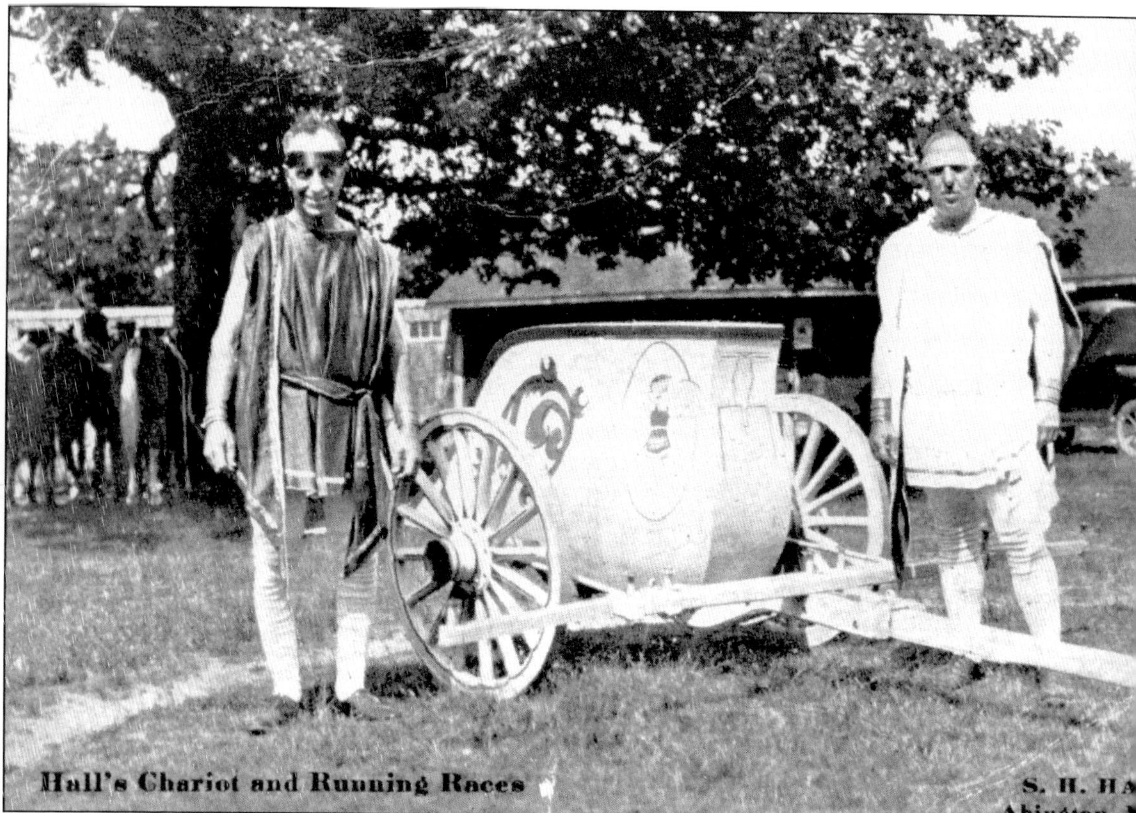

Oftentimes, the people of Abington presented a photographer with a unique photo opportunity, as in the case of Sam Hall and his blazing chariot.

Introduction

If you were setting out to create your own line of postcards of Abington today, where would you go and what would you photograph? No doubt you would head straight for Island Grove for starters. But what beyond that would you imagine would appeal to postcard buyers?

The question is somewhat unfair when taken in the context of this book. Today, cameras are readily available. Some, in fact, are disposable, made to be thrown away after one use. Try explaining that concept to the average Abington citizen of 1910. The unfairness of the question comes from the fact that most Abington residents a century ago did not have access to a camera, and few had photo albums. Photographs as keepsakes were not as easy to come by then as they are today.

The postcard, the mass merchandising of selected photographic images, was the answer for most people. By offering a wide choice of photographs to patrons, postcard publishers covered all the bases. Whereas today we might think of five or six images in town we would consider postcard worthy, in 1910, photographers snapped everything. Abington residents therefore gained access to entire collections of images and could build their own scrapbooks with scenes that meant something special to them in their lifetimes.

Thanks to the modern-day collectors at the Dyer Memorial Library and within the membership of the Historical Society of Old Abington, file boxes full of postcard scenes of Abington exist for all to see and learn from. The cards in the collections range from pastoral to industrial, well defined to marginally recognizable as belonging to Abington, and well photographed to hastily printed. Two main themes pop up over and over again: Island Grove and the Abington Savings Bank block that once stood at the corner of Washington Street and Centre Avenue. Island Grove's images are so extensive that they make up more than one chapter in this book.

That is not to say, though, that we have left much out. We provide a tour of Abington as it looked at the beginning of the 20th century, with a run through its public buildings and churches, a quiet walk through Mount Vernon Cemetery, and a rousing time at the events that made the town famous, from the 1893 railroad riot to the 1912 bicentennial celebration.

But who was sending postcards of Abington in 1910, and who was receiving them? It would be stretching it a bit to call the town a summer resort, although there is no doubt that some folks did come to stay with their families in Abington during the summer, if just to visit Island Grove. But larger forces were at work in those early years.

Due to the influx of foreigners to the United States at that time, many Americans sought to make sure that their children and grandchildren did not forget the deeds of their American ancestors. They organized events like Old Home Week and Heritage Days to attempt to draw their young loved ones home from the big cities, where many had gone to seek adventure or employment. A stirring image on Island Grove Pond could tug at the heartstrings of even the most cynical young man or woman, sending pangs of nostalgia pounding through the breast.

On the other hand, with the factories growing as they did, when Abington was in the heart of the shoe-manufacturing district, many of the employees working in the area had come from other towns, and some had come from other countries. A postcard sent to a loved one far away could soothe any discomfort created by the distance.

But then, just to be able to send a short message to a friend on the back of a card must have been a novelty in itself. Postcards were the e-mails of the early 20th century.

We hope that you enjoy this book, which includes a wonderful primary-source collection for research on 20th-century Abington history. We also hope that if you have any postcards of Old Abington you will consider donating them to the Dyer Memorial Library or the Historical Society of Old Abington, the protectors of Abington's past. But for now, let us start the journey. All we need are a pen and a whole mess of stamps.

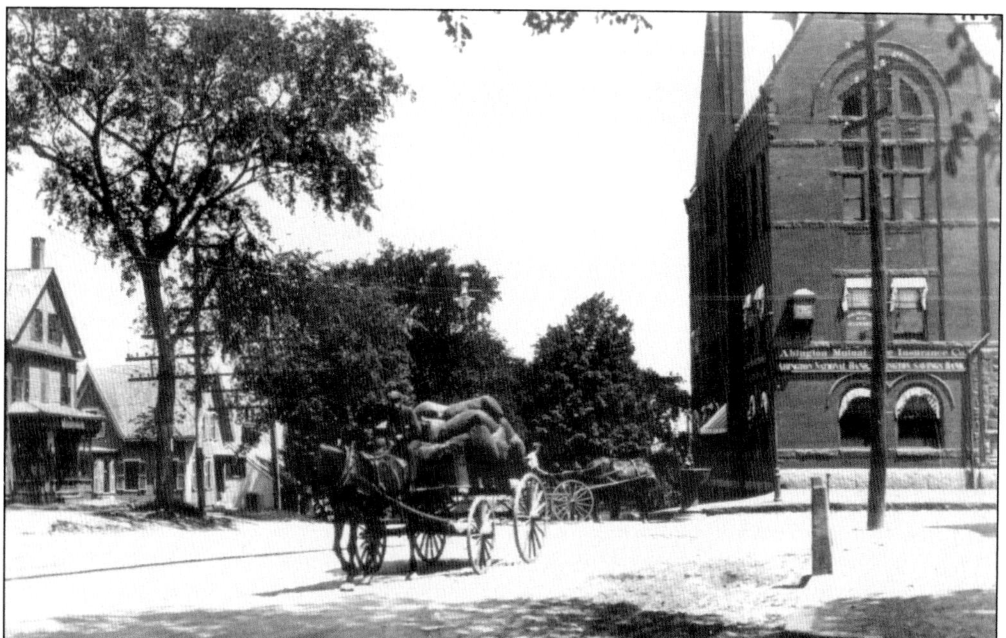

Most Abington postcards revolved around two themes: the Abington Savings Bank and Island Grove. Let us take a ride down memory lane.

One

Around Abington

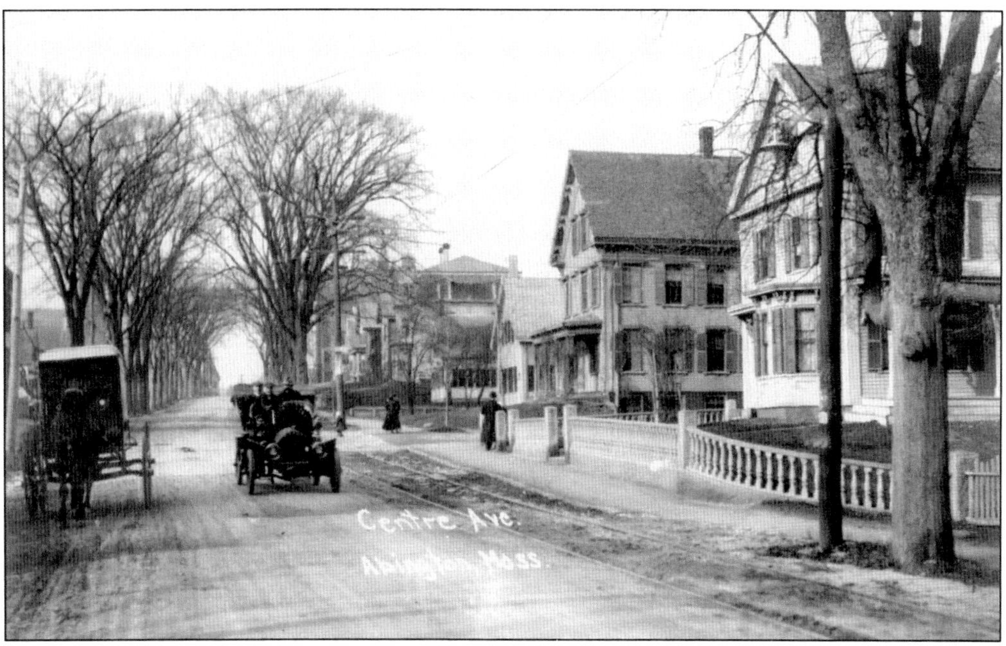

This photo postcard was taken *c.* 1912 on Centre Avenue looking west, just down the road from Post Office Square. The first house on the right is No. 78, just one house up from Island Grove Pond and the northeast corner of Lake Street. The next house is No. 68 on the northwest corner of Lake Street. The house with the mansard roof is the house of Gen. Henry Dunham. You can see the savings bank building at the top of the street on the right side. Note the electric arc light on the right, the woman with the pram, and the little girl just about to go into the street.

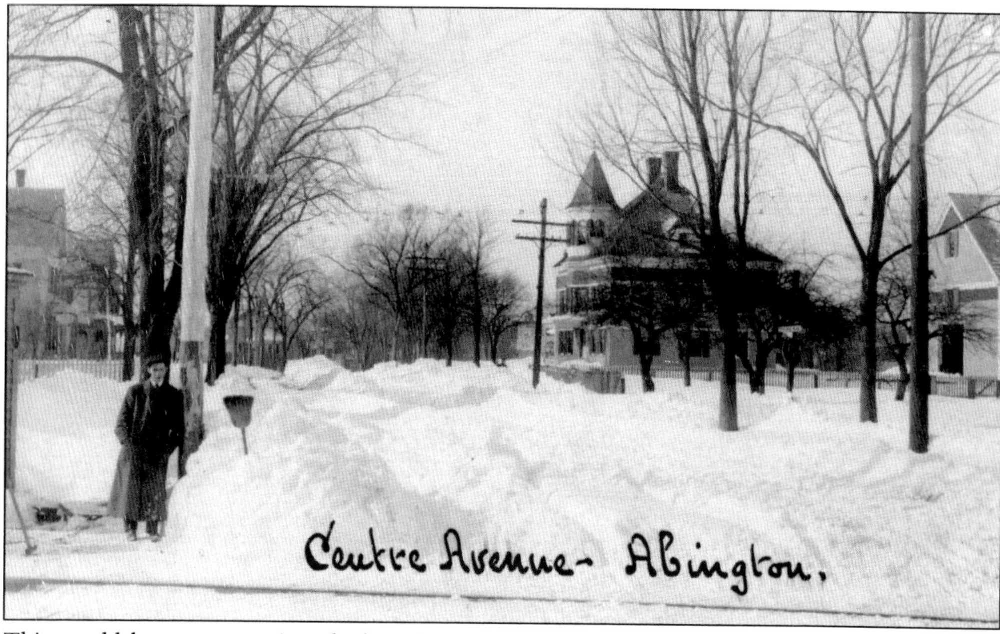

This would-be commuter is in luck. While it looks like nothing is moving on Centre Avenue, the train tracks are cleared, and someone has also cleared a place on the sidewalk. Ezekiel Reed built the house on the right *c.* 1797. The house was extensively remodeled in the 1880s by, we believe, the great-grandson of Ezekiel, George Reed. At that time, the roof got its high pitch and the tower was added. The rooms have round corners in order to make cleaning easier and to prevent the spread of germs.

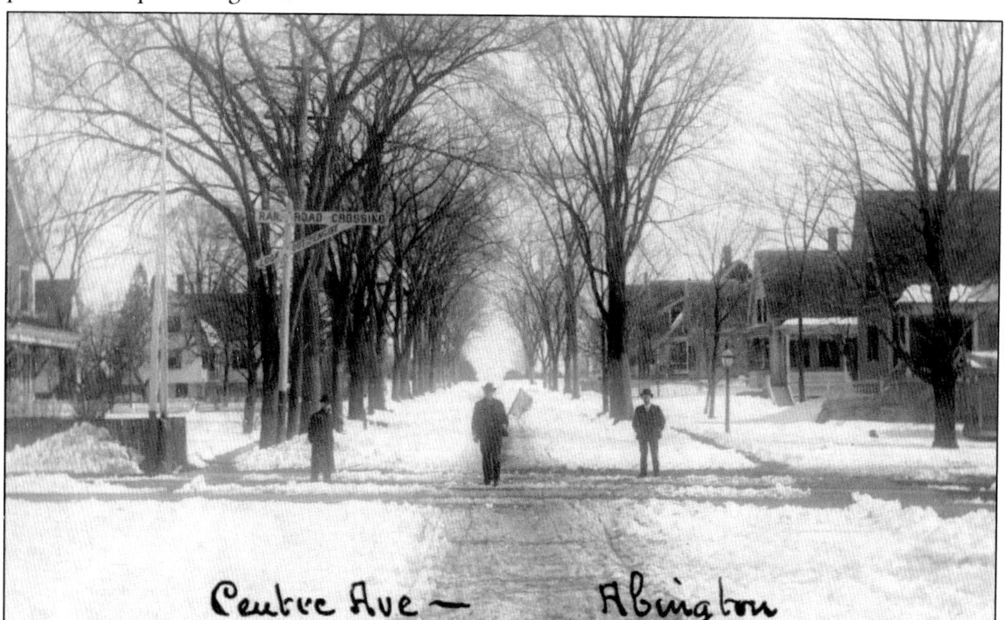

In this view looking west there is a flagman. Perhaps there is some work being done to the tracks, for this is a gated crossing. It appears the snow has been on the ground for a while, as there is a well-worn area in the center of the street and the sidewalks have been cleared. There are no visible electric wires in the photograph, but there is a gas lamp on the right sidewalk.

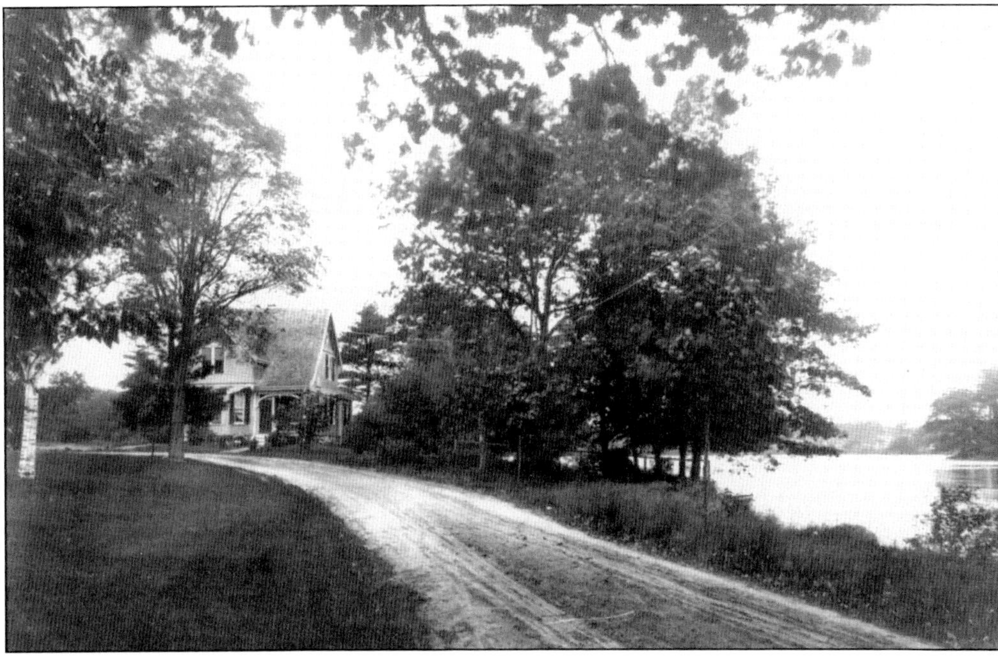

This is Lake Street before the memorial arch and bridge were built in 1912. The photograph was taken *c.* 1904. The house is the home of L. W. Attwood. This card is a good example of a picturesque view of Abington in the early 20th century.

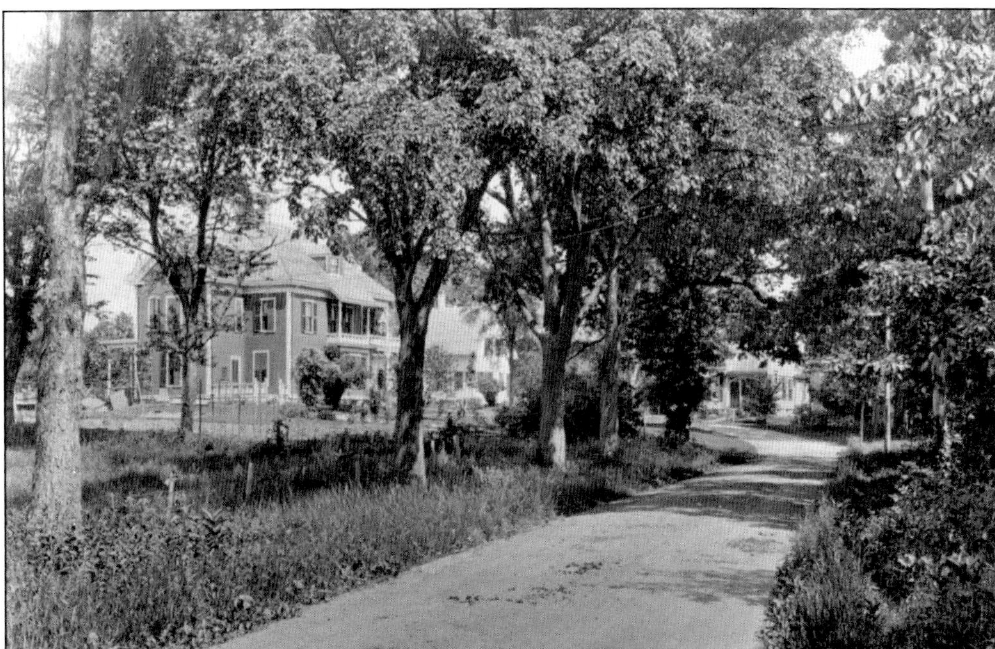

This is another view of Lake Street in the early 20th century. The large house on the left is the home of Billy Dick Nash at 1236 Lake Street. Nash and his brother ran the grocery store in the old Daniel Ford building at Vaughan's Corner.

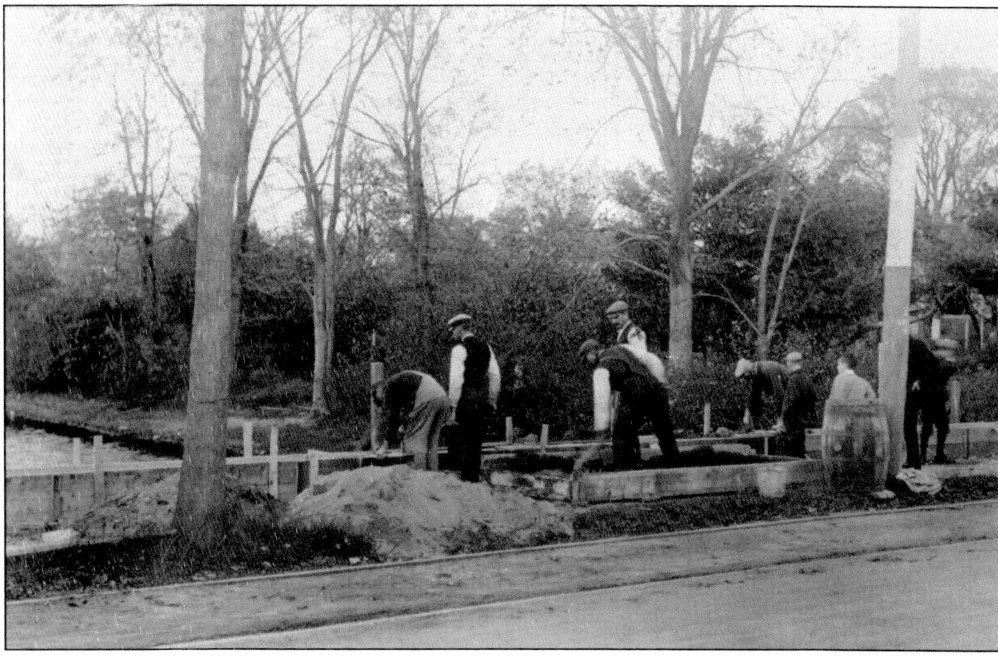

This is the sidewalk on the section of Centre Avenue located at the edge of Island Grove Pond. It appears that work is being done on both the sidewalk and the grass border. The men are quite formal in their work clothes. The only one without a cap is the boy who is watching the work.

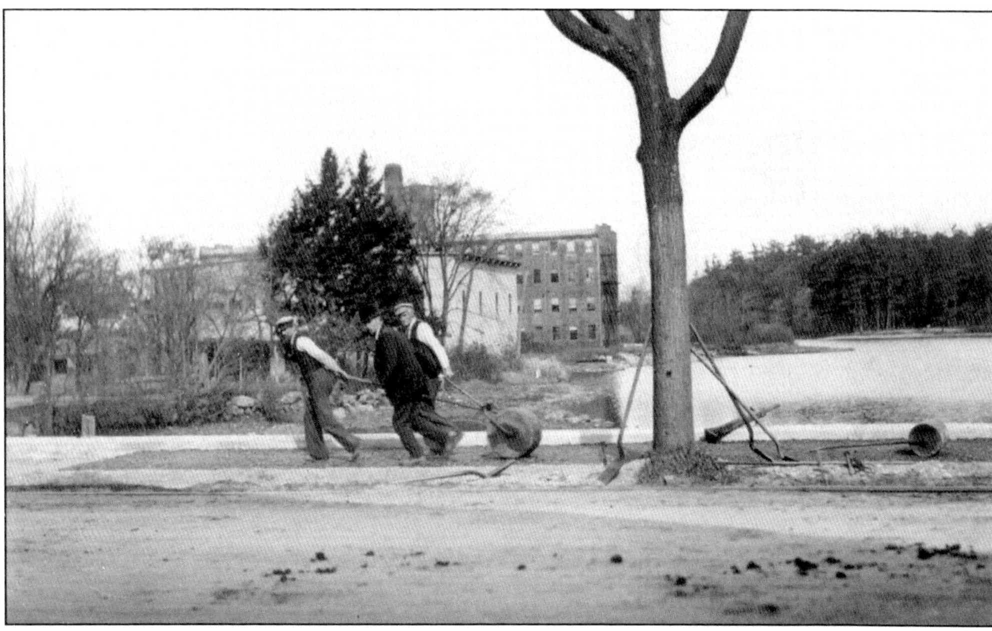

The pavement is all laid out, and it seems the only work left is rolling out the earth in the landscape strip, or perhaps putting down some grass seed. The man in the black hat is the boss, who is lending a hand in the rolling. The buildings in the background are the street railway power station and Alden Shoe Company on Lake Street.

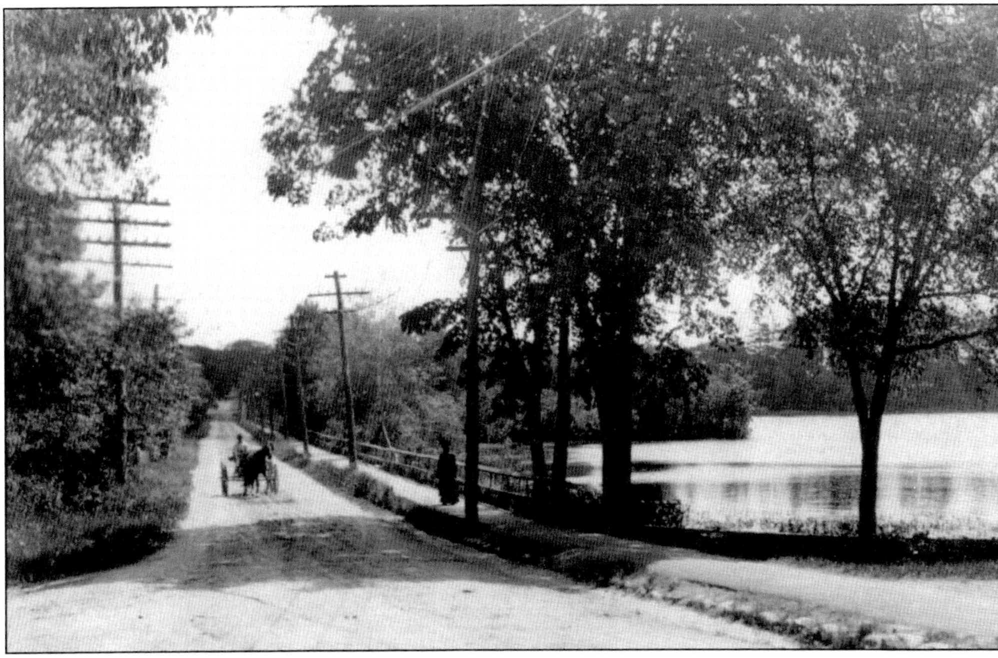

Seen is a pleasant summer day on Central Street in a time when life was slower and summer dress was more formal. This postcard view is just the thing to send to arouse pleasant feelings of Abington in the early 1900s.

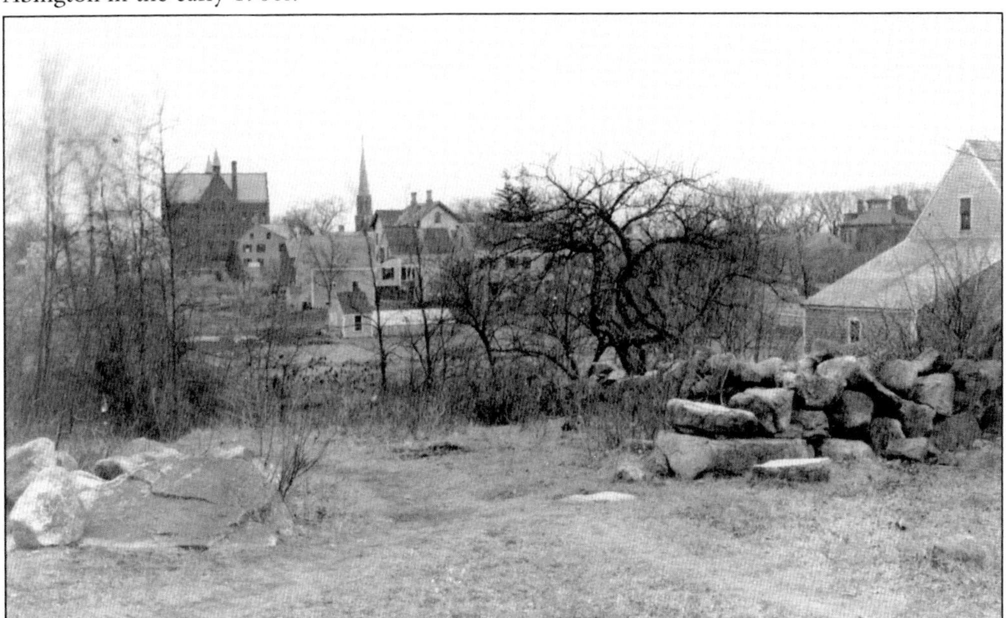

The notation on the back of this card says the photograph was taken from "the big rock in Sproul's field" on Everett Street. In Europe, cathedrals and castles dominate village and town views. In Abington, when this photograph was made, it was the savings bank block, which housed business and town government, and the Church of the New Jerusalem that dominated the views. This is certainly one of the most picturesque views in the collection. The view conveys a certain prosperity and stability, as well as a sense of the survival of Abington's rural character.

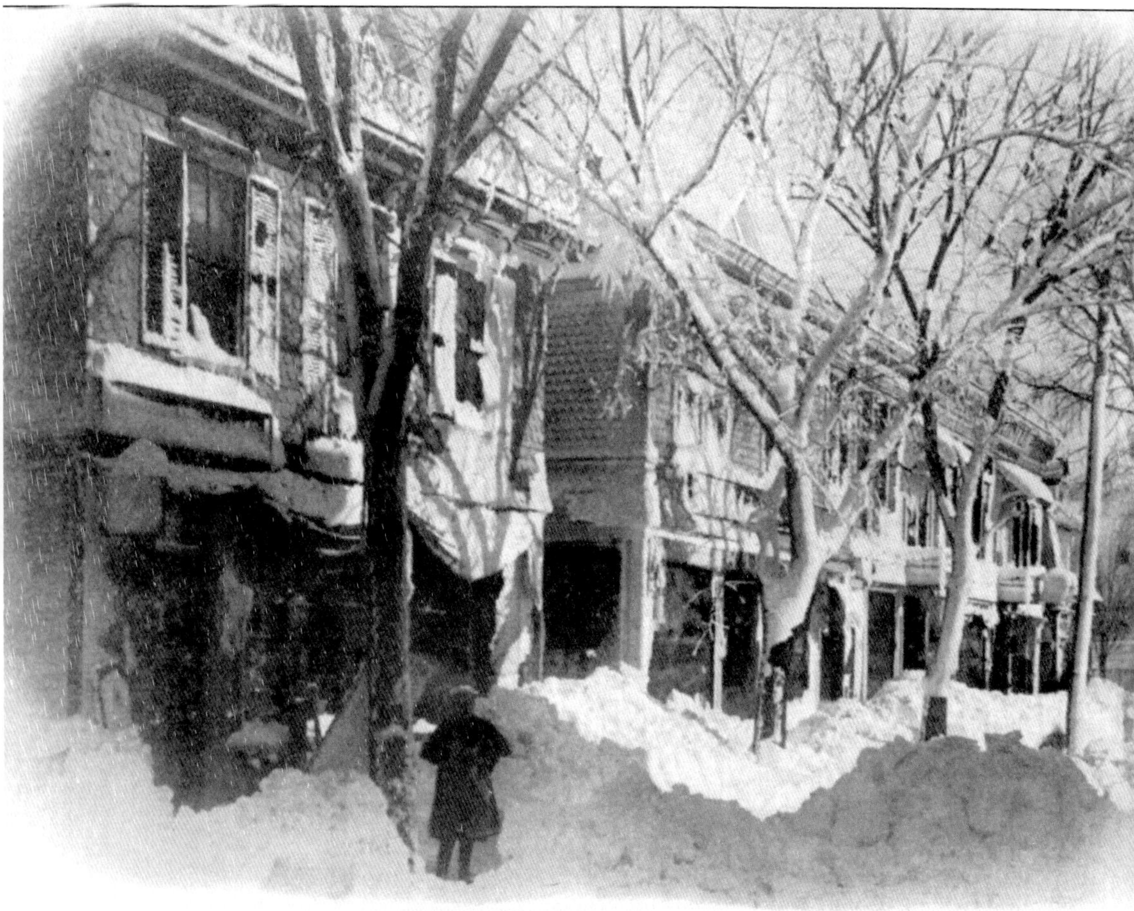

NORTH AVENUE, NOVEMBER 28, 1898, NORTH ABINGTON, MASS.
Issued by W. J. SHEEHAN NEWS CO.

November 26, 1898, is remembered as the date of the Portland Gale. The nor'easter lasted for 24 hours and caused the sinking of the side-wheeler *Portland* with all 192 passengers and crew members. The storm was a collision of two storms, one coming from the Great Lakes and another from the South. When it was over, 24 inches of snow had fallen on Abington. The storm's wake left 500 people killed and 300 vessels lost, with more than 30 vessels lost in Boston alone. This is North Avenue on the day after the storm.

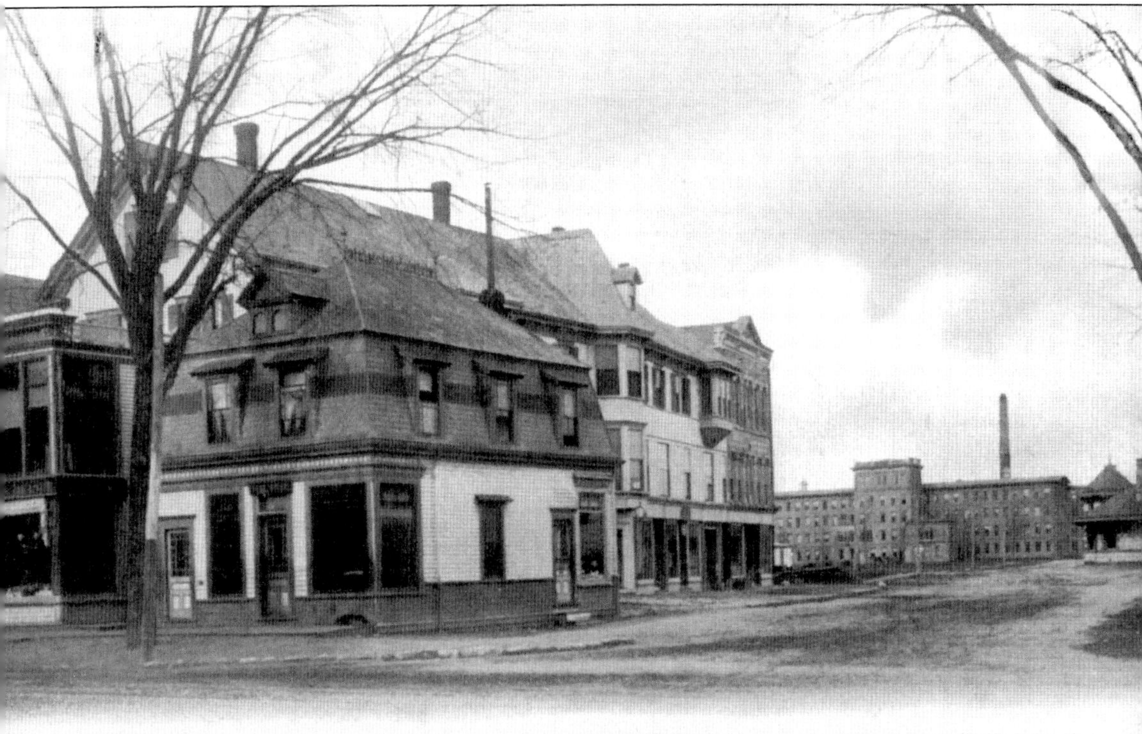

CORNER OF NORTH AVENUE AND RAILROAD STREET, NORTH ABINGTON, MASS.
Issued by W. J. SHEEHAN NEWS CO.

This postcard view of Railroad Street shows one of the most pleasant places in North Abington. In the background is the Arnold Shoe factory. Unlike most other shoe factories, this well-proportioned building was built of bricks. The bricks at the cornice line, the small arches at the top of the windows, and the balustrades at the top of the central portion give this building an understated quality that make it one of the landmarks of industrial Abington. On the right side is the North Abington train station, another beautiful and highly praised landmark, built in 1894. On the left side, the first building with the mansard roof is the old North Abington post office, built in 1885. The last building in the block on the left is the Peerless Theatre at 84 Railroad Street, built in 1894 as a harness and saddle store by Henry G. Crossley. His initials are in the pediment in the front. In 1915, this building became a theater; it was a very popular place in the golden age of the neighborhood movie theaters.

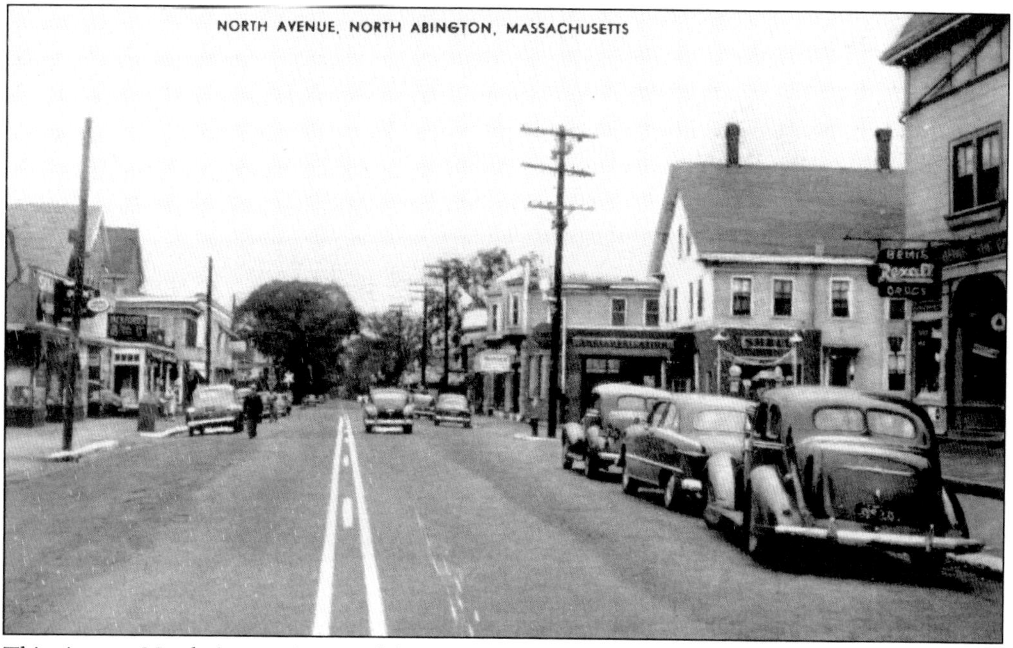

This view on North Avenue is one of the latest in the book, dating from the early 1950s. The three cars parked on the right are in front of Standish Hall, the location of Bemis Drug at that time. Bemis Drug eventually moved to the next building down, which in this view is a Shell gas station.

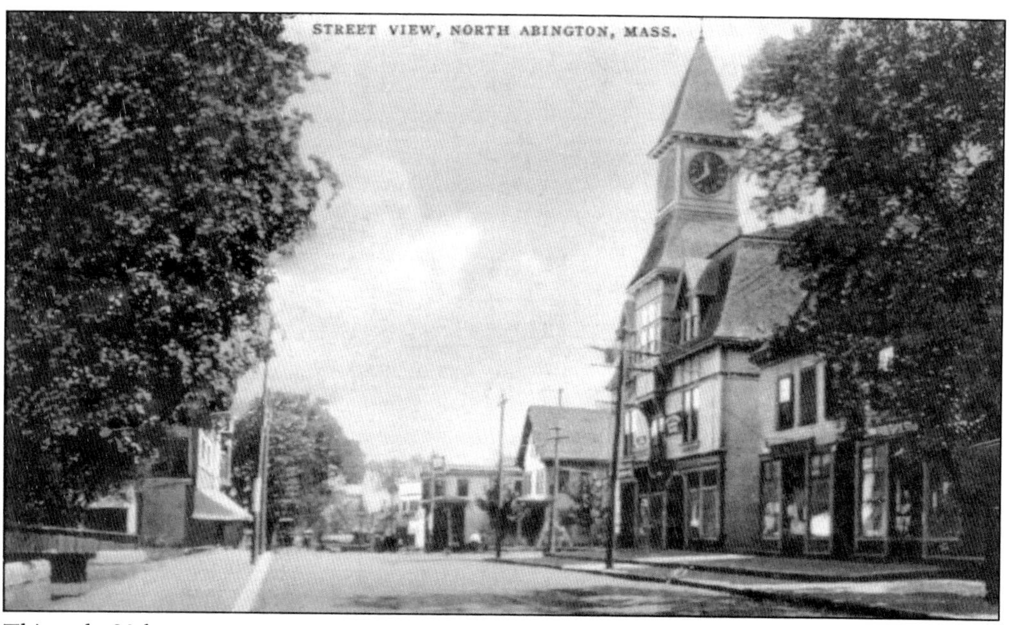

This early 20th-century view is of North Avenue, the retail center of North Abington. The first building on the right is the Winthrop, and next to it is the Standish building (with the clock tower), built by the Standish Hall Association in 1880. The most notable tenant on the first floor of the Standish building was a drugstore. The first pharmacy was Spiller's, established in 1885 by Fred M. Spiller; it was followed in 1905 by Bemis Drugs. In 1969, Bemis moved just down the street to the building seen beyond Standish Hall.

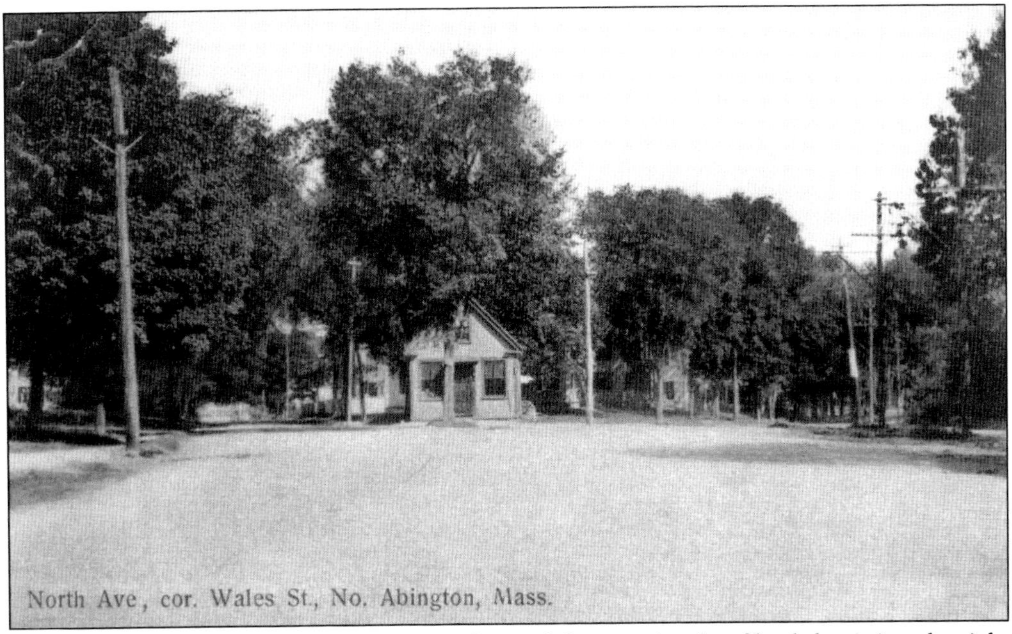

North Avenue and Wales Street come together and form a triangle of land that is just the right size for building a corner store, once a staple in every neighborhood. The store was built *c.* 1860. The store's meats and provisions are what Eugene Llewellyn Chapman and his wife advertised in the 1905 directory. A bakery and, later, a barbershop occupied this building.

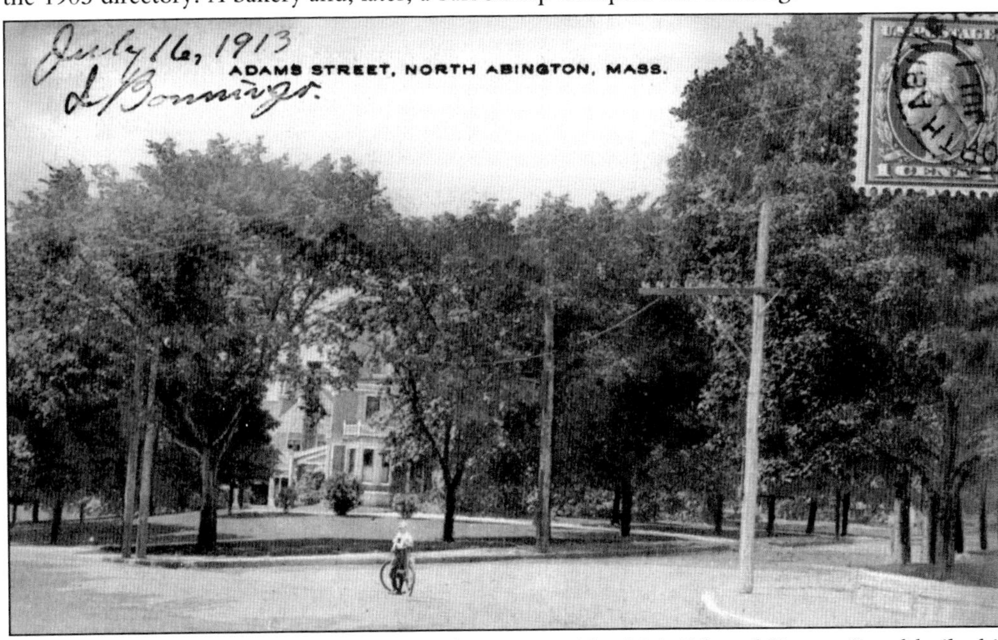

This postcard has the date and stamp on the picture side. Maj. Edward Payson Reed built this Queen Anne–style house in 1882 at 262 Adams Street. Major Reed, a Civil War veteran, was president of the Rockland and Abington Street Railroad Company. The directors of the streetcar company met here on the night of August 15, 1893, to make their plans for the crossing of the Old Colony Railroad's tracks that led to the notorious North Abington Riot. This house was destroyed by fire on December 28, 2003.

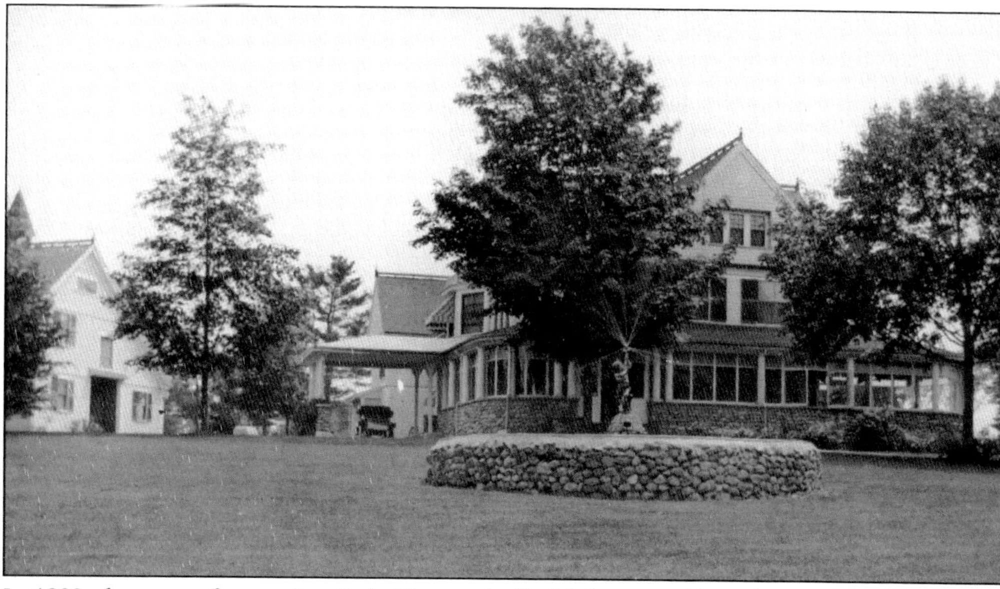

In 1888, shoe manufacturer Lewis A. Crossett built this house at 125 Adams Street. In 1910, he moved to a new house at 262 Adams Street. W. Percy Arnold bought the house, and his family remained there until the early 1940s. The house has an ornamental cresting on its roof typical of the Queen Anne style. The large wrap-around porch and carriage port give this house grandeur. The large stone-walled fountain on the front lawn, complete with a figure holding a spouting rod, gives this house a different presentation than others of the time. The barn was destroyed by fire on October 8, 1963.

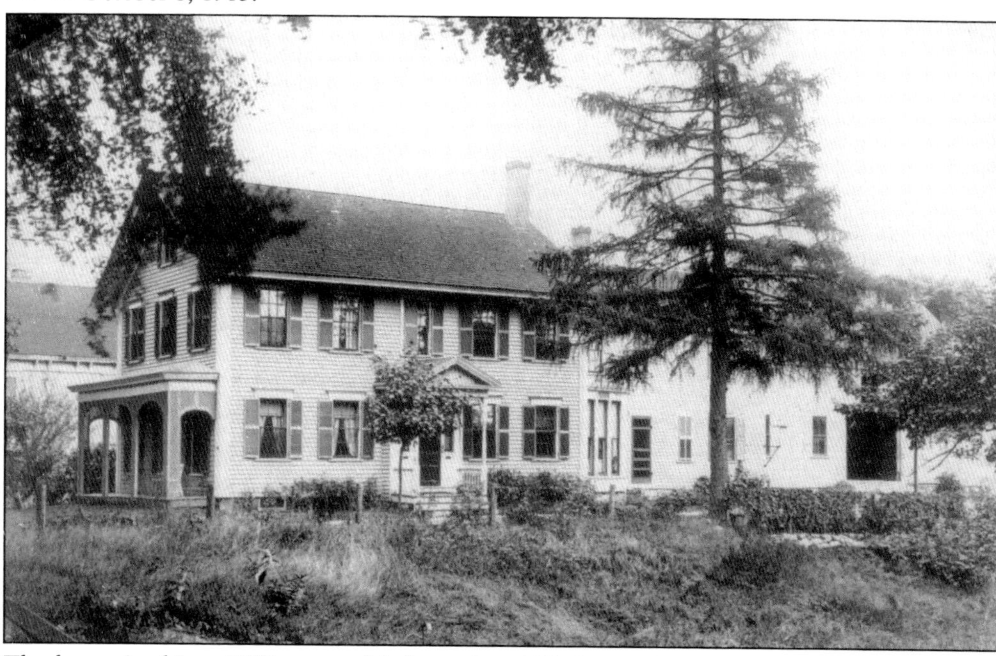

The house in this *c.* 1903 postcard is located at 155 Centre Avenue and probably dates from the Federal period. The end chimneys, the central entrance, and the side lights all provide hints of this period. This was the home of Charles F. Dudley, the owner of Abington and Whitman Ice Company.

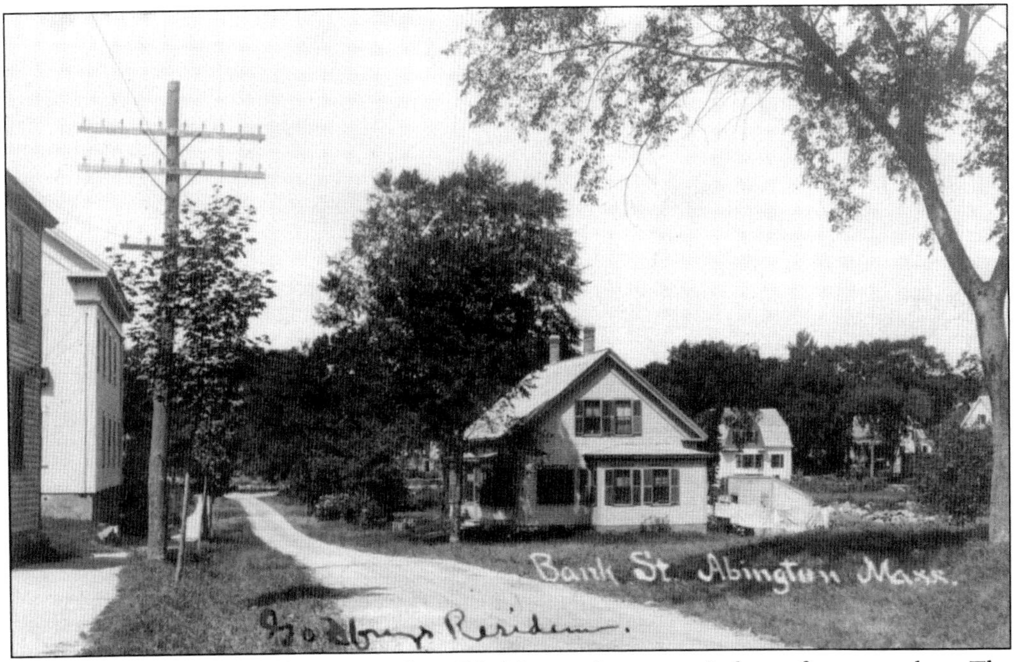

This view of Bank Street, facing west from Washington Street, reminds us of a country lane. The second building on the left, with the turn backs at the ends of the gables, is 73 Bank Street and was a school. This was the principal school for the center village from 1854 to 1874. The house in the center is a duplex, Nos. 66 and 68 Bank Street. This house was moved in 1998 across Washington Street to 99 Bank Street and was made into a single-family home.

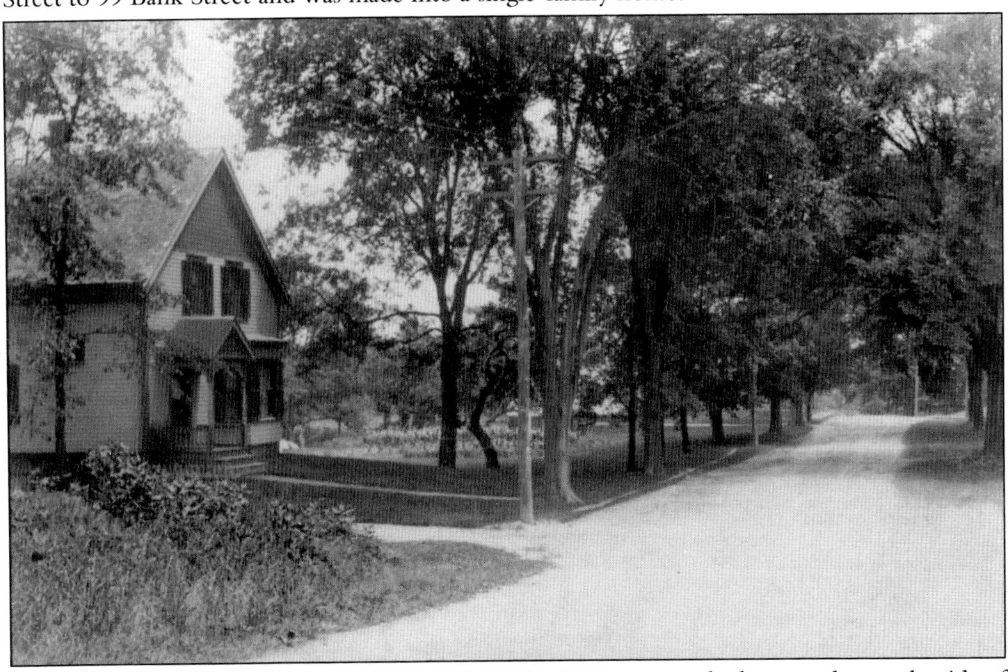

This view of Washington Street at Summer Street looks east. Note the large garden on the side of the house. This card would have the most appeal to people who lived in this section; it is a rare view of a side street in a collection of postcards of main roads.

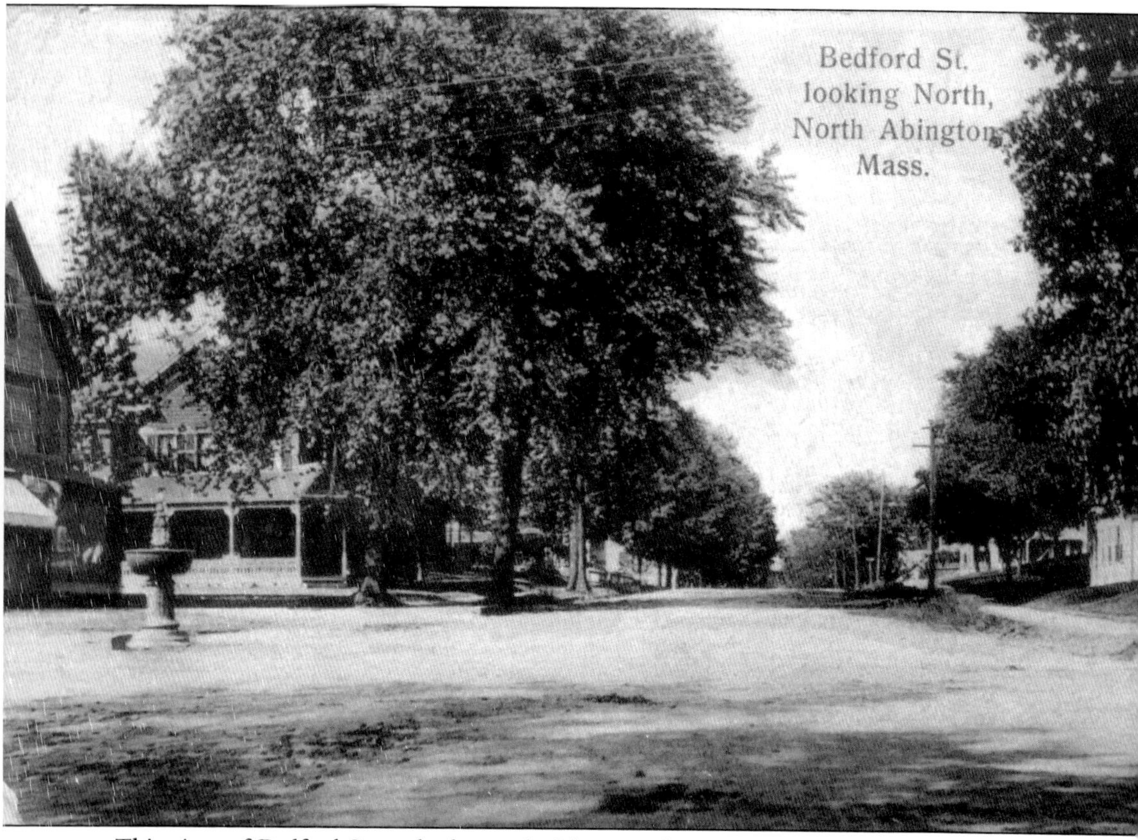

This view of Bedford Street looks north. The urn-shaped water trough for horses is similar in design to the one in Post Office Square. Note the line of trees. On the left, the trees are smaller and set back from the road, no doubt because of the power lines on that side. The trees do not seem to have the wineglass shape of elms; they may be maples.

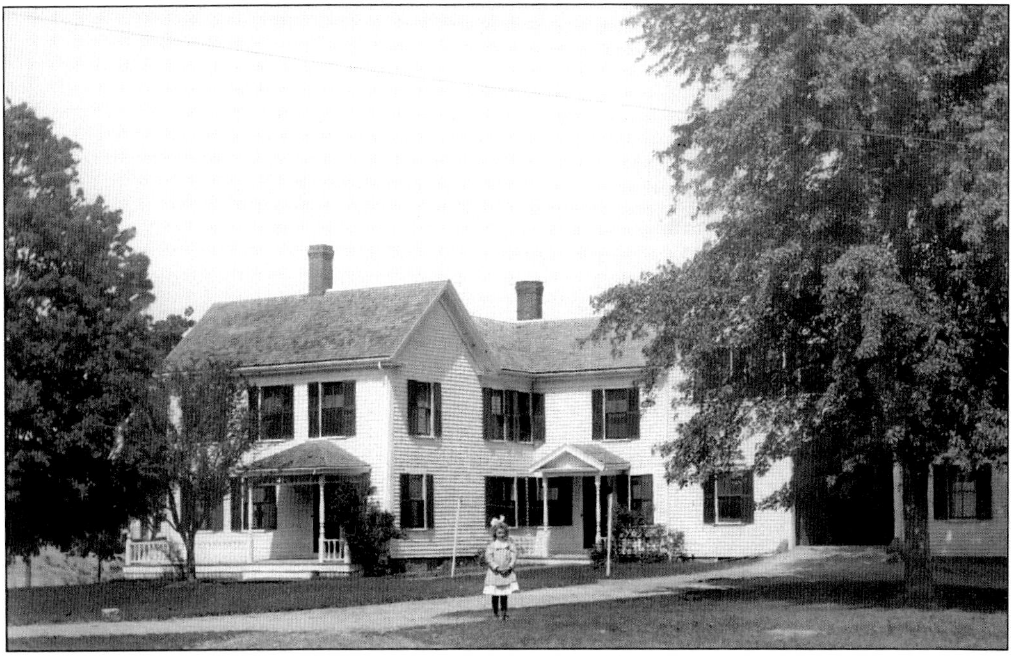

This house is known as the C. H. Russell home at 637 Bedford Street. Perhaps a Russell daughter dressed up so she could be in the postcard view of her home.

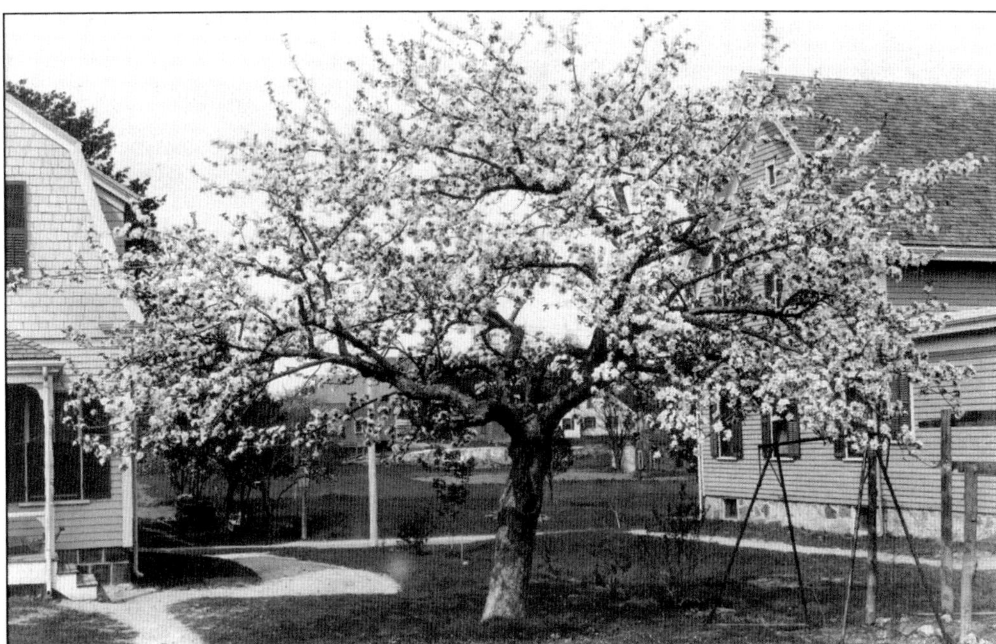

This is a lovely photograph and an ideal postcard. This springtime view shows a backyard on Everett Street.

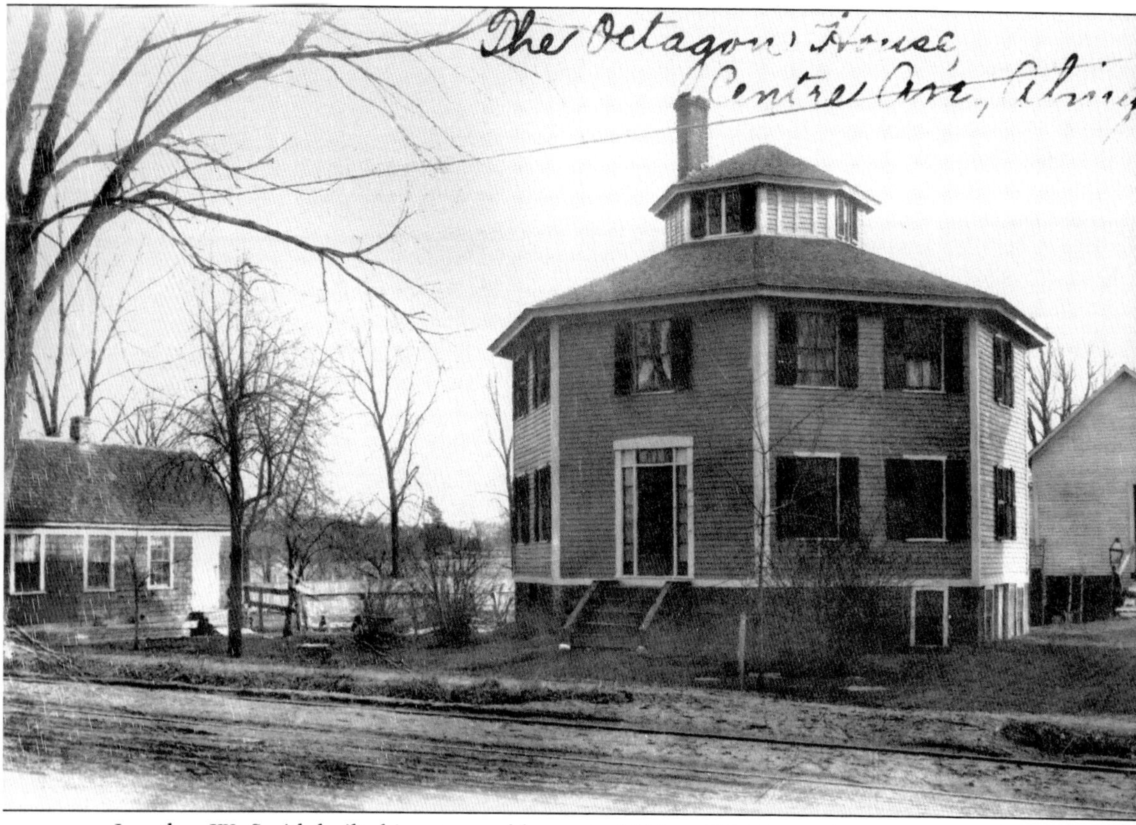

Jonathan W. Smith built this octagonal house in 1869 at 195 Centre Avenue. Using the octagon shape for home building was an alternative that appealed to some people from the 1840s to the 1860s. The concept for this home design is based on the book *The Octagon House: A Home for All of the Nineteenth Century* by phrenologist Orson Squire Fowler (1809–1887). Fowler advocated that this type of house was healthier and more efficient than houses shaped as squares or rectangles. The cupola is a good example of these characteristics; it ventilates and lets in light at the same time. These houses were often decorated in the prevailing styles of their period (Greek Revival and Gothic Revival, for example). The one in this postcard is very plain in its style. In the 1960s, a survey was made of octagonal houses in the United States, and 21 were identified in Massachusetts. This house was taken down on June 11, 1997, to make way for a small apartment house. Abington is lucky—there is another octagonal house on Brighton Street.

Two

The Savings Bank and Washington Street

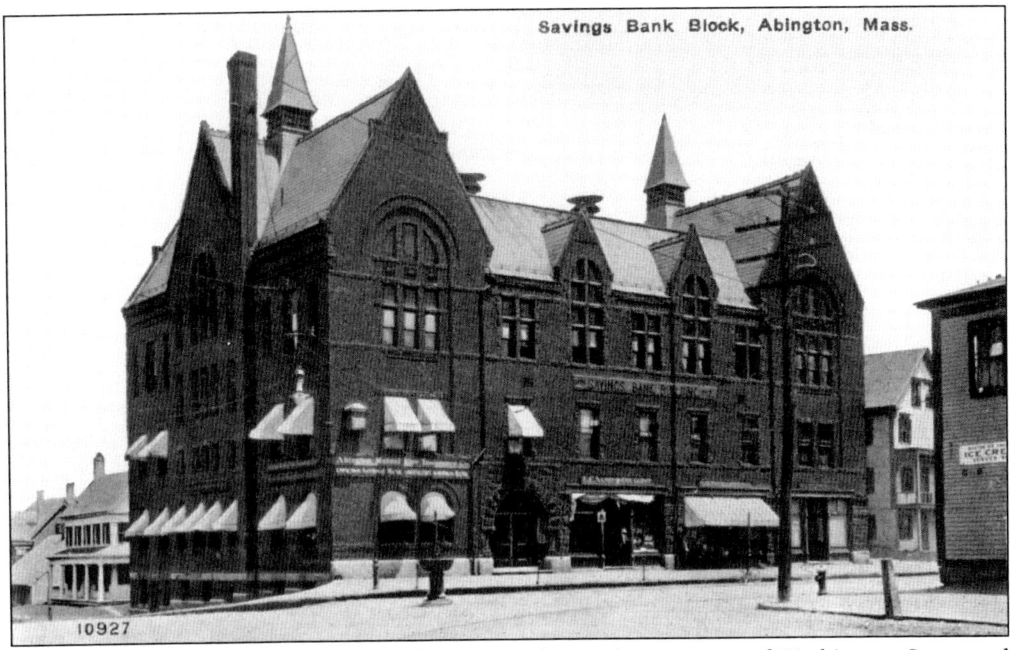

The Abington Savings Bank block was located on the northeast corner of Washington Street and Centre Avenue. The bank built this building in 1883 on the site of Nelson Beal's 1847 house. The arches on the gables and dormers, the arch in the principal stone doorway, and the building's steep roofline reflect this building's medieval style. The building was home to the savings bank and the Abington National Bank (both on the first floor), the town offices, the Franklin Hall, and the Franklin Club. Dr. Samuel Ring and Dr. John W. Chessman, both dentists, had offices on the second floor at various times, and retail establishments such as Nash's Drugstore, Packard's Groceries, and Godfrey's Dry Goods were located on the ground floor. This building was a favorite subject of postcard publishers of Abington. In this view, Nelson Beal's house is just left of the savings bank building, where it was moved to make room for the bank. The bank block was destroyed by fire on November 26, 1956.

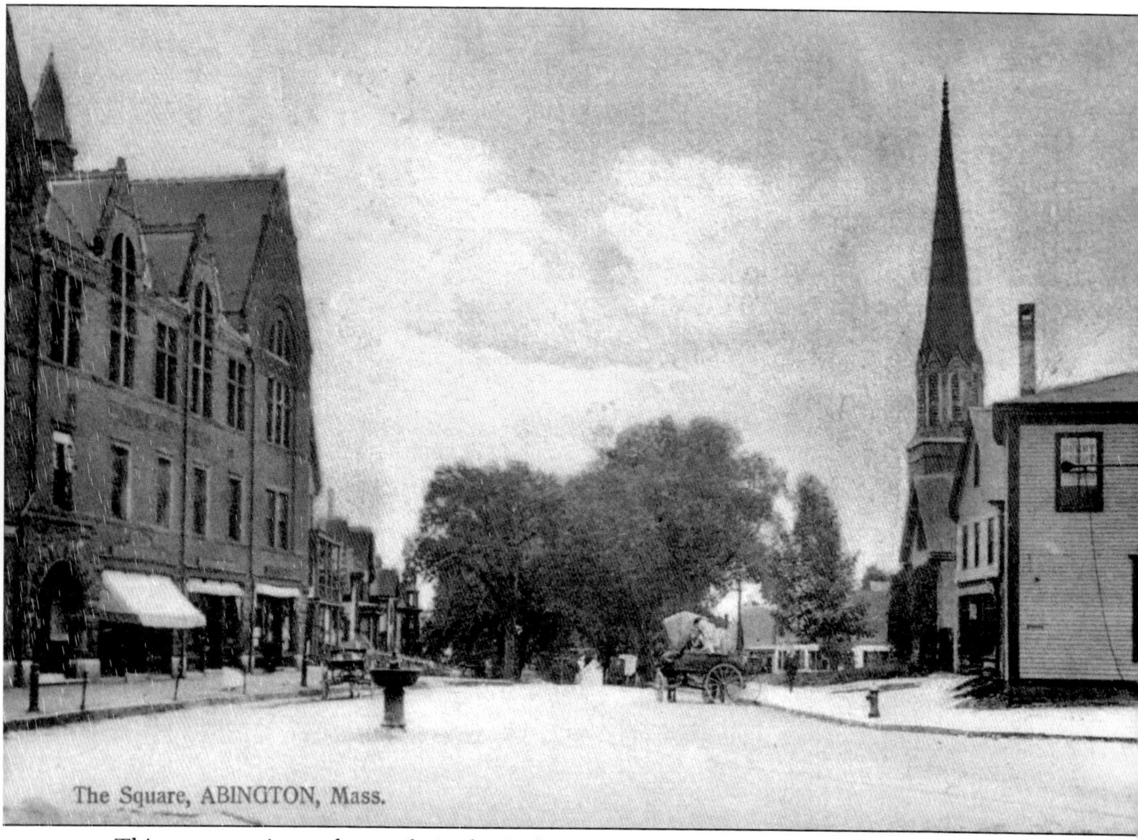

This summer view, taken early in the 20th century, looks down Centre Avenue. The house next to the savings bank building is 18 Centre Avenue, built by Z. Whitmarsh *c.* 1850. The first floor served as a barbershop and housed stores of various kinds, including the Golden Slipper Country Store, which closed in the 1970s. The next two houses, dating from the mid-19th century, were taken down to make way for the Dyer Memorial Library in 1932. One can make out the tower of 48 Centre Avenue. This is the mansard-style home of Gen. Henry Dunham. This house was taken down in 1950. On the opposite side of the street, the first building dates from the Federal period. This location is known as Vaughan's Corner for Joseph Vaughan, who owned most of the land on this block. The next building, attached to the corner building, served as a store. Behind that building, the spire of the Church of the New Jerusalem, built in 1832, is visible. The Cape on the corner of Centre Avenue and Dunbar Street still stands.

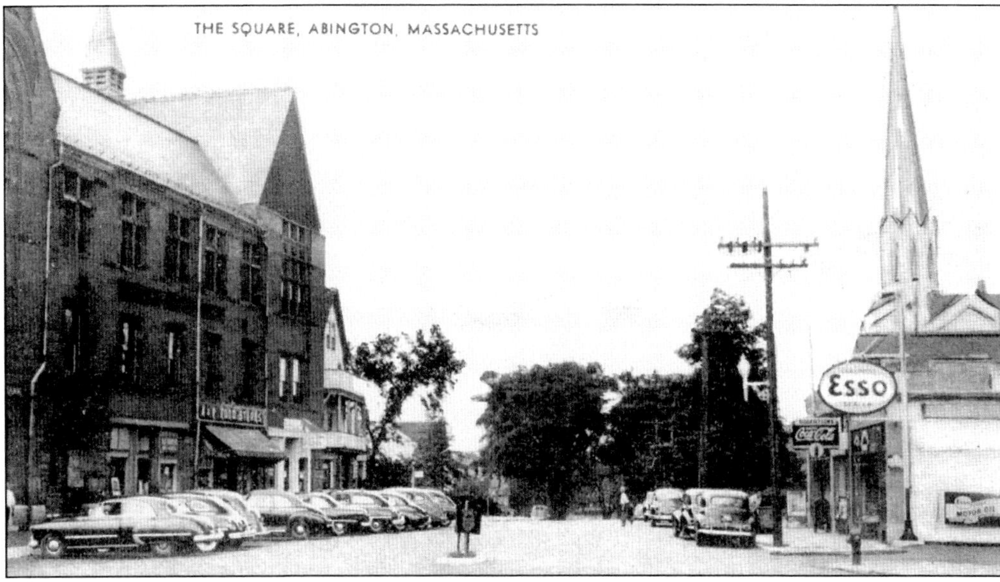

By the mid-20th century, the view down Centre Avenue had changed. On the right, an Esso gas station and a block of stores have replaced the buildings at the corner, although in this view the church is still there. The trees seem to be the same ones seen in the earlier view, but appear to have been cut to accommodate wires. The left side of the street is about the same, except the Dyer Memorial Library has replaced the earlier buildings and is just out of sight beyond the tree. By the turn of the 21st century, more buildings had disappeared from this neighborhood.

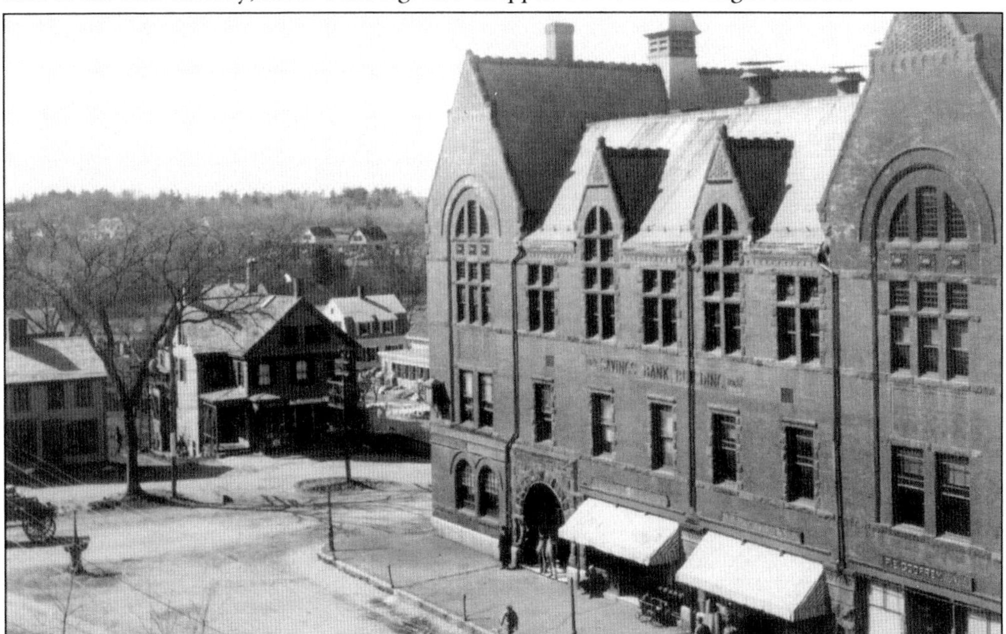

This view was taken from the steeple of the Church of the New Jerusalem. The front of the bank gives a districted, urban look to the scene. The lack of traffic and the openness to the west makes the large building look a little out of place. The building across the street was the location of a drugstore as well as a painting company.

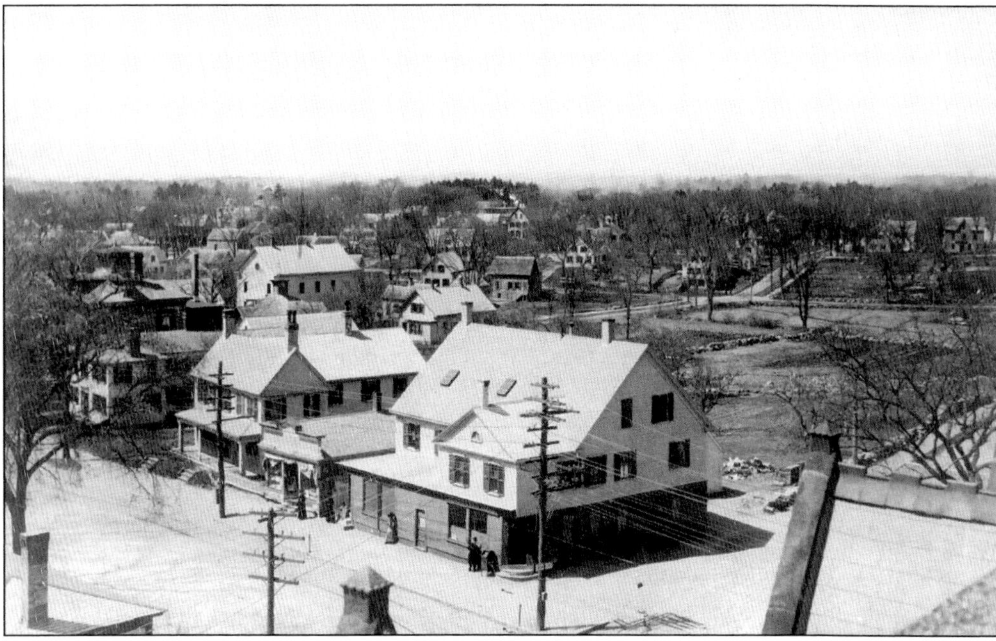

This photograph, which looks south, was taken from the savings bank building. Although the center of town included a five-story commercial building, there were still a lot of open fields behind Washington Street and off Orange Street in the early 20th century. Shoe manufacturer Joshua Nash's house is the fifth from the right. You can see the cupola. The large building behind Nash's house with the three windows on the side was a school located on Bank Street.

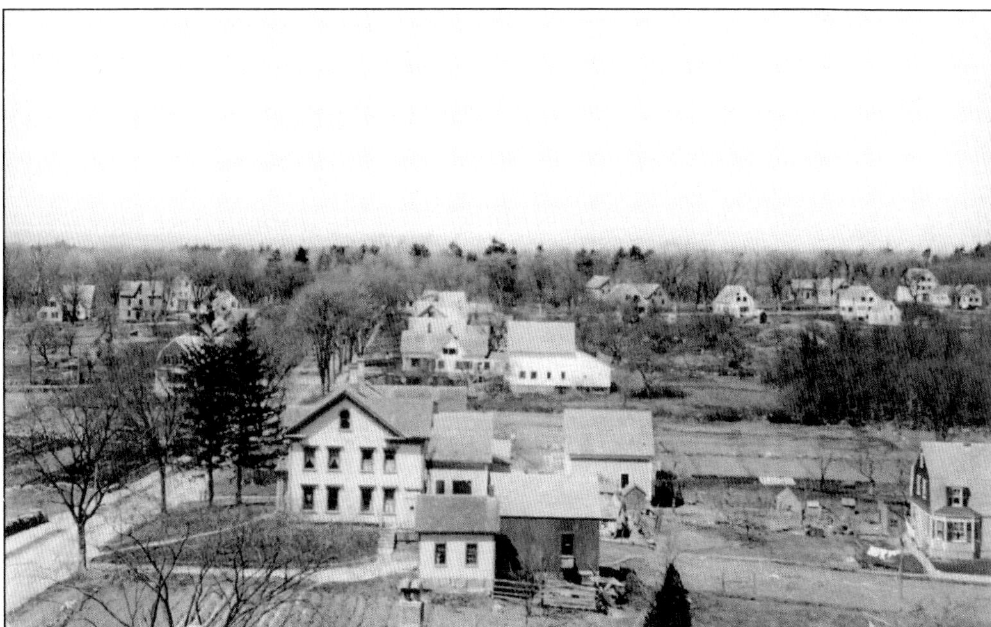

This view of Orange Street was taken from the savings bank building. The house in the foreground is 11 Orange Street, and the one in the background with the extended barn is 69 Orange Street.

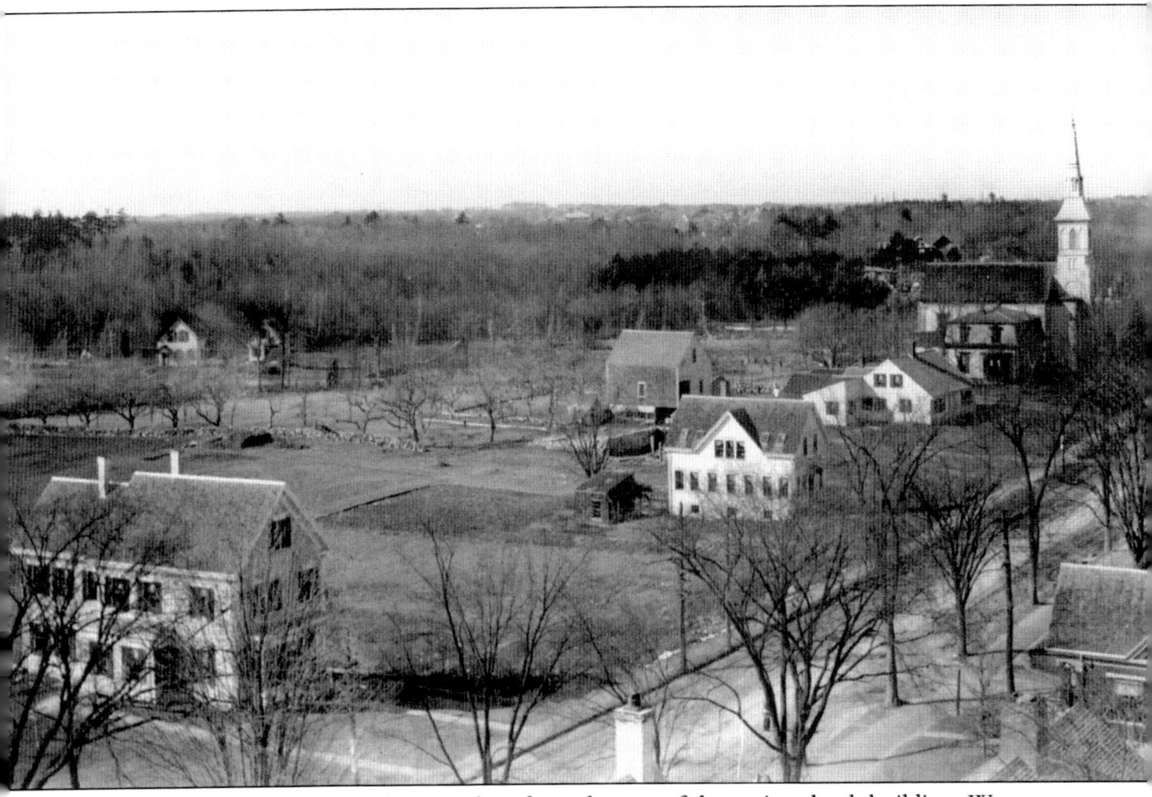

This postcard view, looking north, was taken from the top of the savings bank building. We are looking upon a landscape of Abington that reminds us of Thornton Wilder's play "Our Town." This play describes a fictional New England town in the same period, when most of the postcard photographs were taken. On the left is 608 Washington Street, at the corner of Everett Street, once the home of James Claflin, a barber. Carlos P. Faunce, in his 1949 remembrances at age 88, recalled seeing his first baseball game on an open field in this vicinity. He described the game as similar to the modern game, although the pitcher pitched underhand and the catcher did not wear a mask. He stood a distance back of home plate and caught the ball on a bounce. Faunce remembered that the Abington team was called the Pilgrims. The next house is the site of the Lilliputian Shoe Factory. Next is a Cape with its barn at 644 Washington Street that dates from 1827 and was built by Nathaniel Nash. The house with the mansard roof is at 256 Washington Street and was built in 1869 for George E. Curtis. The church at the corner of Washington and West Chapel Streets is Universalist. It was taken down in 1967.

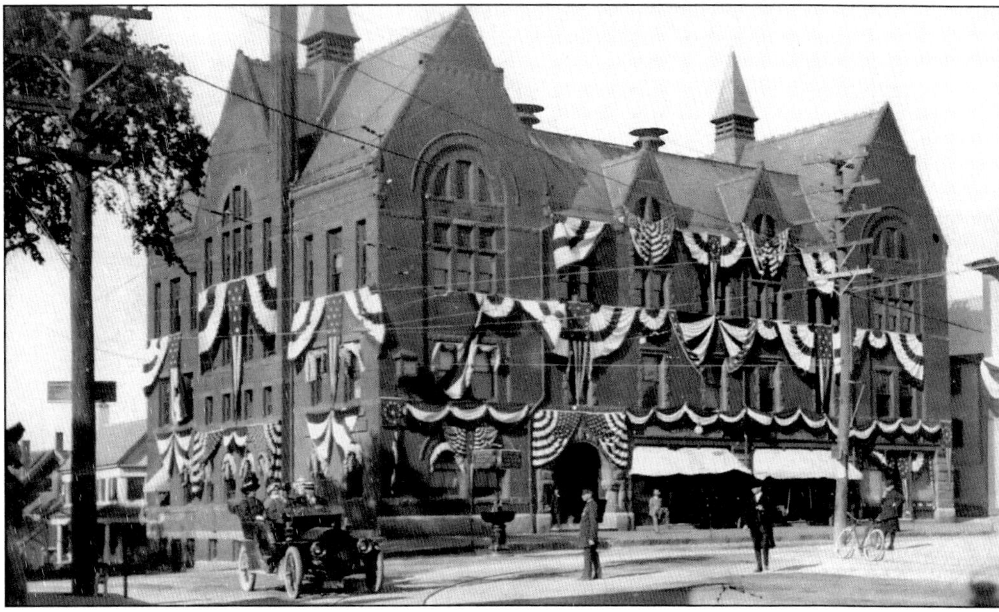

The Abington Savings Bank building was decorated in its finest for the 1912 bicentennial celebration of the town. This postcard must have been a favorite for a long time after the big celebration. Buildings of this type became instant landmarks. They gave status to the banks and the town at the same time, and for a while they were good business. Times do change, and by the mid-1950s, these buildings became obsolete. For a short time after the fire that consumed this building, the first two floors looked as though they might be saved, but they were not.

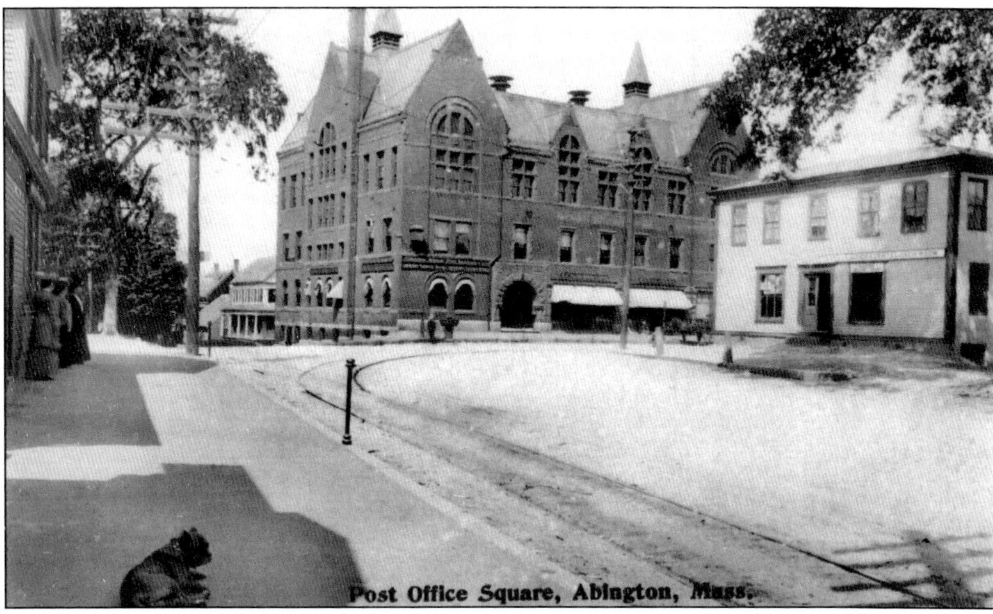

This is Post Office Square as it looked in the early 1920s. The ladies waiting for the trolley and the dog in the foreground are in the afternoon shade of what looks like a warm summer's day. The first floor of the building across the street at Vaughan's Corner has been remodeled several times. We see it with a central entrance, which is different than in earlier views. The signs on this building read "Ladies & Gents Lunch Room" and "Rockland Waiting Room."

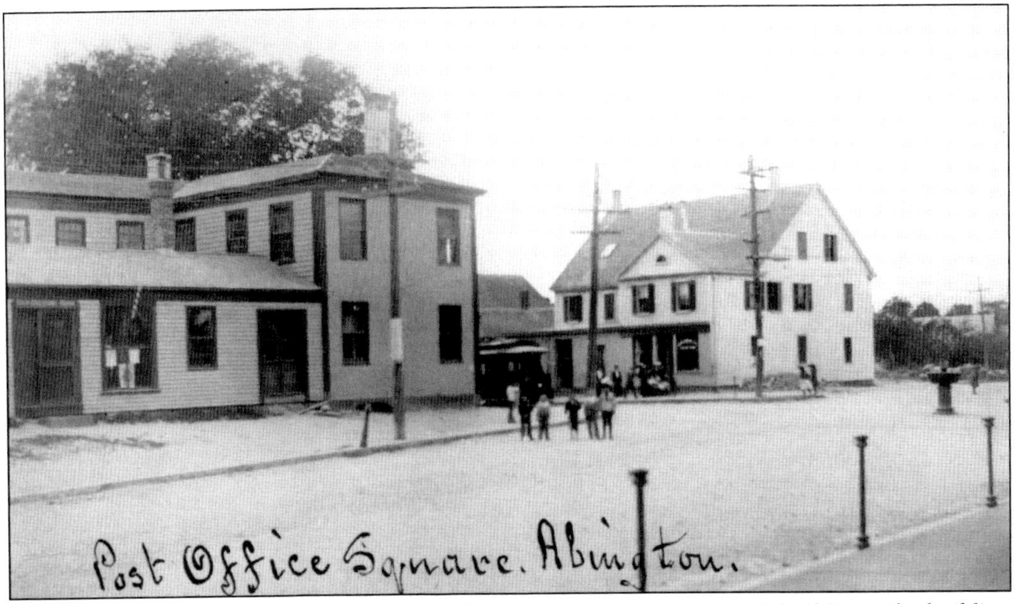

This photograph was taken from the sidewalk in front of the savings bank building. The building in the background is the post office. Rebecca B. Turner, a milliner, had a shop on the second floor of this building, where she also ran a lending library. In 1878, the public library was established and her books were purchased to become part of its collection. We can see the brick side of the building at Vaughan's Corner. The shed addition was a printing shop, and the *Abington Standard* was printed here between 1855 and 1874.

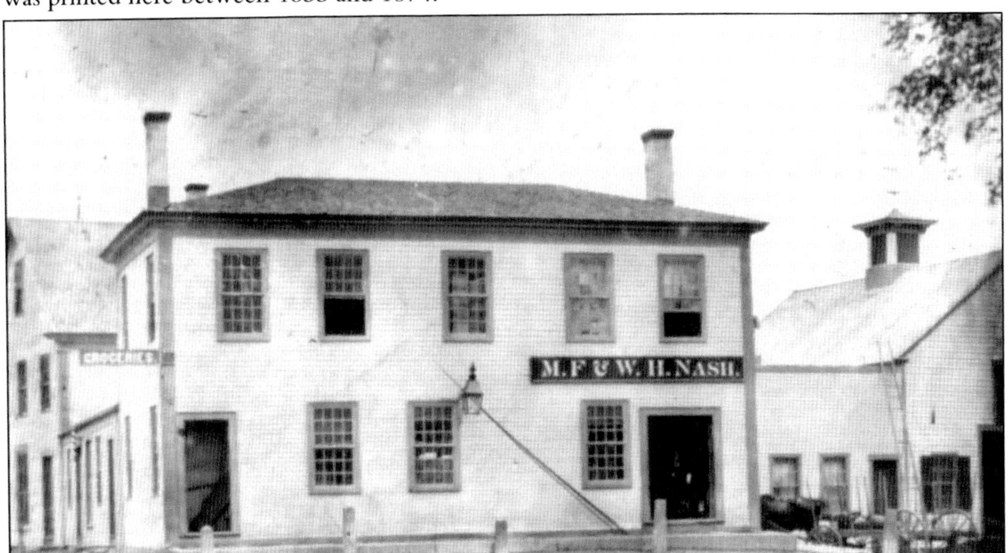

This is the earliest postcard view of the building at the corner of Washington Street and Centre Avenue; it was built by Daniel Ford in 1815. The building is typical of houses of the Federal period in that it has a low hip roof and chimneys at the sides. Ford used the building as a shoe factory in 1816 with his son-in-law Joseph Dunbar. Joseph Vaughan acquired the building and much of the land on this block and continued to manufacture shoes until the building was sold.

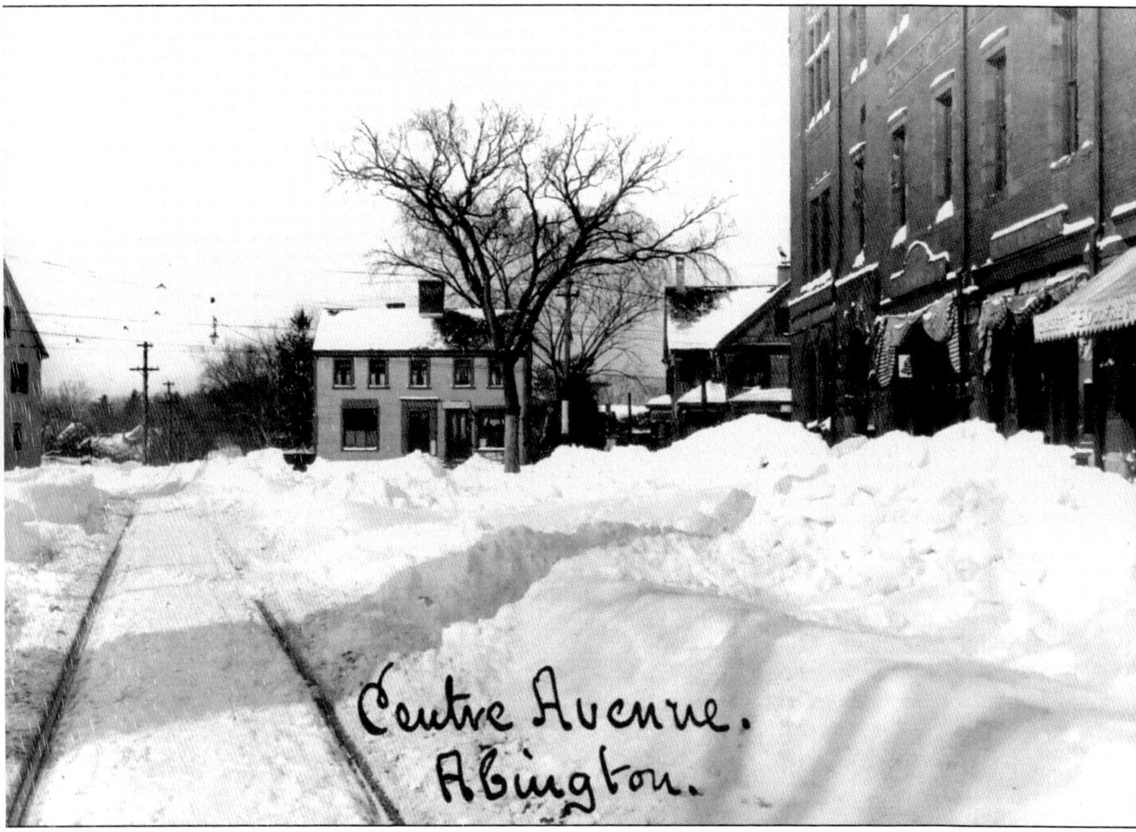

This view of a winter morning near the beginning of the 20th century gives the impression that, except for the trolley, not much is able to move with the snow so high. The building in the background is on the northwest corner of Washington and Orange Streets. When this photograph was taken there were two stores on the corner. The store on the left is a Chinese laundry. The store on the right sells hardware and has cut a new door for an entrance.

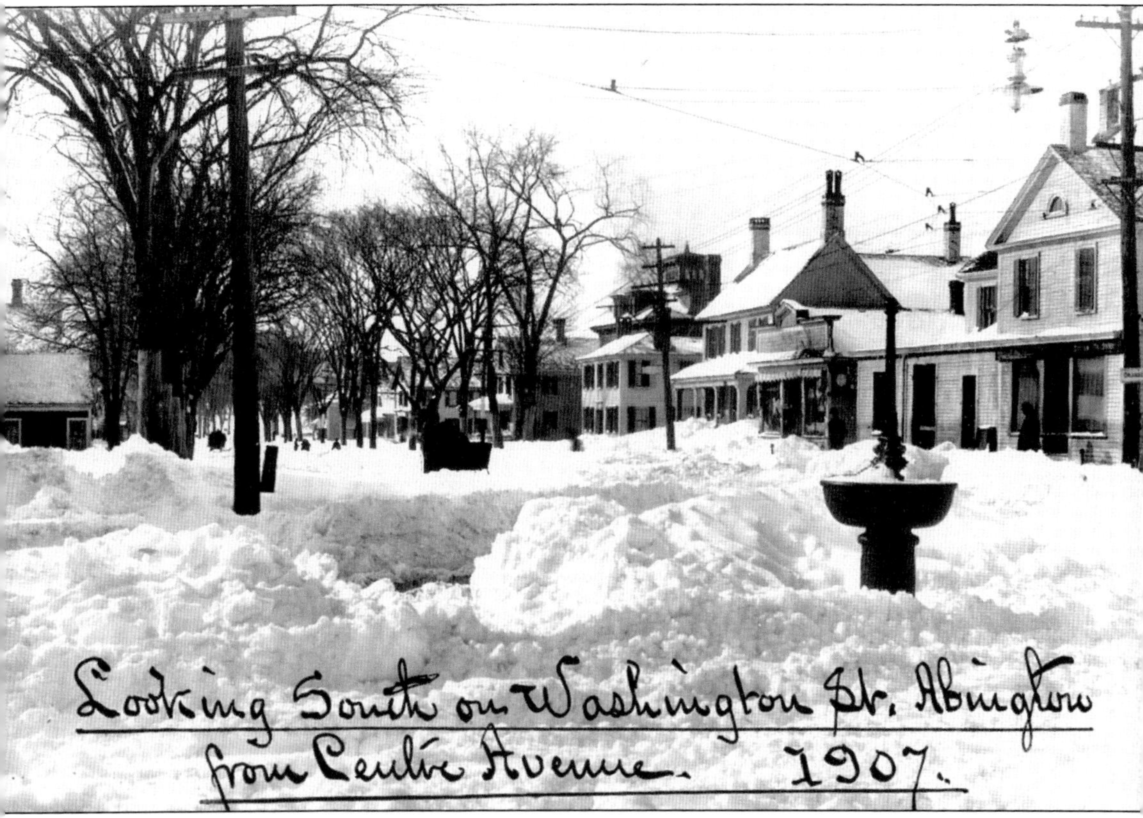

A postcard like this, sent to a person from Abington spending the winter of 1907 in Florida, had to bring a smile to his face. On the right above the post office is an electric arc light of the type that was commonly used in Abington. The fifth building from the right is the residence of Joshua L. Nash, who was a shoe manufacturer. While all the other structures in the view are either from the Federal or Greek Revival periods of architectural style, Nash's house is in the Italian villa style. You can see the cupola in this view.

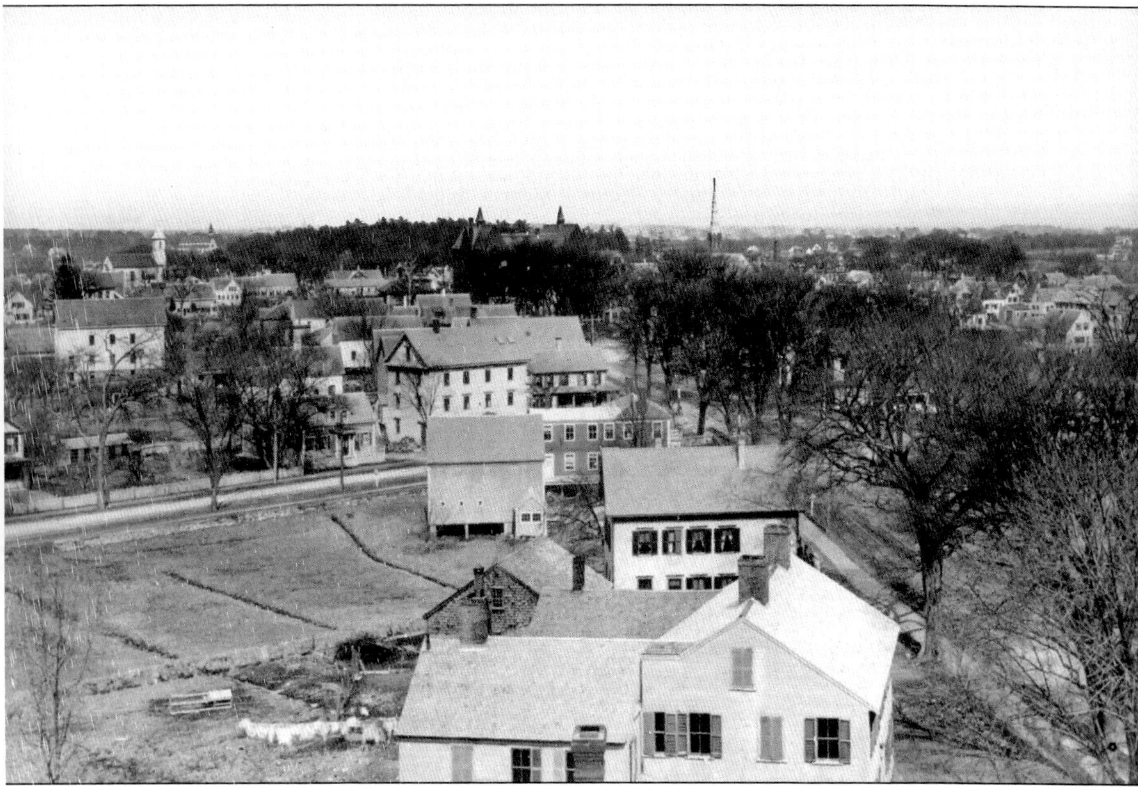

This view from the Masonic building provides a good panorama looking north. On the left in the background is the steeple of the Universalist church at the corner of Washington and West Chapel Streets. To the right of the Universalist church is St. Bridget's on Central Street. To the right of St. Bridget's is the savings bank building at Post Office Square (near the center of the photograph). The next tower to the right is the Church of the New Jerusalem on the corner of Centre Avenue and Dunbar Street. On the far right is the firehouse at the corner of Dunbar and Bank Streets. In the center of this view is Brockton Avenue, spanning from left to right. The building just behind the barn is the Lucius Faxon shoe factory. To the right of the factory is the Faxon home. The large building with the three windows on the second floor was a school located at 73 Bank Street. The Dunbar Street School replaced it, and in 1874, the Odd Fellows bought the building. The house in the foreground is the Thaxter brothers' home at 440 Washington Street.

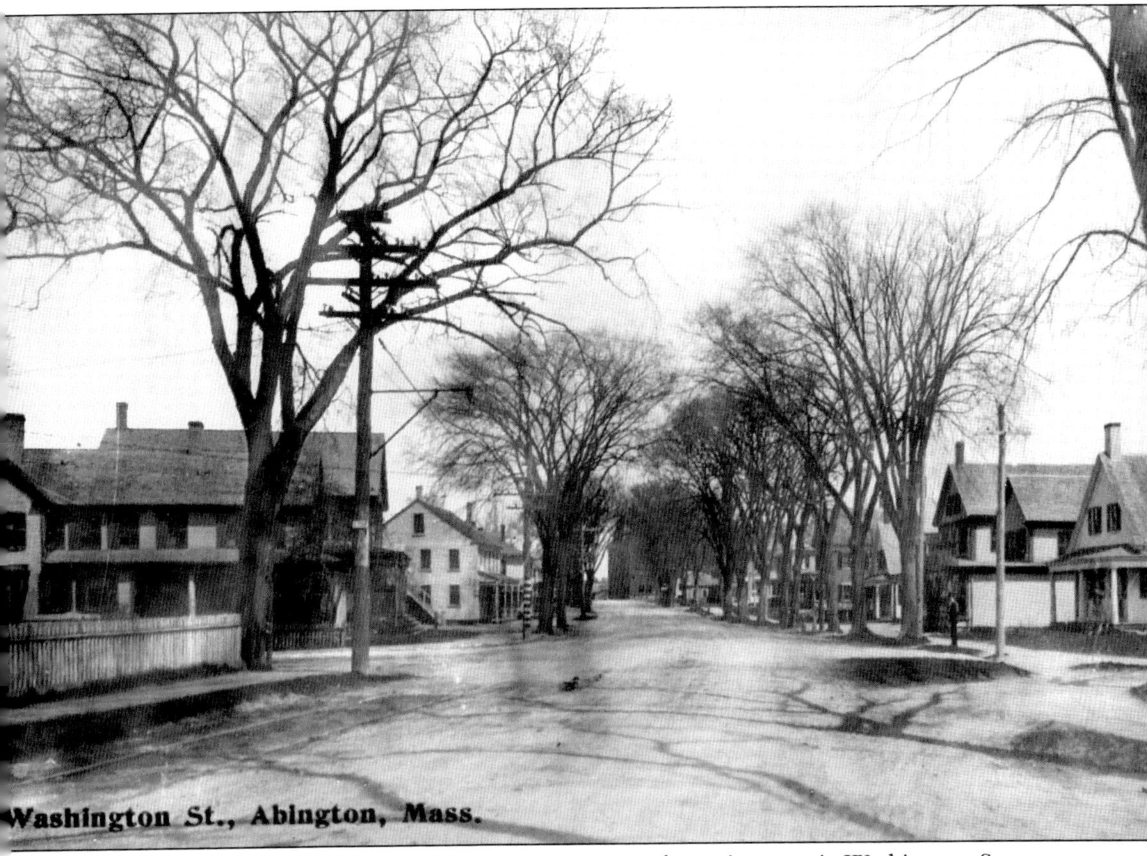

In this view, looking south from Faxon's Corner at Brockton Avenue, is Washington Street. The first building on the left, at 492 Washington Street, is Lucius Faxon's house, built in 1845. The next building, at 500 Washington Street, is William Ripley's hardware store, built in 1855. The next building, at 506 Washington Street, dates from *c.* 1850. The hotel next door may have used it as a stable. It was converted into a shoe factory in 1850 and eventually was remodeled into a store. For a long time, the store was Blanchard's Market.

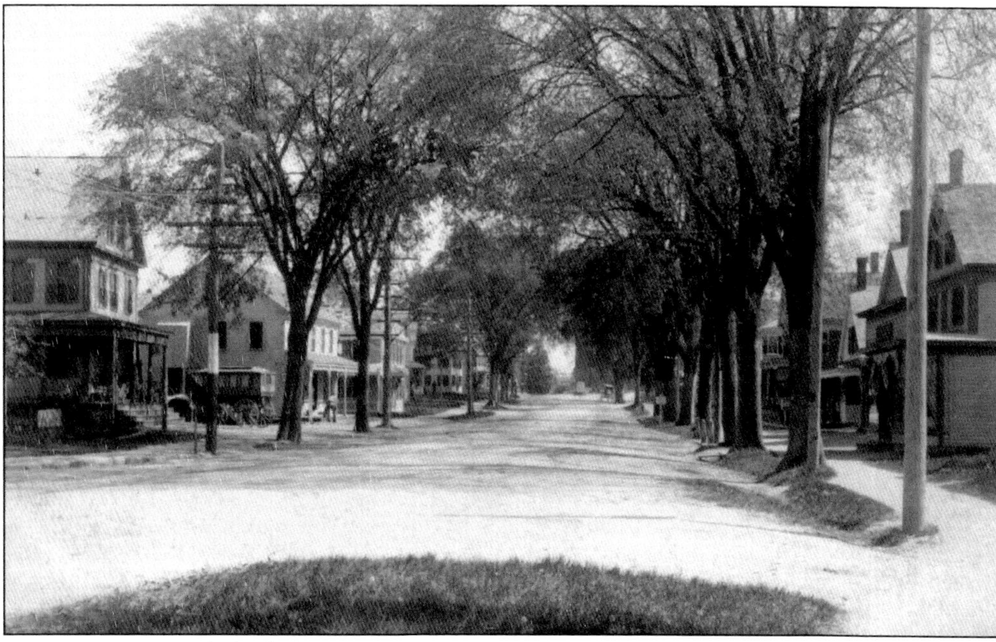

This view is just a little farther down Washington Street. The first building on the left is 500 Washington Street, a hardware store. Blanchard's Market is the next building, at 506 Washington Street. The stagecoach, driven by Bernie Blanchard, has pulled into the side yard of the market. Blanchard took the kids from West Abington to school in the morning, worked in the market during the day, and took the kids home again in the afternoon.

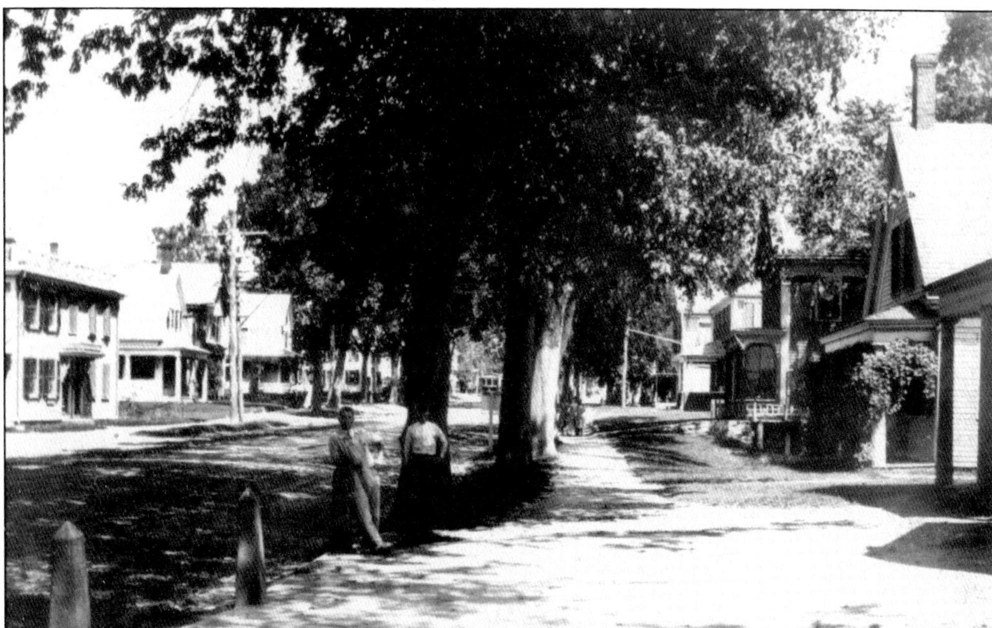

These fellows are across the street from a building used as a hotel starting in the 1830s. The hotel was known as the Colson House in 1852, the Centennial House in 1877, and, by the time of this 1903 postcard, the Wilson House. In 1929, this building was moved to the back of the lot. It was eventually converted to housing. Note the girls walking down the street on the right.

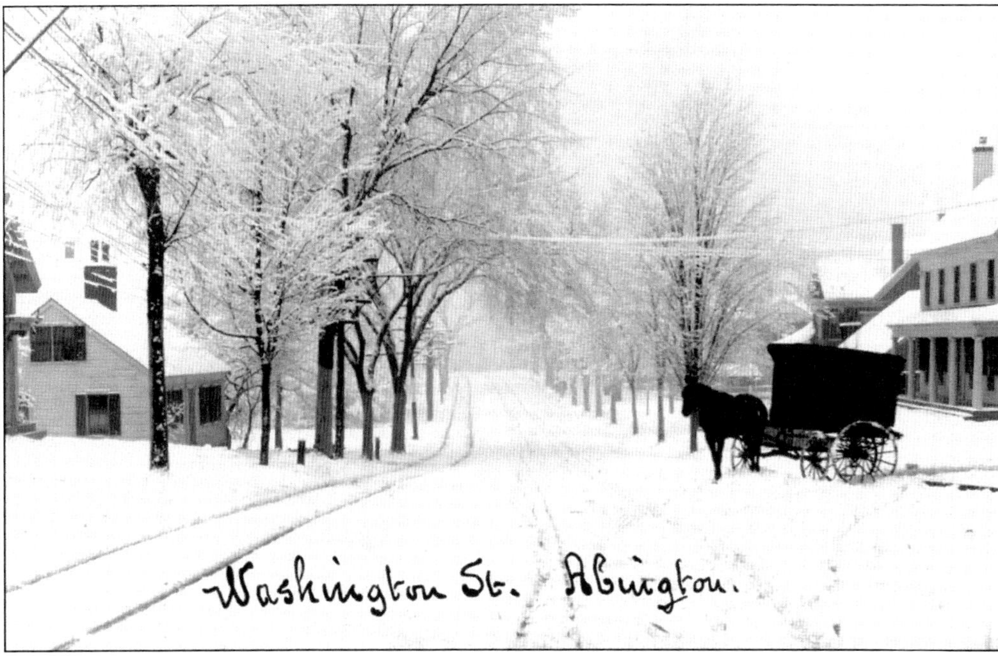

This is Washington Street just north of the savings bank building in the direction of North Abington. Nelson Beal built the house on the right on the site of the savings bank building in 1843. It was moved to this location in 1882 to make way for the bank. It was taken down in 1953. Delivering milk and other goods was not easy on a snowy morning in the early 20th century.

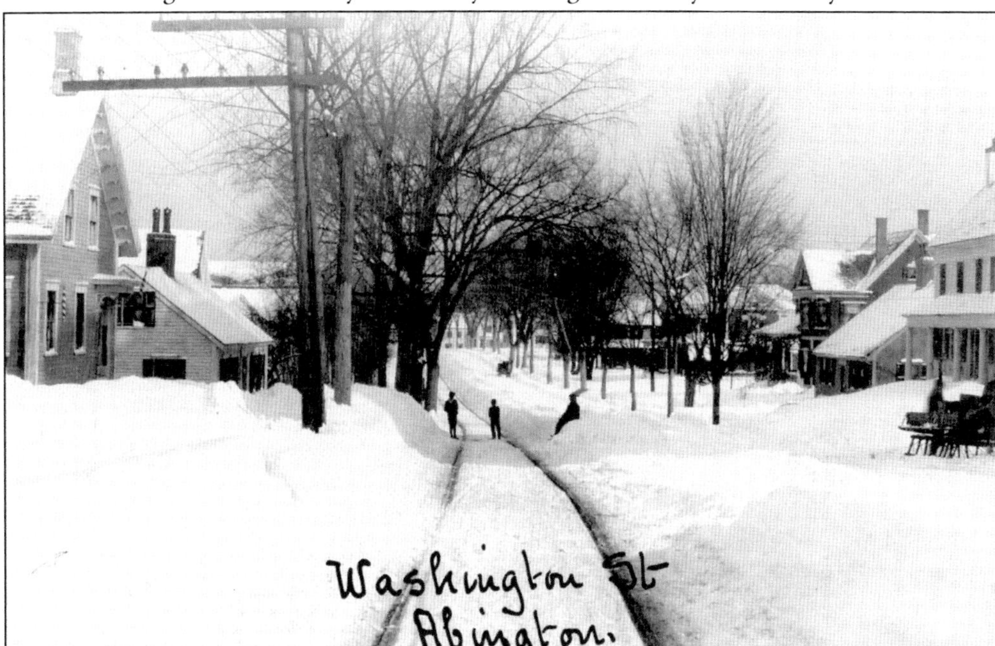

This photograph was taken near the same spot as the previous one, but things have changed a little. There is a vehicle with snow runners in the driveway of the Beal house. It looks like some boys have come out to enjoy the snow. The postcard scenes of snow were of the storms that many grandfathers told tales about.

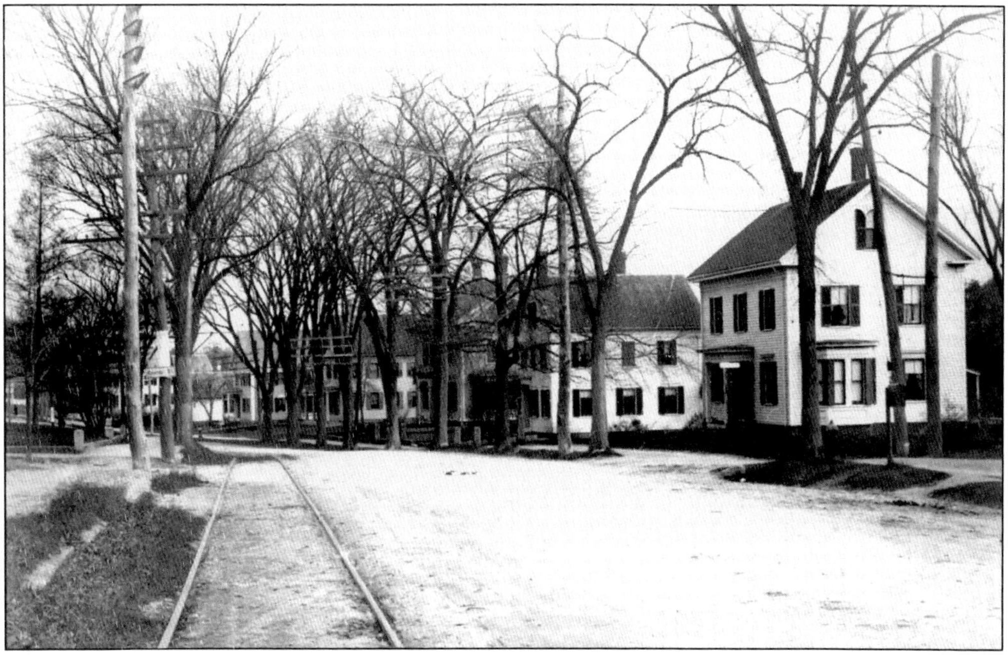

This view of Washington Street is just opposite West Chapel Street. You can see the street sign in the left center of the photograph. The American elm was a favorite shade tree on America's main streets in the late 19th and early 20th centuries. This is evident in this view as well as in other views in this book. Because of the lack of foliage, a photograph taken in winter showed more of a streetscape than a photograph taken in summer .

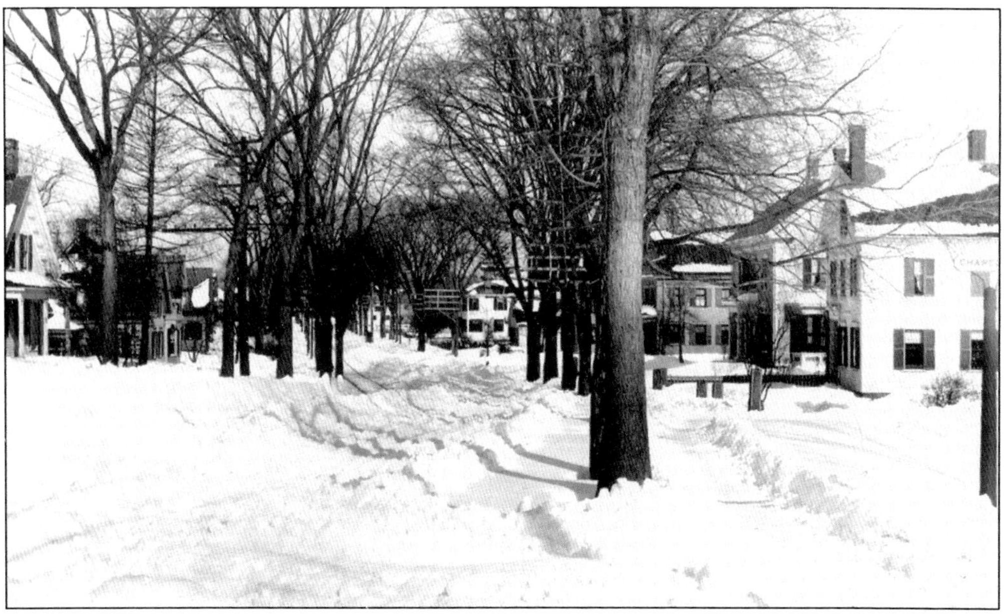

This view is just beyond Chapel Street. The sidewalk has been shoveled, but the street looks as if nothing could pass and nothing has been done to clear it.

Three

Abington Businesses

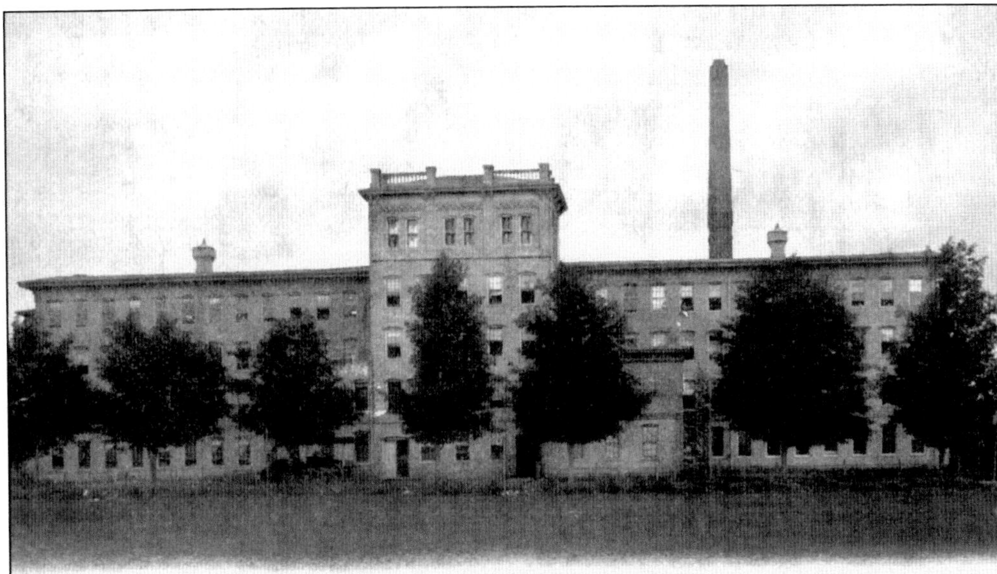

M. N. ARNOLD & CO.'S SHOE FACTORY, NORTH ABINGTON, MASS.
Issued by W. J SHEEHAN NEWS CO.

Soon after Moses N. Arnold returned from the Civil War, he returned to work as a shoemaker, a profession at which he had been trained as a youth. After a year's time working "on the bench," according to historian Charles F. Meserve, Arnold dabbled in larger-scale manufacturing. His business acumen and drive eventually led him to the 1875 construction of his factory at 200 Wales Street, where he continued in the business for more than 50 years, turning out as many as 2,000 pairs of shoes a week. With the surrounding towns—Brockton, Whitman, Hanover, Rockland, and others—Abington helped provide shoes to one-quarter of the American people in the 1920s. Business in Abington meant big business.

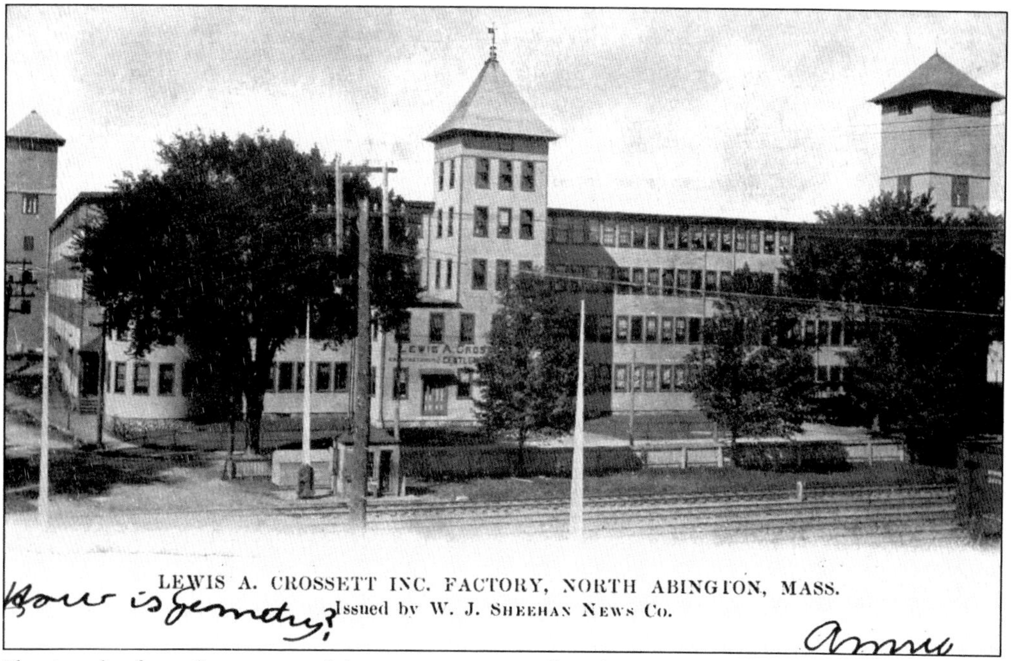

Shoeing the feet of a quarter of the country was a tall order, so Arnold had help. The Lewis A. Crossett Shoe Company turned its product out at its 2.75-acre site at 10 Railroad Street. Crossett, originally from Pelham, built his factory in 1888 and stuck with it until his death in 1926. His son ran the company into the 1930s but was forced to close the factory during the Great Depression.

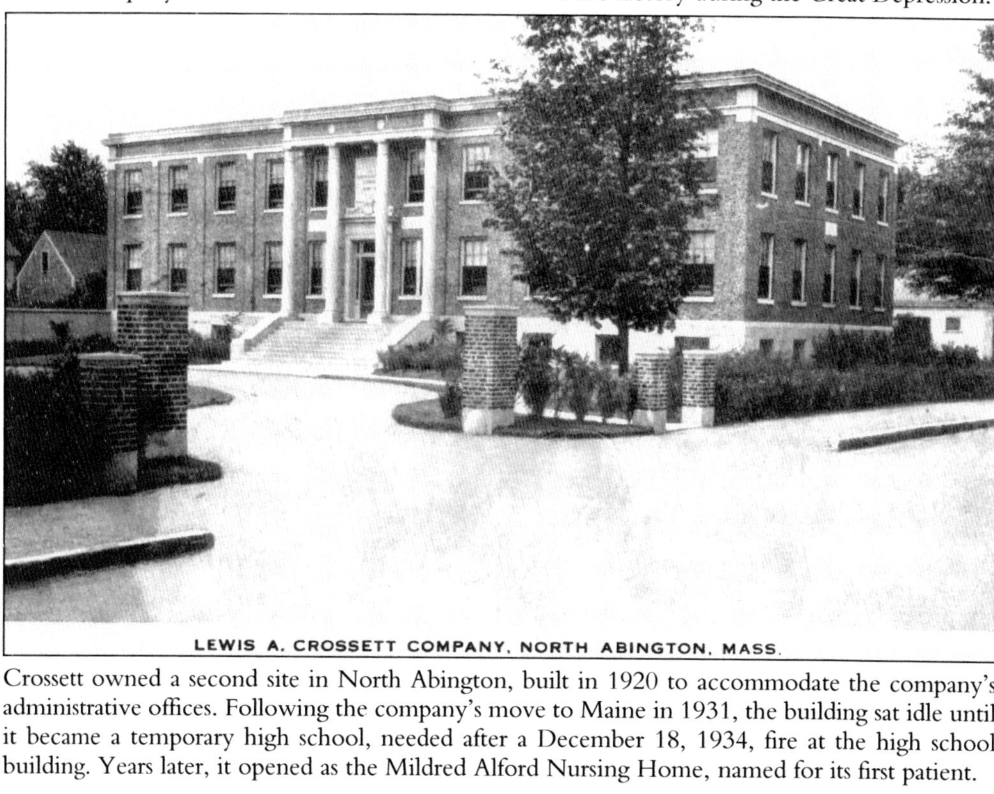

Crossett owned a second site in North Abington, built in 1920 to accommodate the company's administrative offices. Following the company's move to Maine in 1931, the building sat idle until it became a temporary high school, needed after a December 18, 1934, fire at the high school building. Years later, it opened as the Mildred Alford Nursing Home, named for its first patient.

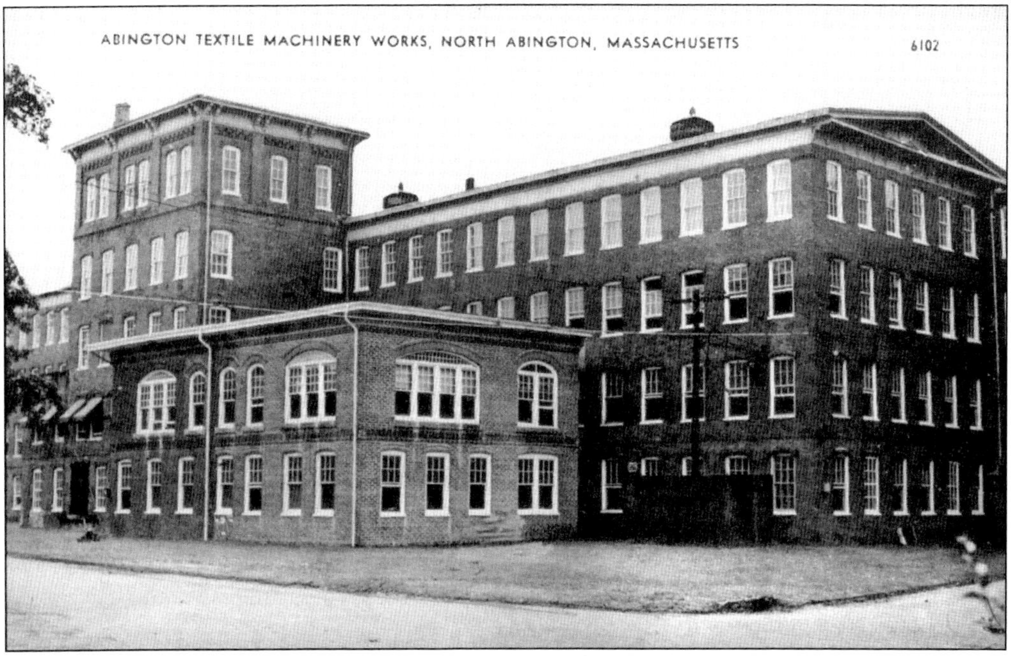

Some buildings offered multiple uses over the years. After Arnold's shoe company left its famed factory during the Great Depression, selling out to rival Stetson Shoe of Hanover, the building remained a shoe factory for a few more years. In later years, it became an antiques warehouse and the home of the Abington Company, manufacturers of vacuum cleaning systems for textile factories.

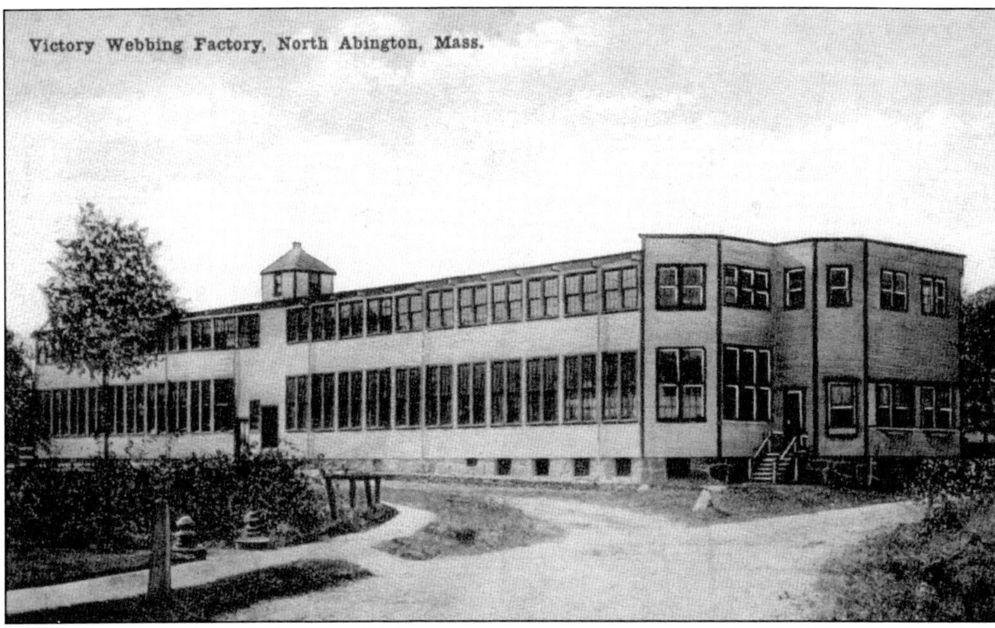

Tacks were needed to hold shoes together, and wooden boxes were needed for shipping. Oftentimes, businessmen could get rich by manufacturing the attendant items needed for larger products. Such was the case with the Victor Webbing Company (the spelling on the card is incorrect) at 38 Bates Street, where weavers produced narrow woven material for different uses in relation to shoemaking.

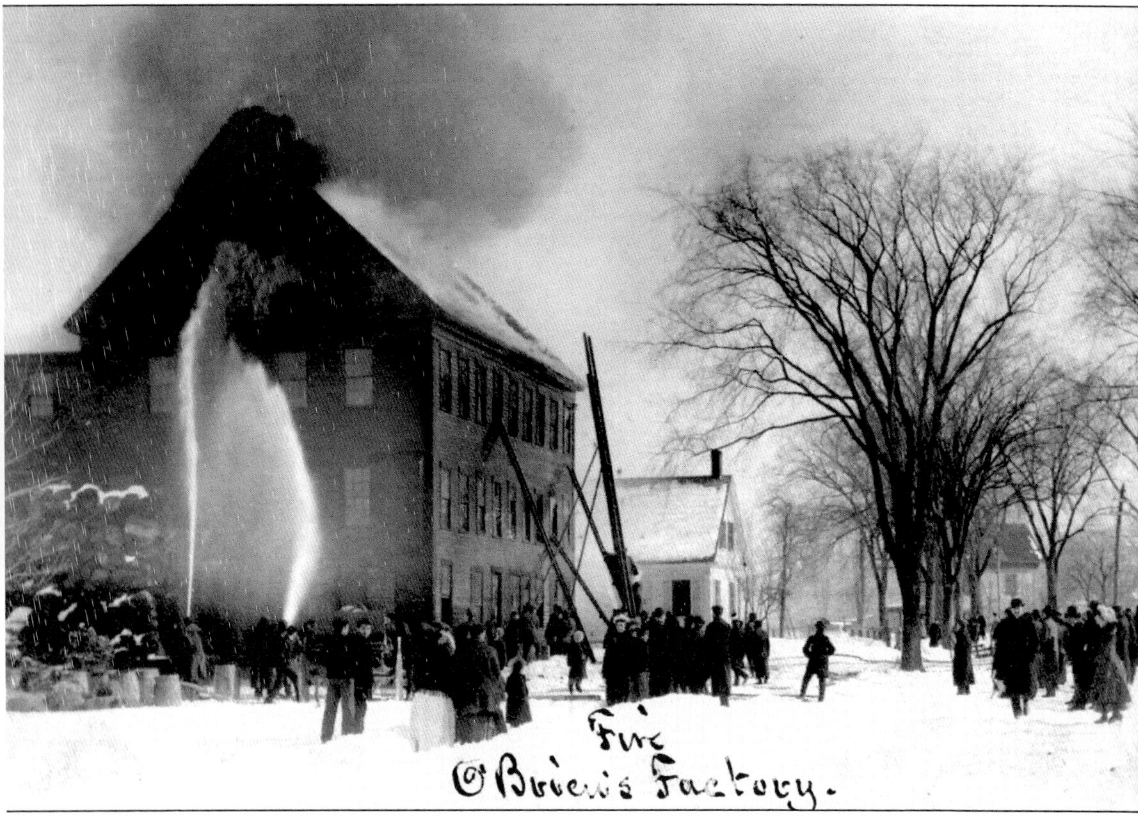

Heel manufacturers abounded around town. According to the research of Martha Campbell, Worthy C. Dunham had started the process by 1874 around the site of what is today 603 Hancock Street, as had James S. Sharp on Washington Street on Church Hill. Within 10 years, J. Ellsworth Dunham had joined the business at 214 Adams Street, as had Robert Meserve near today's 116 Washington Street and William S. O'Brien at 11 Rockland Street. O'Brien's factory out-produced them all, even after surviving a fire that caused it to lose its top floor. With the local shoe industry thriving through the 1920s, O'Brien kept making heels into the Great Depression. Sensational events such as fires made for highly sought-after postcards because, prior to the widespread use of cameras, they were tangible reminders of the events that took place in a person's life.

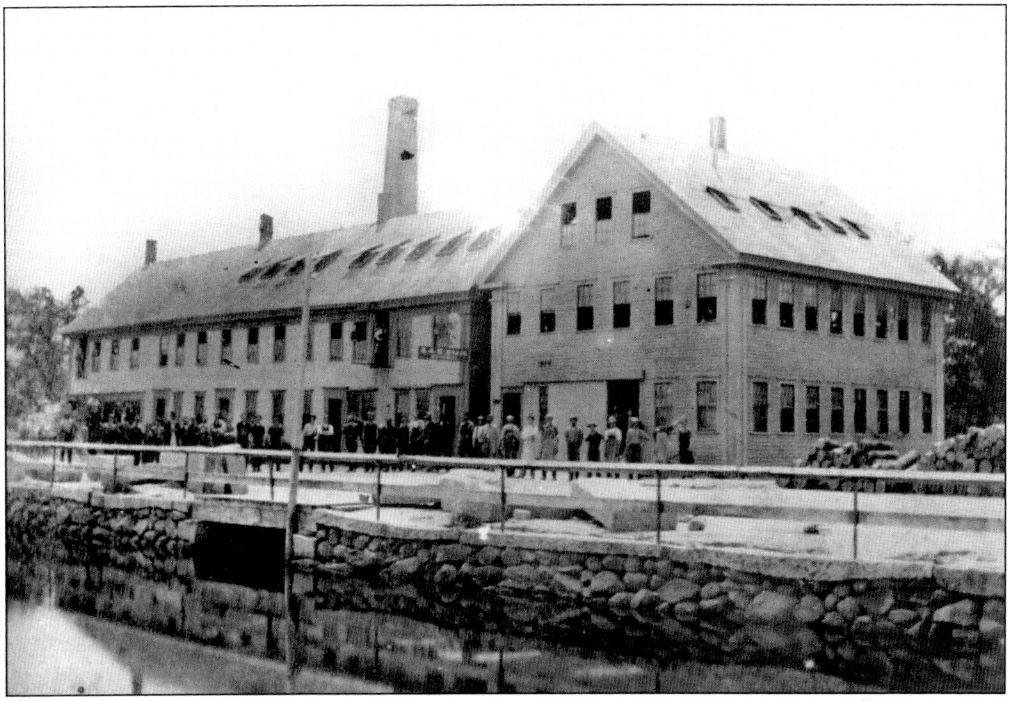

Jesse H. Giles built the factory on the right for the manufacture of lasts, the wooden forms on which shoes were assembled. The building stood on Centre Avenue, across from the Island Grove Pond dam.

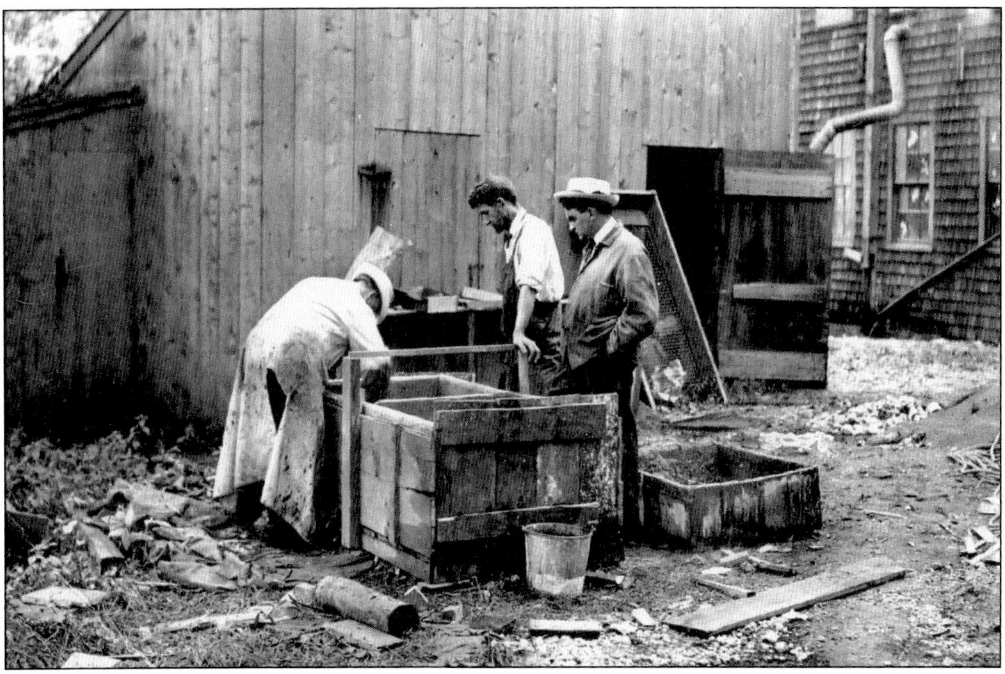

In later years, the Giles factory converted to make dry plates for photography. Standing at the center and supervising the work is Thomas F. Giles. To the right is the ubiquitous Henry Claflin, the postcard publisher, observing.

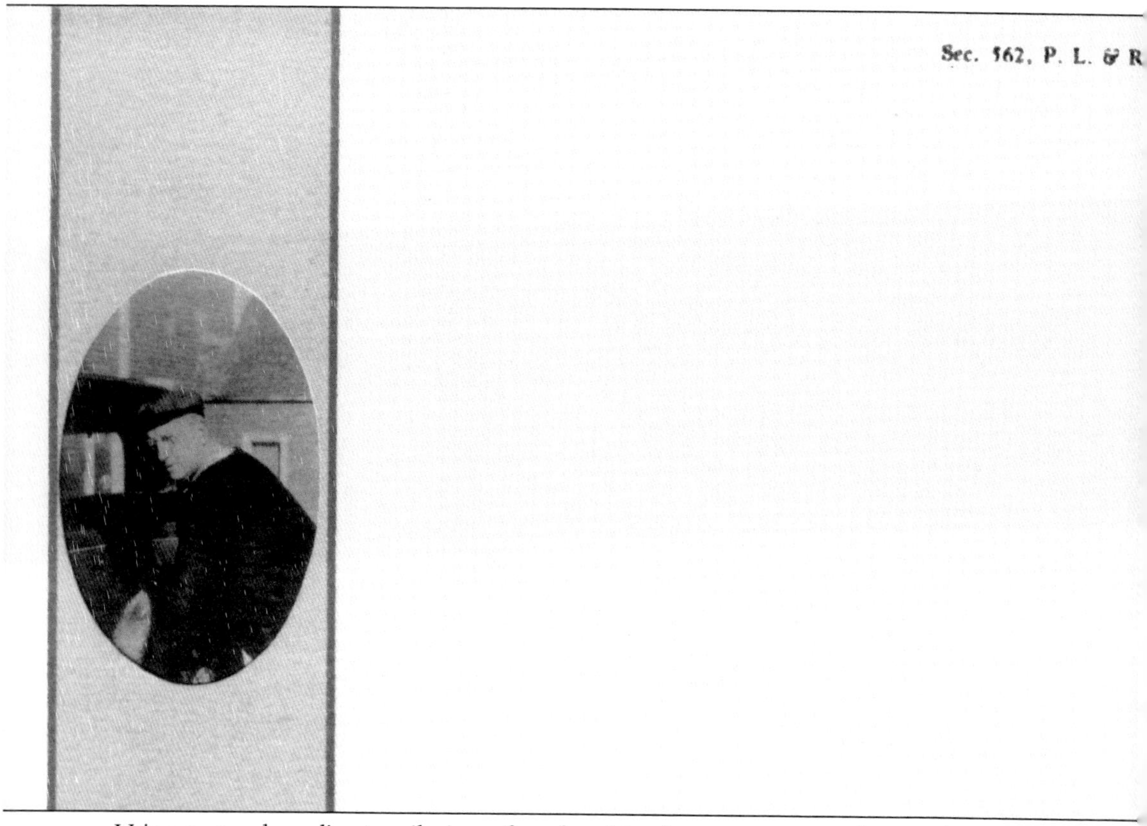

Using postcards as direct mail pieces for advertising became commonplace as the 20th century moved on. Some businesspeople became quite creative with their advertisements as well, as can be seen by the folded and unfolded images of the Black and White Service Station's mailer on this and the following page.

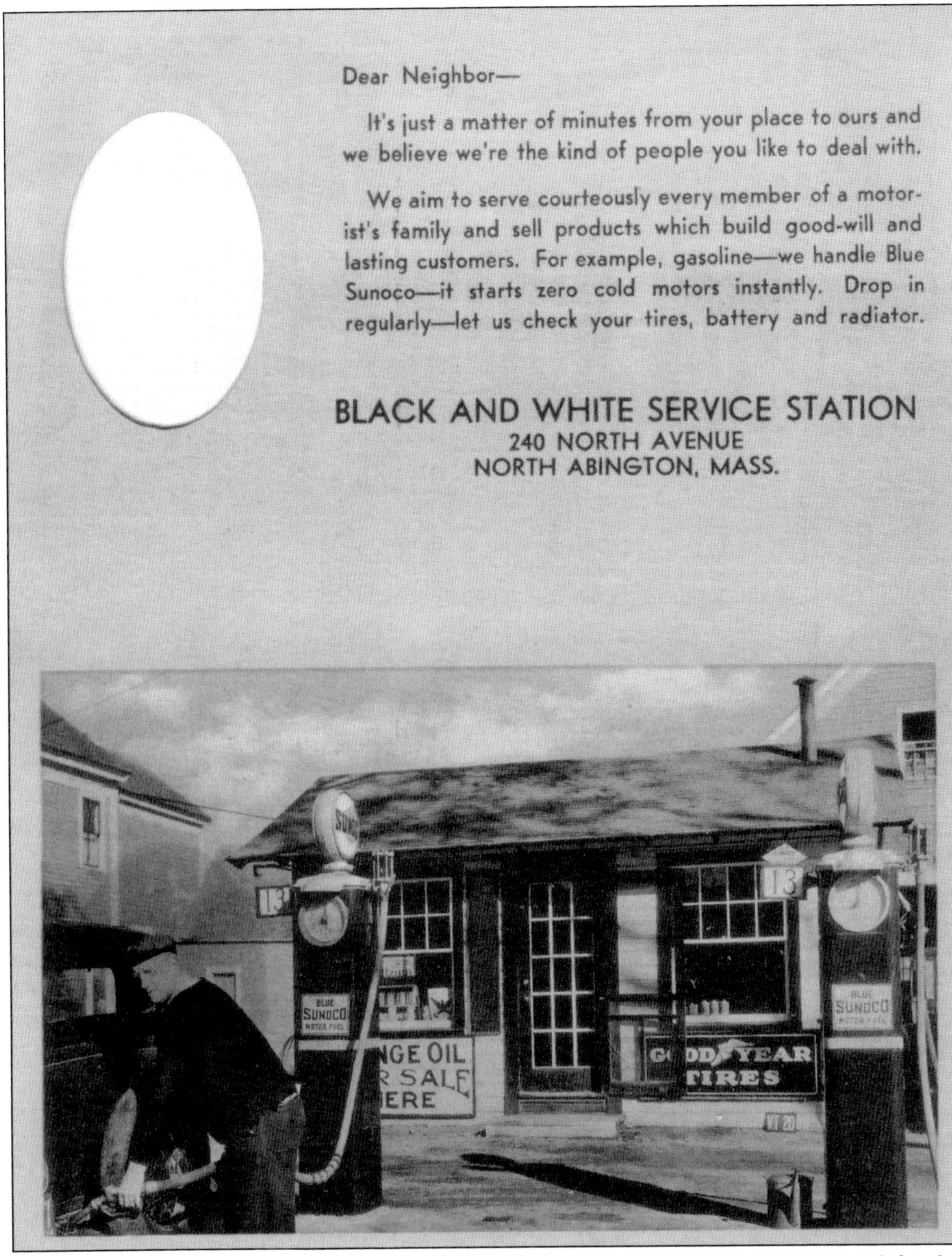

Oftentimes, businesses tried to create idealized visions of their product. Here, the card for the station at 240 North Avenue includes an attendant pumping gas and advertisements for both tires and oil. The image sends the message that all that a motorist needs can be found at this one location. And the text above the image, of course, says that as well.

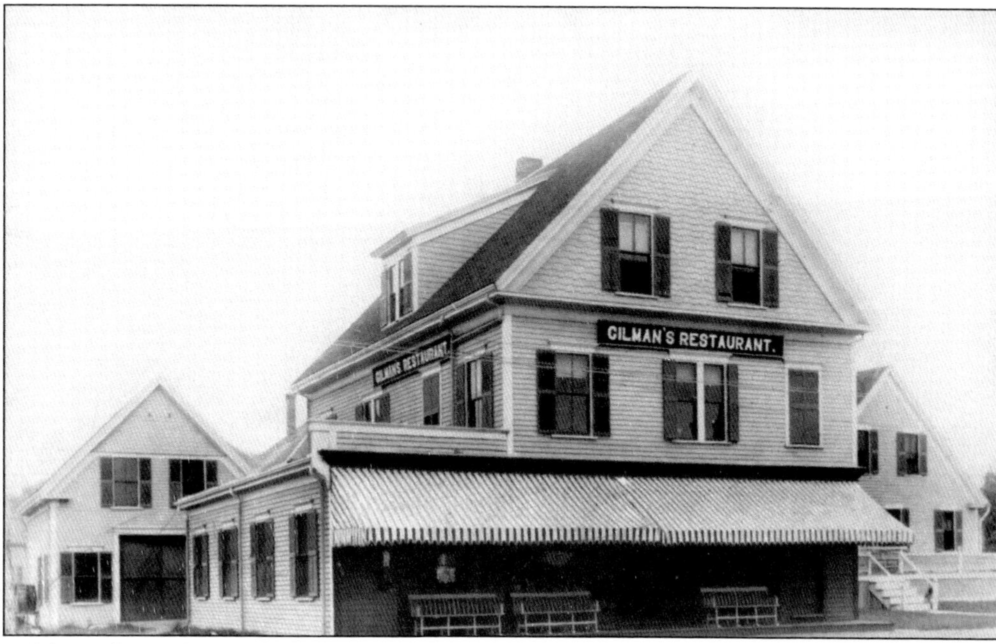

Caleb Dudley Gilman promised that "Regular and transient boarders will find good board and prompt service at reasonable rates" at his restaurant and home bakery at 94 Railroad Street, conveniently located opposite the North Abington railroad depot. In later years, the building served as the millinery of Catherine Badger.

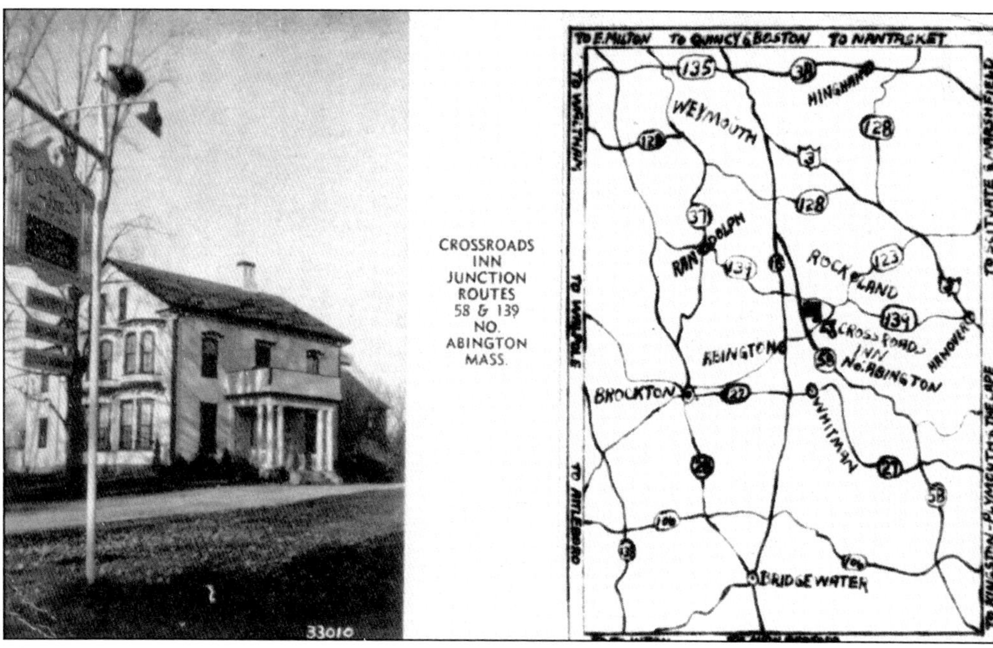

The Crossroads Inn offered the same type of service as Gilman's and included a map showing its location on its postcard.

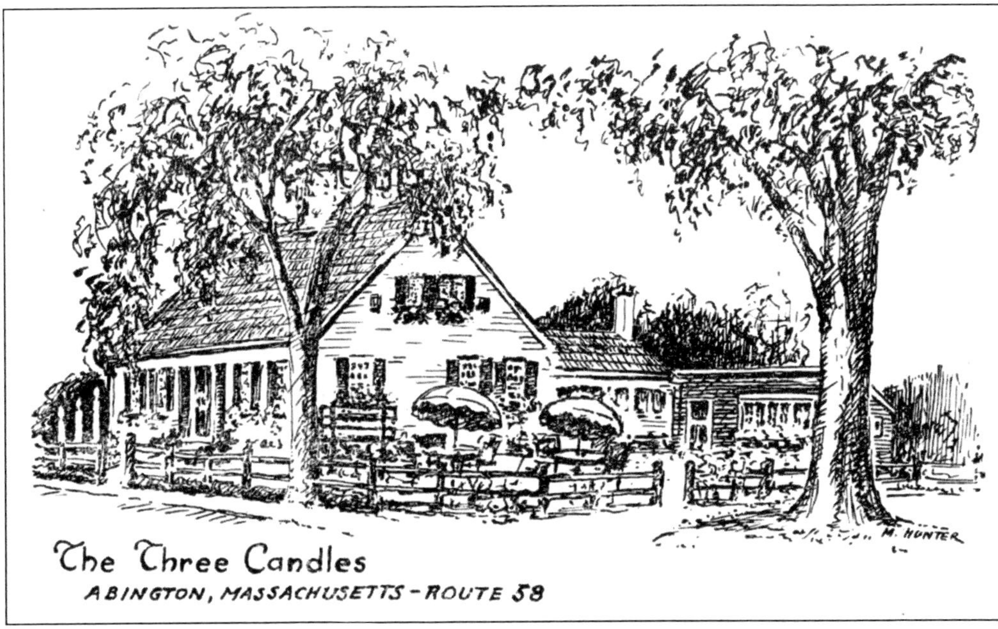

The unassuming 1804 Henry C. Connor house, at 969 Plymouth Street, later served as the Three Candles Restaurant, still remembered by many Abington residents today. The house sat on a stagecoach line (on Route 58) and later on the line of the electric streetcars.

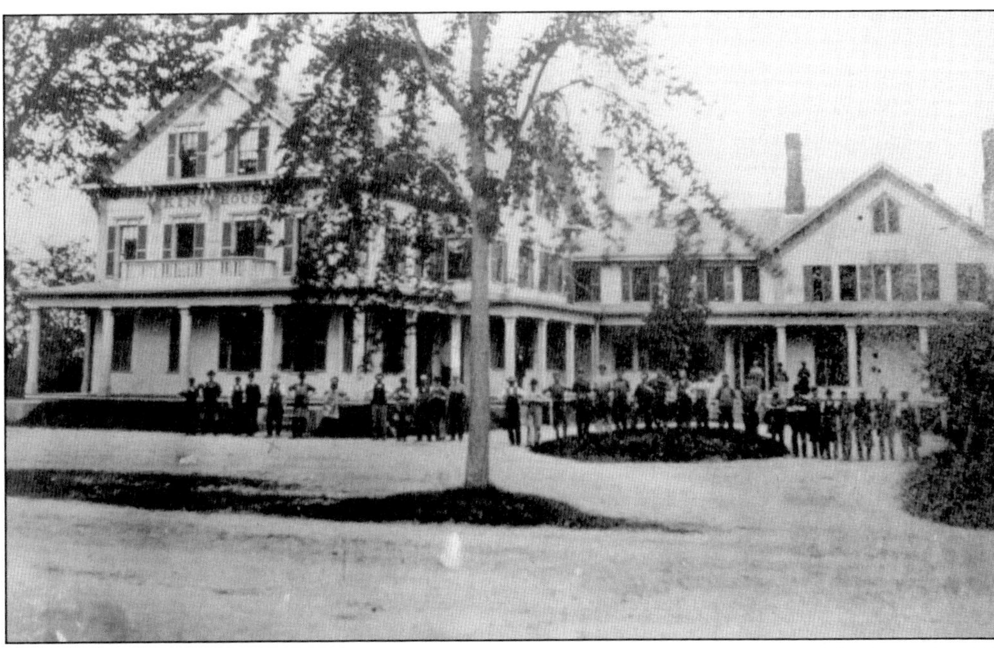
Gen. Benjamin King built his large hotel at 349 Washington Street in 1850. He built on the side of Island Grove Pond opposite the all-important railroad tracks. When his hotel ultimately failed, he sold it to Joshua Leonard Nash, who converted it into a shoe factory. The south wing burned after the factory's closing in 1884, leaving only the original main house standing today.

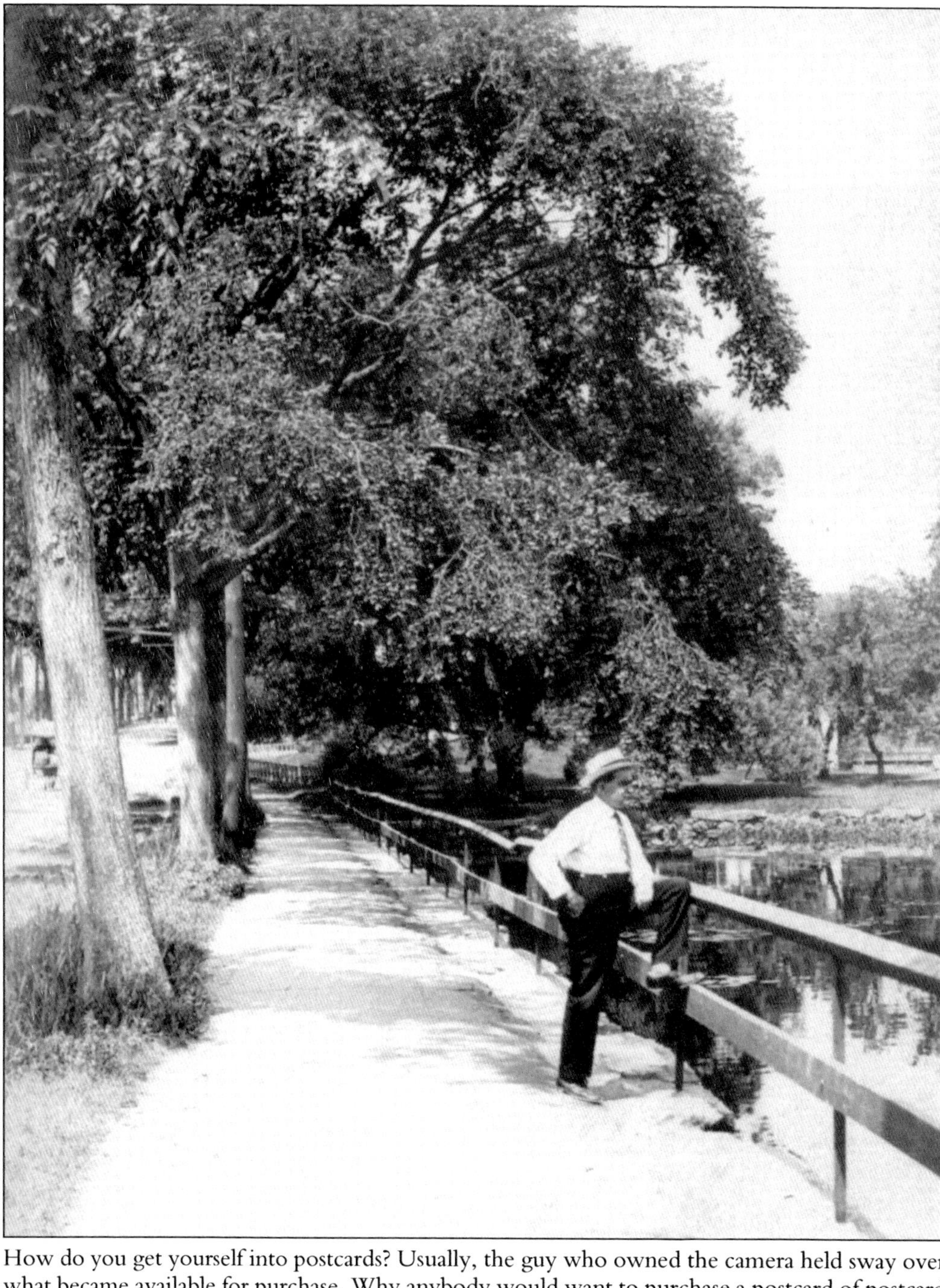

How do you get yourself into postcards? Usually, the guy who owned the camera held sway over what became available for purchase. Why anybody would want to purchase a postcard of postcard publisher Henry Claflin we do not know, but Claflin shows up in quite a few Abington images, fishing, walking through Mount Vernon Cemetery, looking over the shoulders of the townsfolk as they work, and more. Here, Claflin strikes a relaxed pose on the railing along Centre Avenue, gazing out over Island Grove Pond. Whether the postcards sold or not, we thank Henry Claflin for recording these images for posterity, allowing future generations of Abington residents to learn about their town's past.

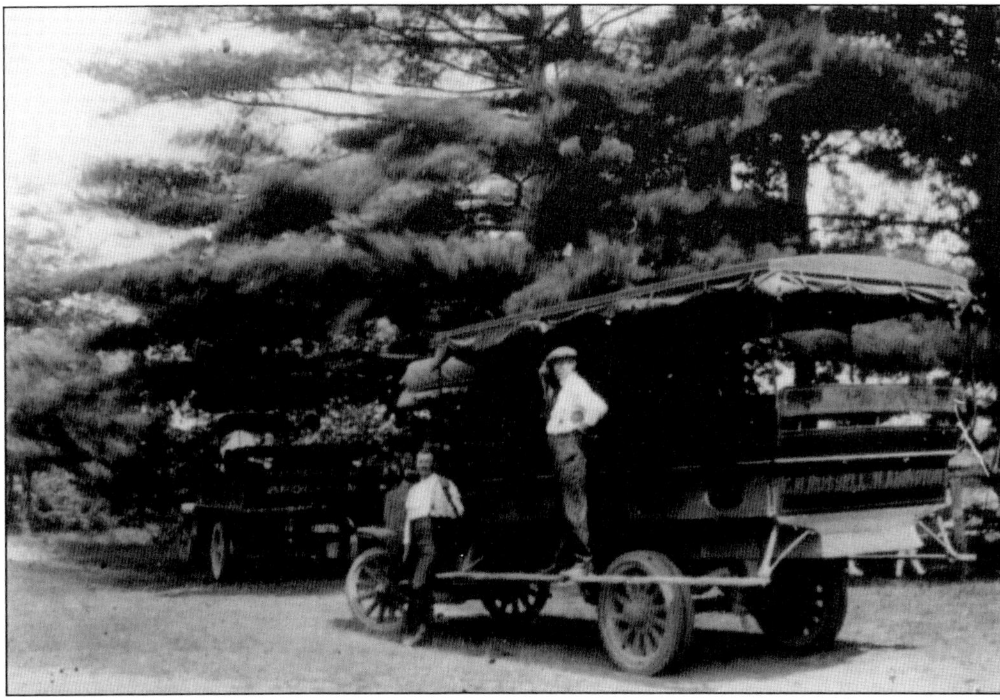

Other hardworking people ended up in postcards as well. Cyrus H. Russell offered up his truck for any purpose, such as hack and livery service, furniture and piano moving, heavy teaming, and general jobbing. If you needed him, he could be found at 18 Brighton Street.

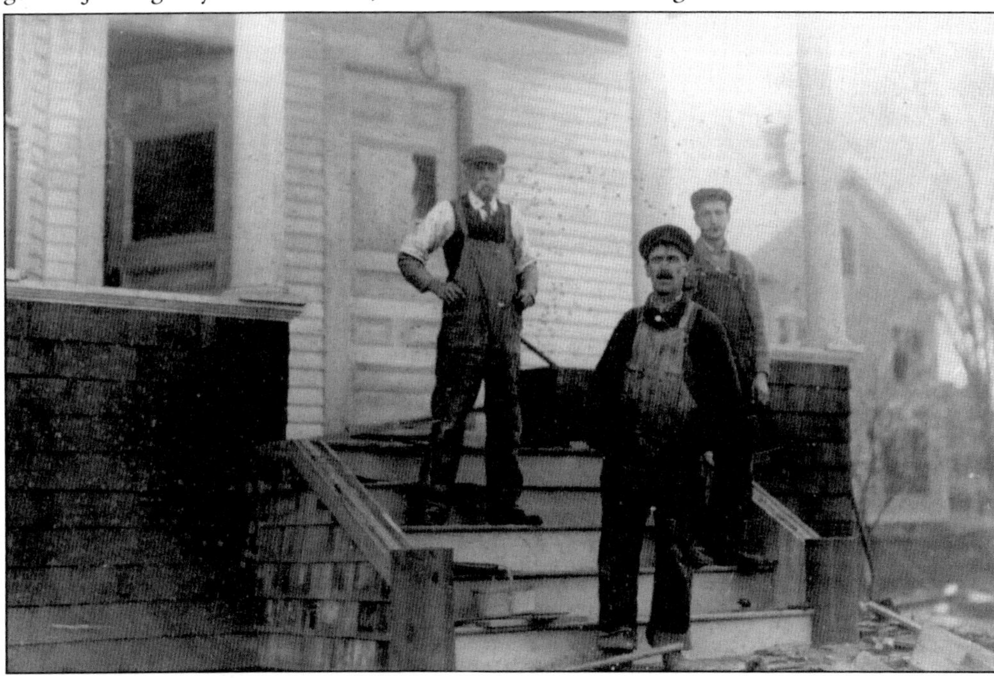

The Leaches—Arthur F. (left), E. Herbert (center), and Joseph W.—worked as carpenters for a living. Here, they stand on the porch of 13–15 Wilson Place *c.* 1910. Postcards like this one show a side of local life not usually glorified by photographers of the day.

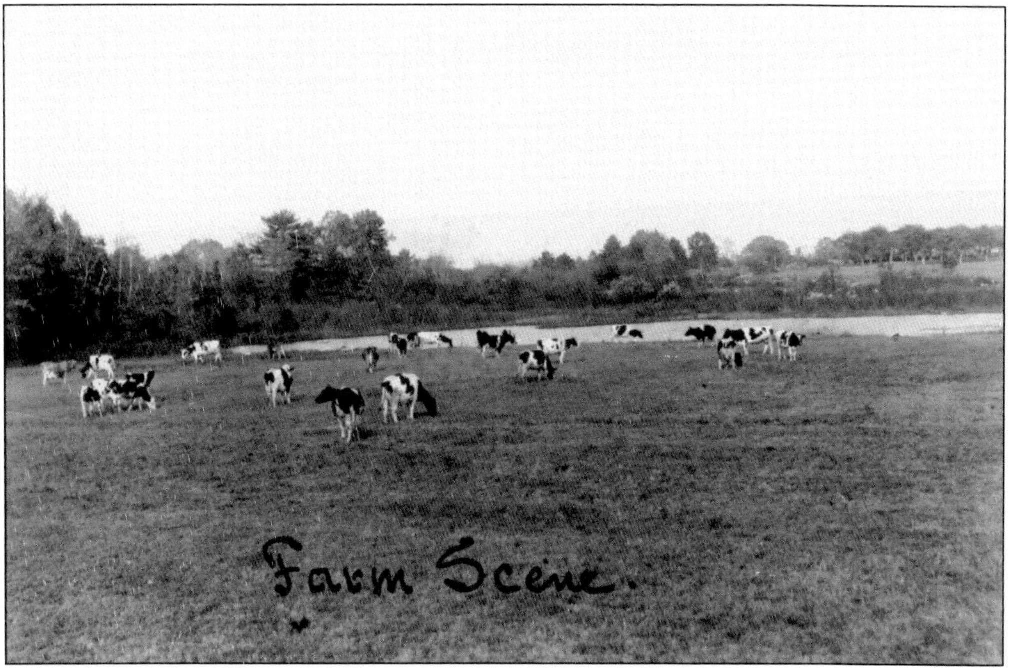

At Ashland Street on the old Trufant farm, the cattle of Philip Trufant, milk dealer, graze on a peat hole *c.* 1910. The business address read 287 High Street. Even with big business dominating the landscape of Abington, agriculture and farming had not yet completely died.

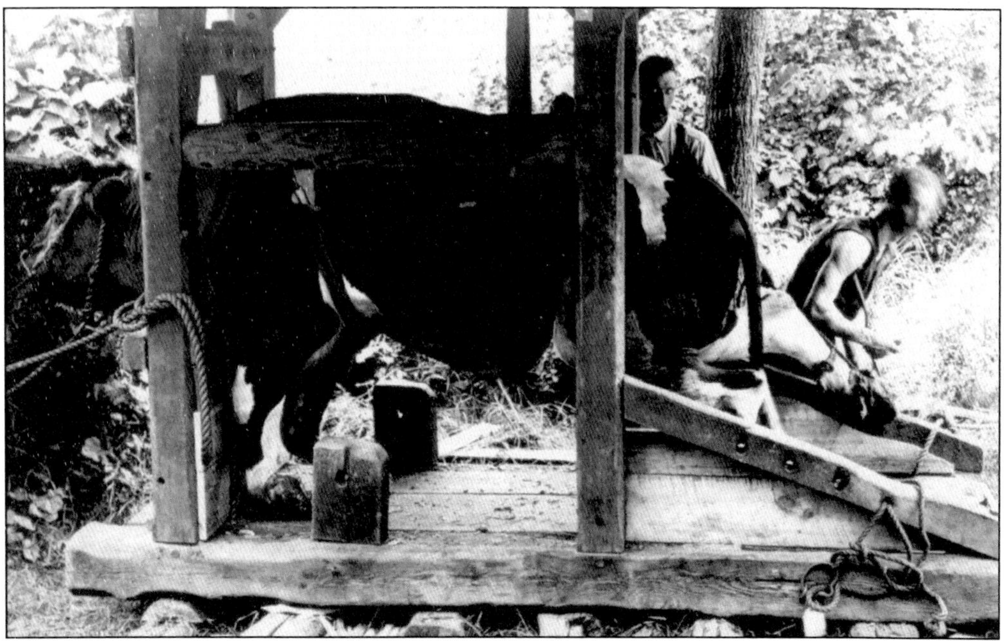
The old skills of the farmer still needed to be taught. Here, an ox is being shod at George Gray's blacksmith shop, just north of the Grand Army of the Republic (GAR) hall on Washington Street. The process must have been carefully undertaken, as one can imagine the wallop an ox could produce if unduly provoked.

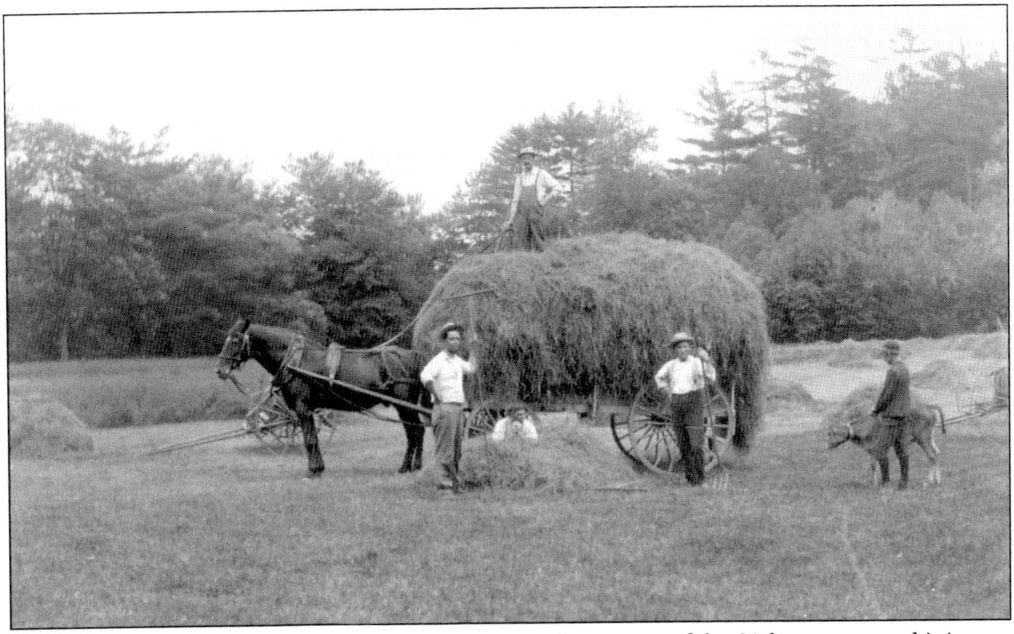

Hay making was still practiced in Abington after the beginning of the 20th century, and it is seen here on the estate of Edward Wright on Walnut Street. On the left is George Wilkes, on the hay load is Sumner Deane, and on the right by the wagon is Frank Bowditch. The man in the hay on the ground and the man holding back the calf on the right are unidentified.

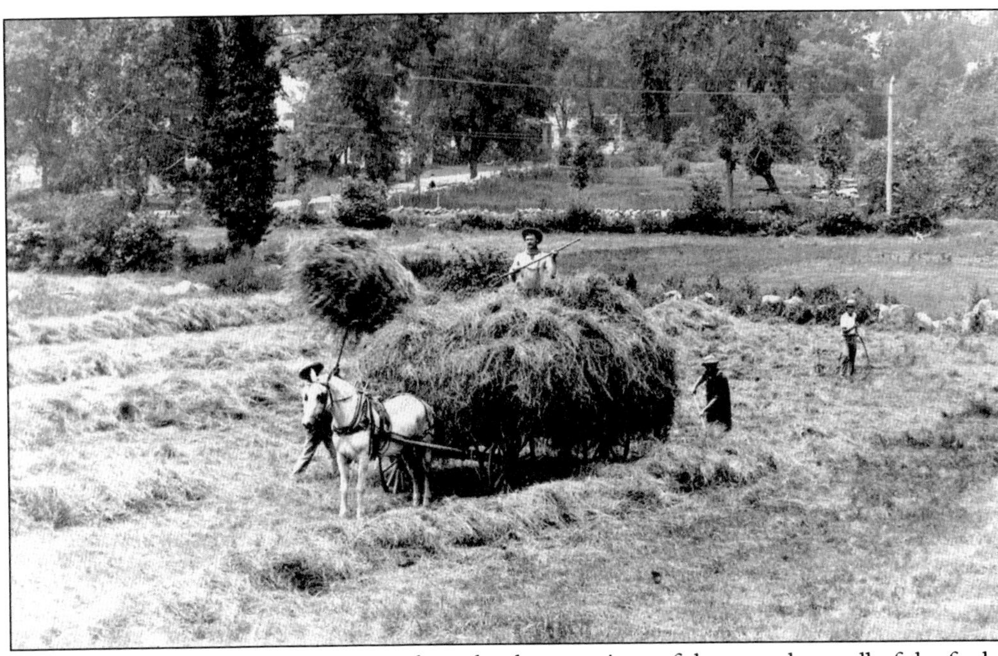

The crispness of the old photo postcards evoke the sensations of the past: the smell of the fresh-cut hay, the sounds of the rickety wheels of the cart, and the shushing sound of the hay being thrown up top. This view is an example of the way Abington looked, minus the electrical wires, for 200 years.

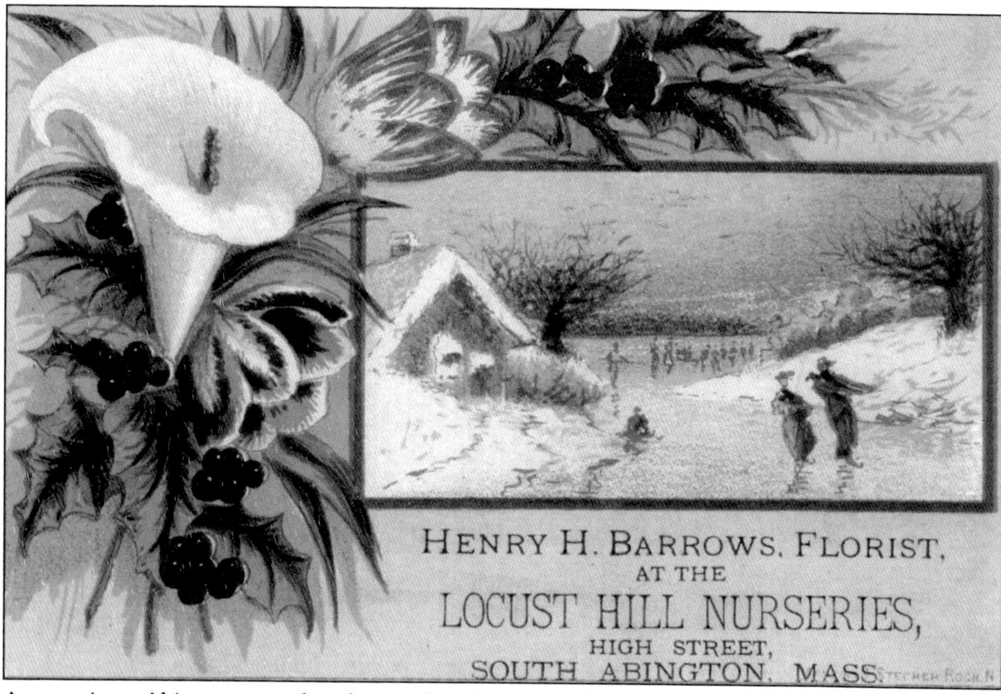

At one time, Abington was the place to be if you were looking for fresh-cut flowers or tips for landscape improvements. Henry Barrows's place was in the southern section of Abington, not the town of South Abington, as Whitman came to be known after its incorporation as an independent community.

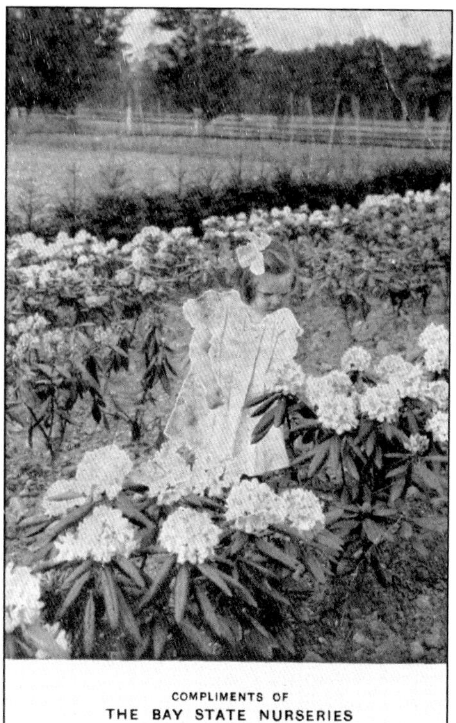

At the other end of the town, Bay State Nurseries sold its products by equating the beauty of youth with the beauty of nature. From the smallest nursery to the biggest shoe factory, Abington's businesspeople understood the value of printed media and how postcards could help spread the word about their services.

Four

A Railroad Runs through It

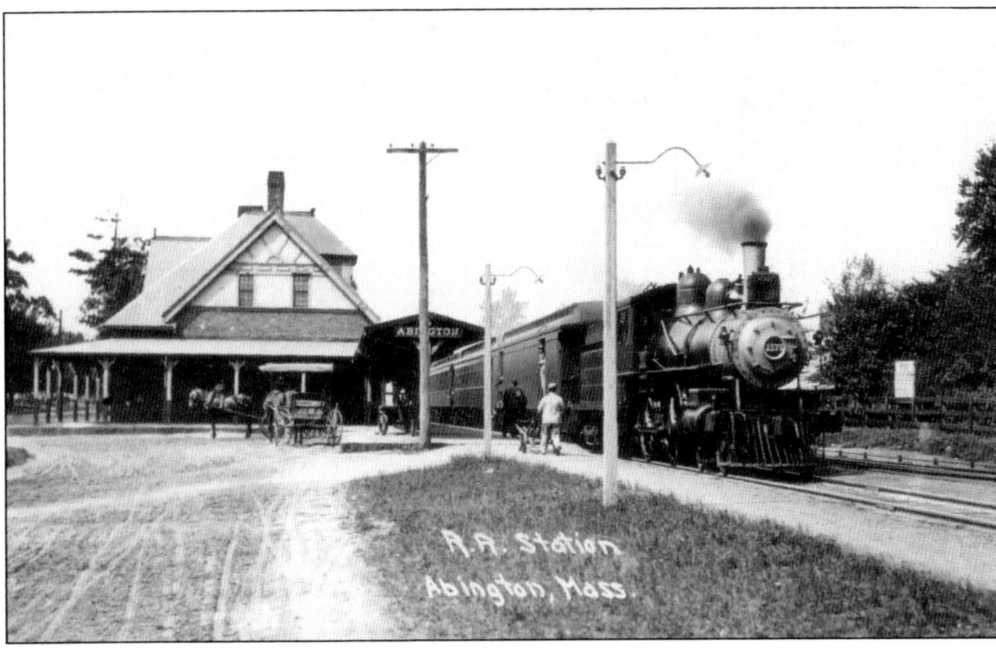

The Old Colony Railroad's Plymouth line was built in 1845. Abington's main station was built on Park Avenue at Centre Avenue, on the opposite side of the street from where the Massachusetts Bay Transportation Authority (MBTA) built a station for the commuter rail line in 1997. This 1911 view shows a southbound train as it stops at the depot. A passenger seems to be looking for his baggage before he takes one of the open carriages waiting at the station. The second carriage at the station may be waiting for the mail, which went to and from the trains by wagon each day. The locomotive is No. 1576. This engine appears in another photo postcard taken at Falmouth in 1911, when it pulled the famous "dude" train, a special charter that took wealthy men to Cape Cod daily in the summer from 1884 to 1916.

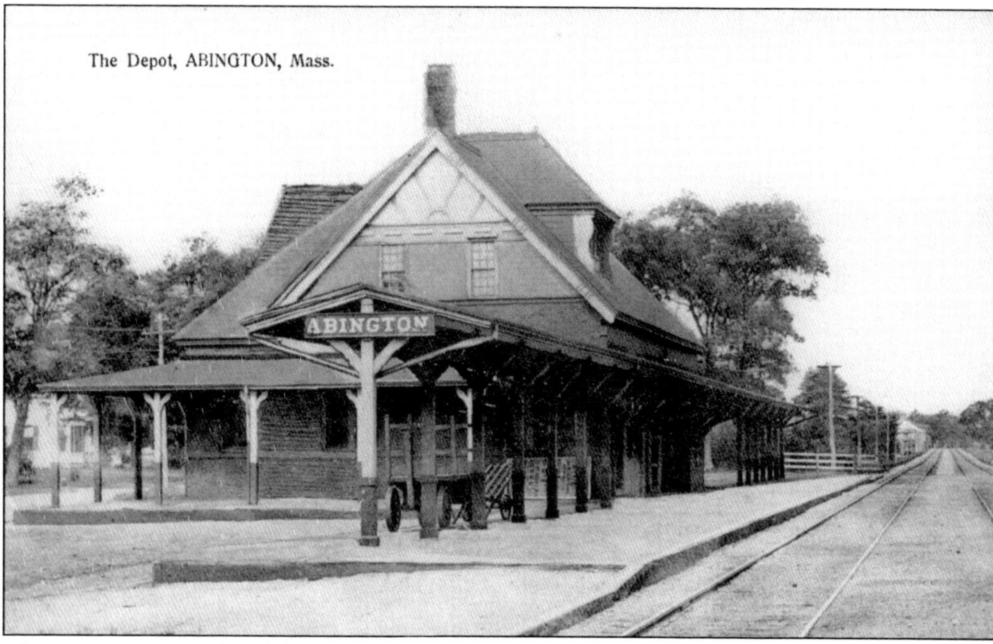

The New Haven Railroad shut down passenger service on the Old Colony line on June 30, 1959. The Centre Avenue depot lasted until 1963 before it was taken down. Coming at the flowering of the Industrial Revolution in the 1850s, the railroad in Abington was a sign of prosperity and convenience, enabling shoemakers to obtain raw materials and easily ship their products throughout the country.

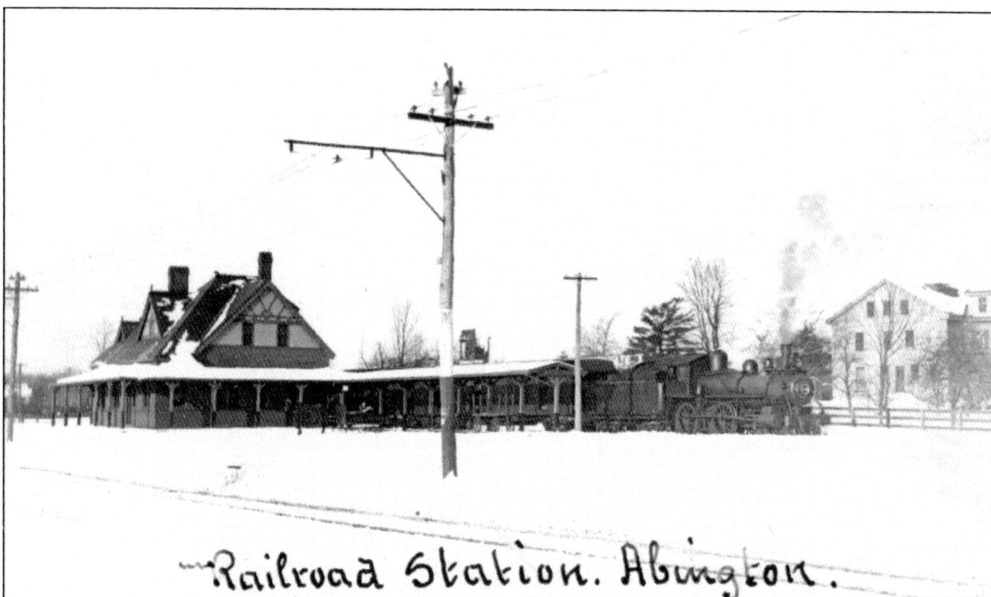

During all seasons, the train brought people, goods, and services to and from Abington. People from the region could commute to Boston, and salesmen from Boston could get to Abington. The train also enabled Boston abolitionists to travel and hold their large meetings at Island Grove. The building in the background is the Cobb and Thomson boot and shoe factory. The locomotive is No. 1592.

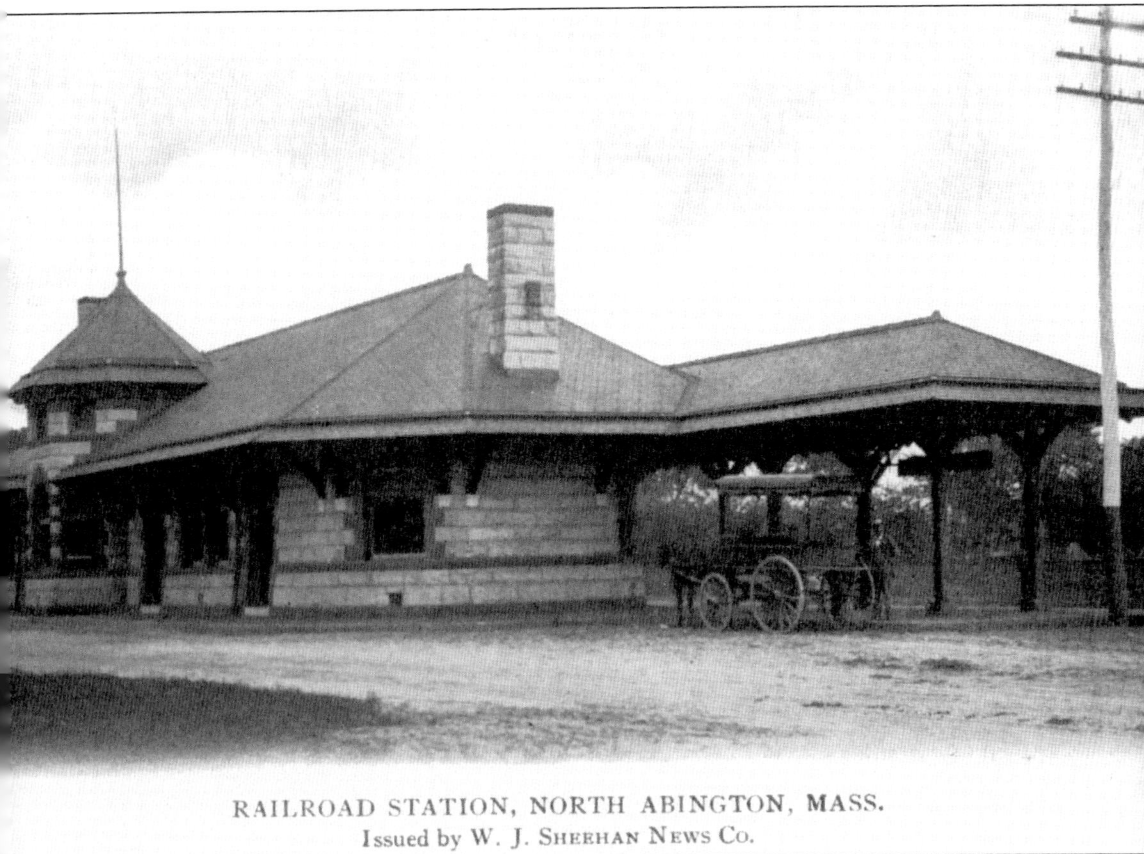

RAILROAD STATION, NORTH ABINGTON, MASS.
Issued by W. J. Sheehan News Co.

The Old Colony Railroad started construction of the North Abington railroad station building in 1893. In 1894, the station was finished, and the Old Colony had merged with the New York, New Haven and Hartford Railroad, becoming part of the New Haven branch. Architect Bradford L. Gilbert designed the station in a style influenced by Henry Hobson Richardson's Romanesque Revival. The Hanover branch line that started operations in 1868 and served Hanover and Rockland ended here. Passengers had to change to take the Boston train. When the service stopped altogether in the 1980s, this station was the object of a great preservation effort. Not even the arson fires in 1979 and 1984 that gutted the station stopped this 20-year effort. The station was rebuilt and used as a restaurant.

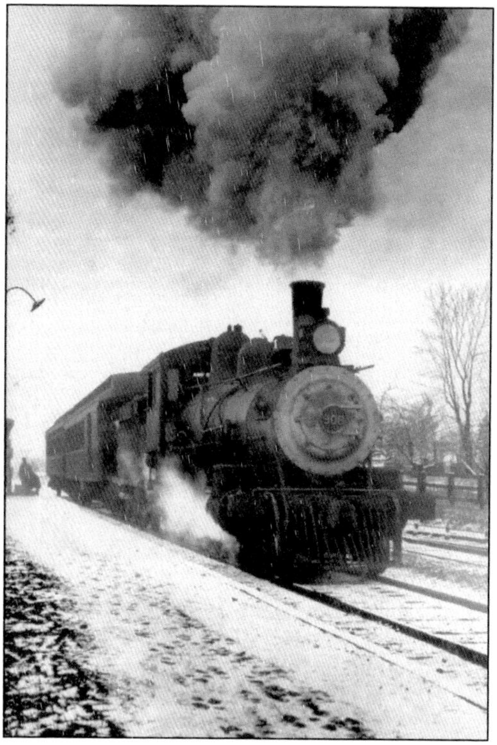

Locomotive 908 is pulling a passenger train south, just leaving the Abington depot. Note the person at the platform with his baggage and the light that angles towards the tracks.

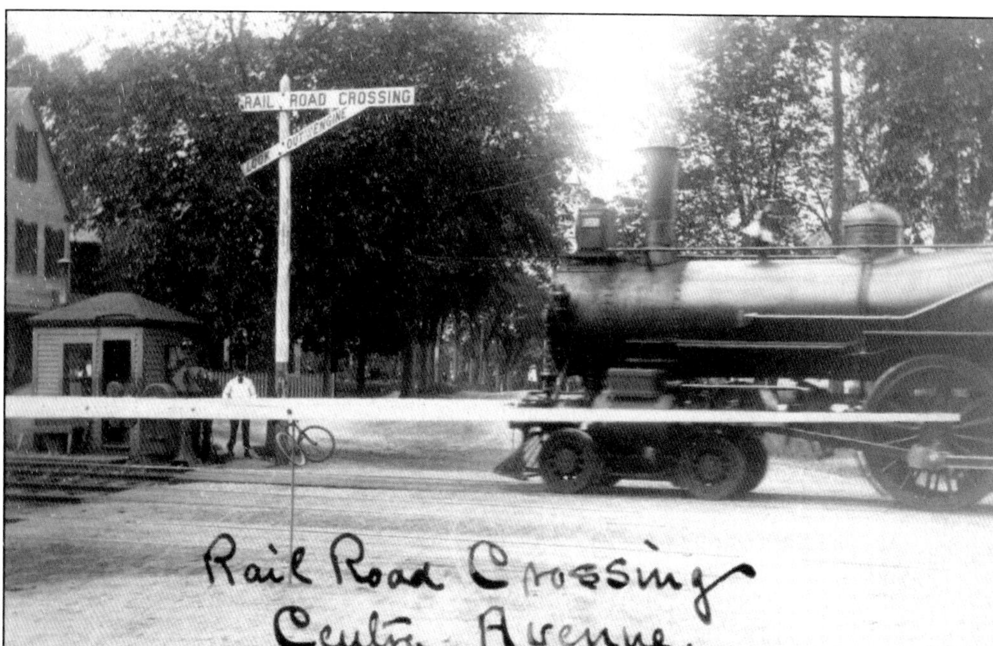

This train is crossing at Centre Avenue. The gateman stands ready to crank the gates up after the train has passed. On the gate stand are crank handles that enable the gates to be put up or down. The shack is for the gateman. The men who worked the gates were fixtures in the neighborhood, known by name, and had many brief visits throughout the day by people on the street.

712 ⁓ Two Hundredth Anniversary of the Old Town of Abington ⁓ 1912

Now Abington, Rockland and Whitman, Massachusetts

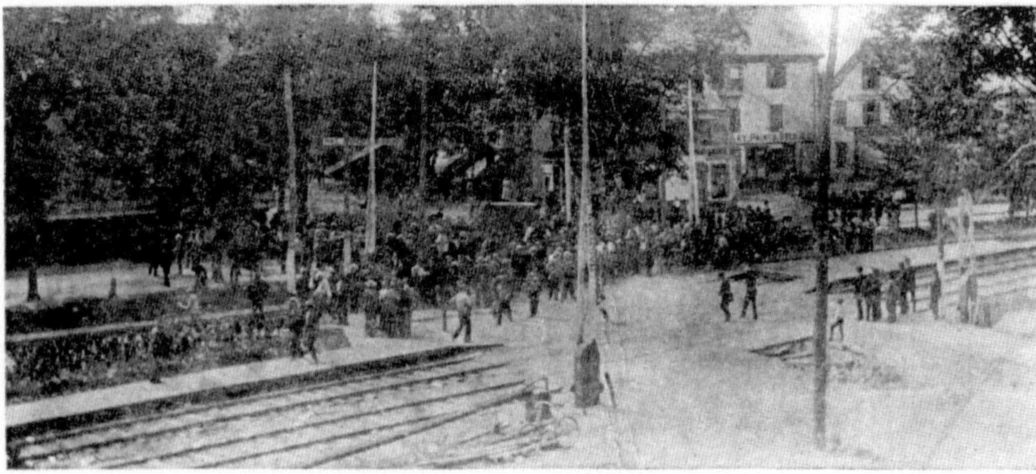

SCENE OF NORTH ABINGTON RIOT AUGUST 16, 1893

Dispute over right of Rockland & Abington Street Railway Co. to cross tracks of N. Y., N. H. & H. R. R. at North Avenue crossing. Pitched battle between constables and citizens and railroad employes.

Compliments of E. P. REED LUMBER CO., North Abington, Mass.

This photograph of the 1893 North Abington Riot was taken by Albert A. Haskell from the second floor of the E. P. Reed Lumber Company building. It was reissued as a postcard by the company in 1912 for the celebration of the 200th anniversary of the town of Abington. The riot occurred after the Abington and Rockland Street Railway Company received permission from the board of selectmen to lay tracks along North Avenue, crossing the New York, New Haven and Hartford Railroad tracks. The railroad maintained that it had a right-of-way and would not let the streetcar tracks pass over it. The town insisted that it owned the street, and the town only gave the railroad permission to make a street crossing with its tracks. On the day of the riot there was a standoff between the railroad employees and the street railway company workers when they tried to lay the streetcar tracks over the railroad tracks. The standoff led to a brawl that sent some to the hospital and others to jail. The fight was finally broken up when a telegram to the railroad boss arrived saying that a superior court judge had issued an injunction restraining the railroad from blocking the crossing over its tracks.

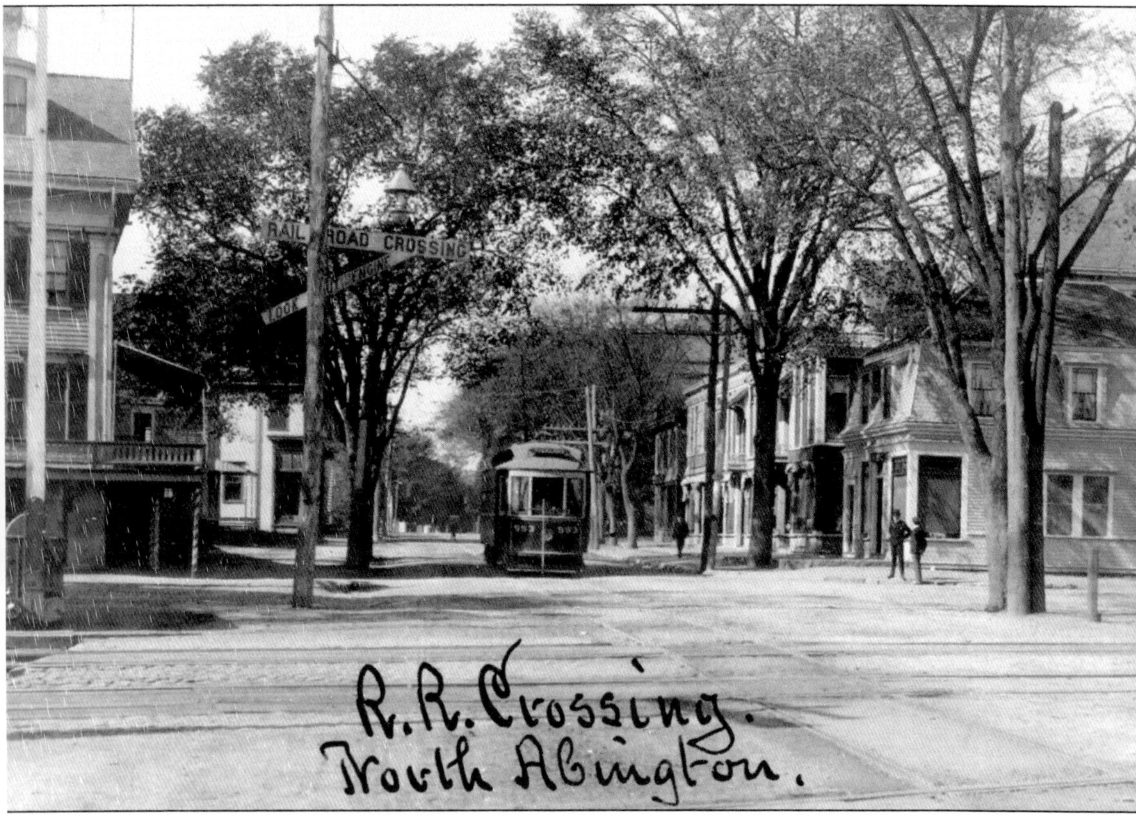

This is the crossing that was the scene of the famous riot in 1893. On this summer day *c.* 1900, the gates are up, and frogs have been installed to ensure the smooth crossing of the railroad tracks by the streetcar, which will peacefully cross without the notice of the bystanders on the street. The Greek Revival building on the left is the Culver House Hotel, at 223 North Avenue. Railroad officials stayed here the night before the riot in anticipation of a problem the next day. During the riot, it is reported that selectmen directed townspeople from the balcony seen in the postcard. The mansard-style building on the opposite side of the street, at 222 North Avenue, is the old North Abington post office, built in 1885. During the riot, the plate-glass windows of the first floor were broken by paving stones. Later, shards of the glass were sold as souvenirs. The round objects at the base of the railroad crossing gates are weights. The gateman could add or subtract weight as required by wind conditions.

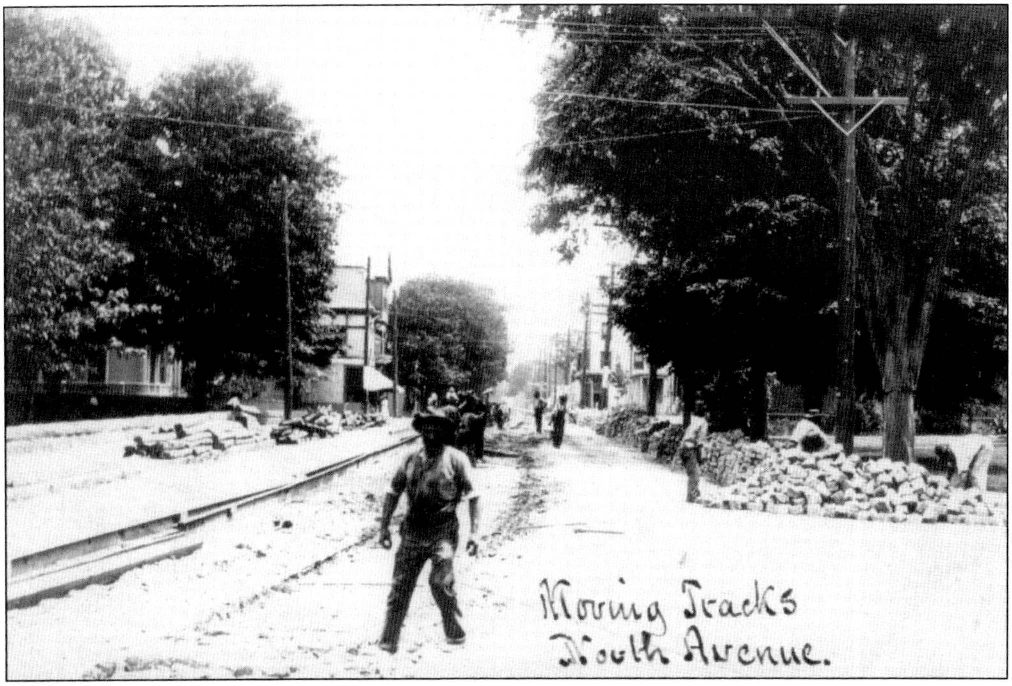

In 1893, the streetcar tracks were put down on North Avenue temporarily until the street was widened. This postcard view shows workers in the process of re-laying the tracks, probably in the summer of 1894. With this connection, trolley service was complete to and from Abington, Rockland, and Whitman.

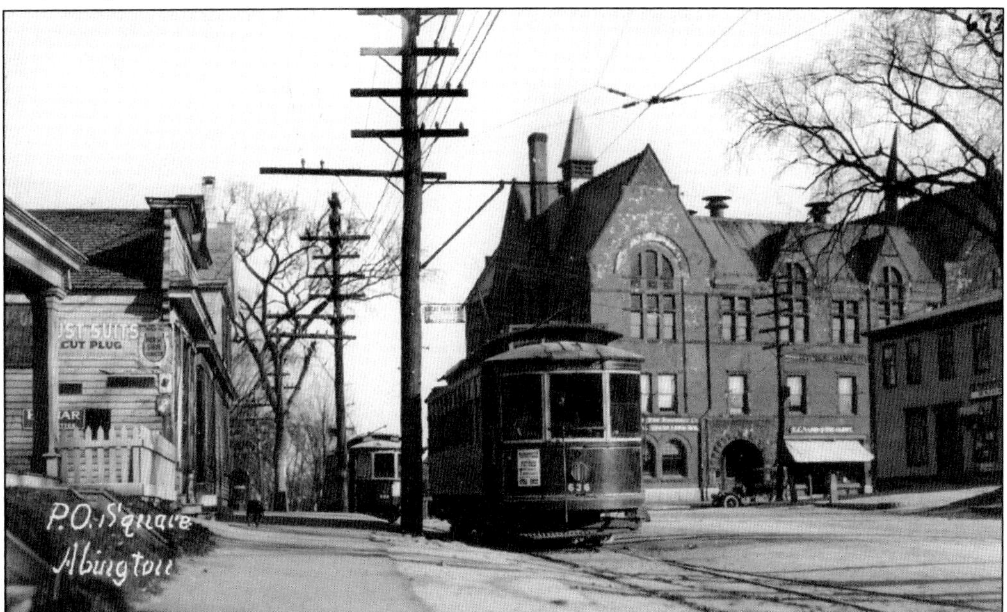

Abington's streetcar service started in 1892 and lasted until 1931. During the height of the street railway period, a person with enough time and transfers could have gone from Portland, Maine, to Washington, D.C. These large streetcars were headed for Brockton. The people of Abington thought it was just great to get to Nantasket Beach by streetcar.

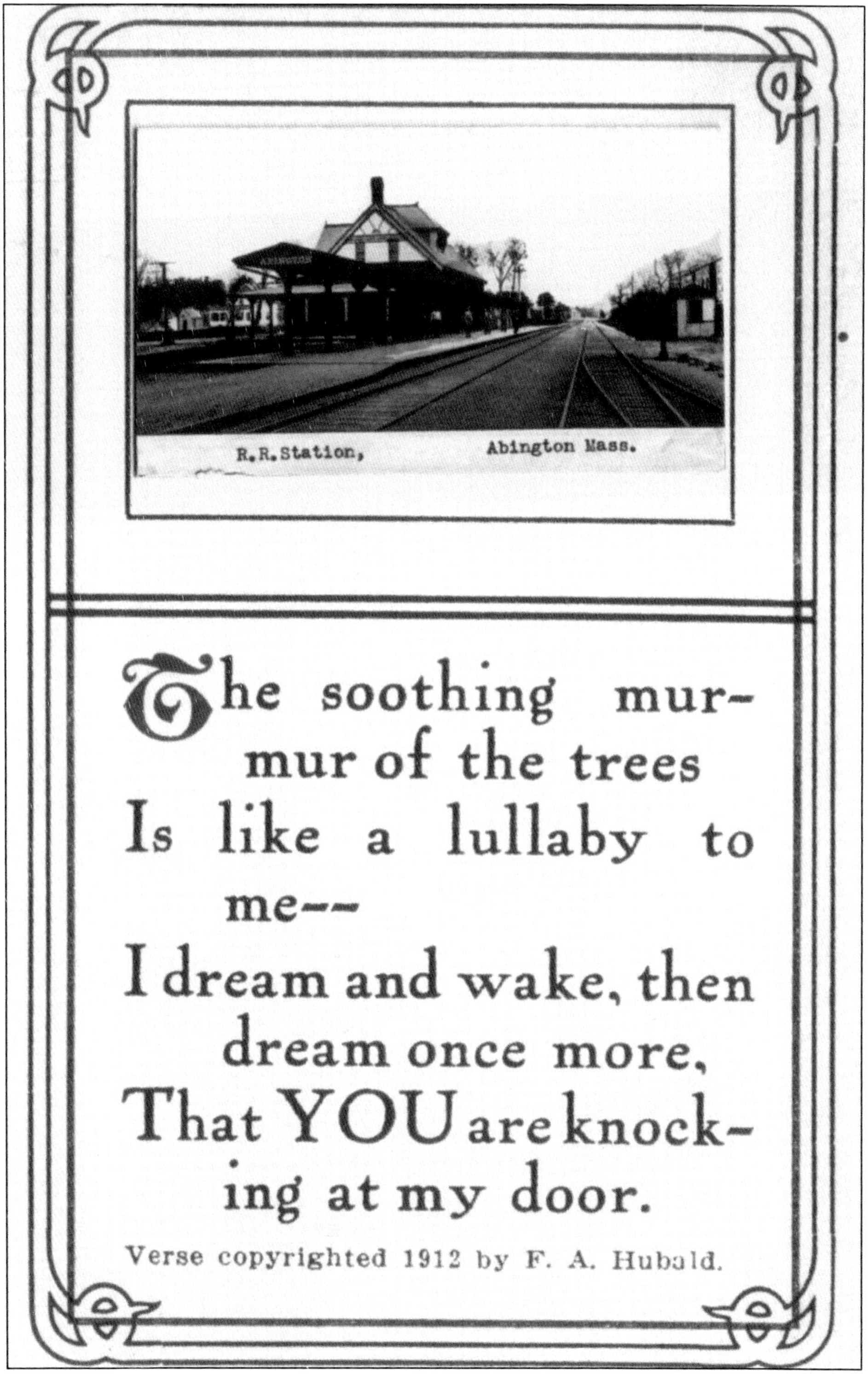

This is a postcard of Abington's main depot. The station looks lonely without a train. The photograph and poem beckon a return visit to Abington.

Five

The Pride of the Community

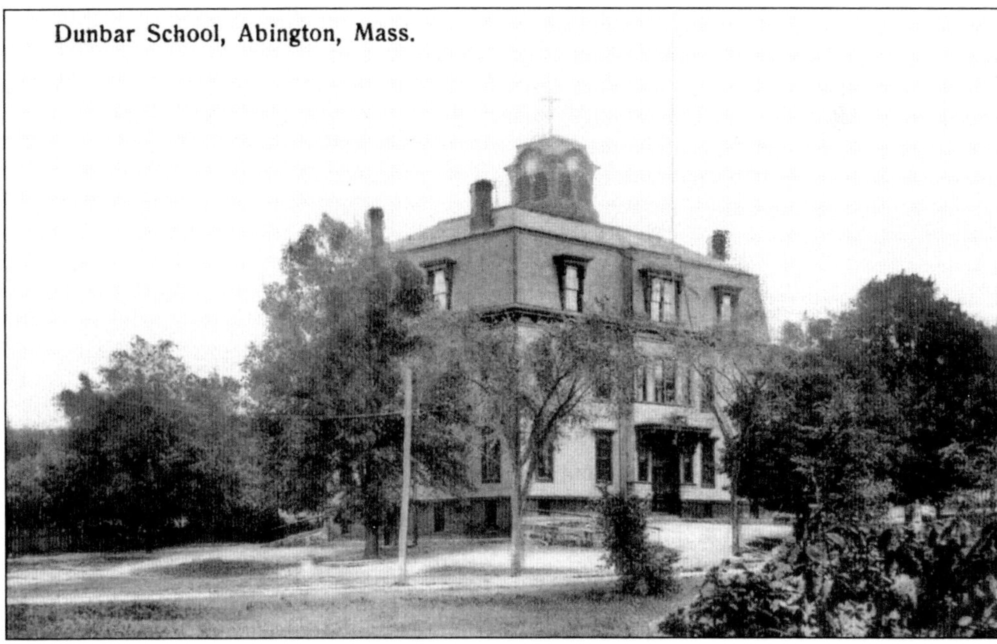

The first school in Abington was built in 1732 and was located near the church on Meetinghouse Hill. By the 1870s, the town was so spread out that three high schools were built, one in East Abington, one in South Abington, and one in Center Abington, each with a budget of $12,000. The schools for East Abington and South Abington came in at budget. The school in Center Abington, which was built on Dunbar Street, was over budget and cost $25,000. This was the last straw for those in East Abington who wanted to separate and form a new town; the town became Rockland in 1874. The Center Abington school was soon known as "the great Mansard abomination." After 14 years as the high school, this building became the Dunbar Street grammar school. Its end was not glorious, as it was finally sold, the top floor was taken off, and the building was converted into a frozen-food warehouse. In 1969, it was taken down to make way for apartment houses.

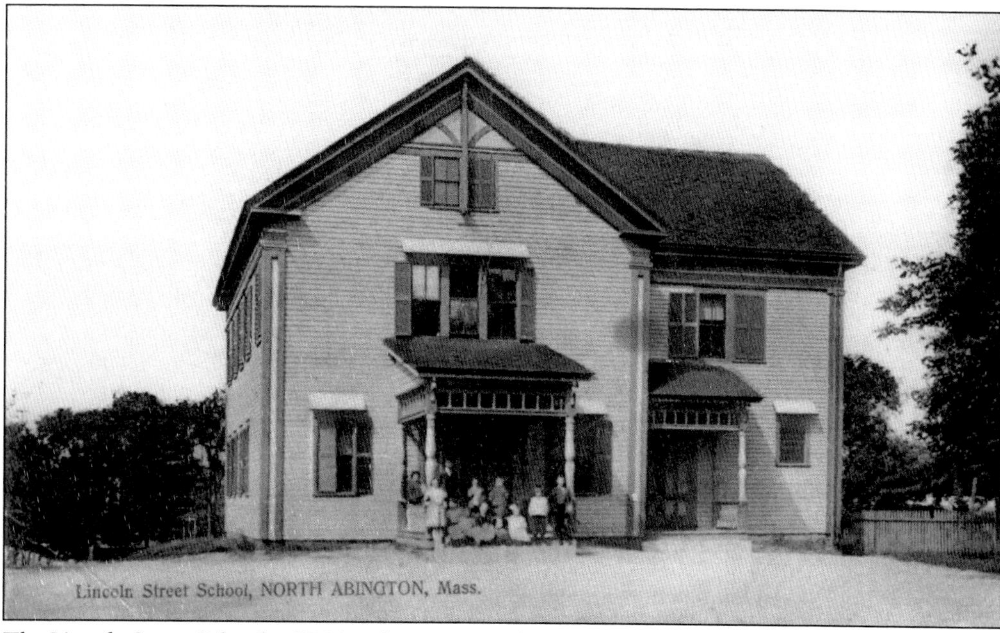

The Lincoln Street School at 77 Lincoln Street was built in 1854 and razed in 1913. Architecturally, it combines the old Greek Revival style, with wide corner boards, the entrance on the gable end, and turn backs at the roof line, and elements of the Victorian period, with porches featuring millwork and trim high up in the gable. This building's style is typical of the neighborhood schools in Abington in the mid-19th century.

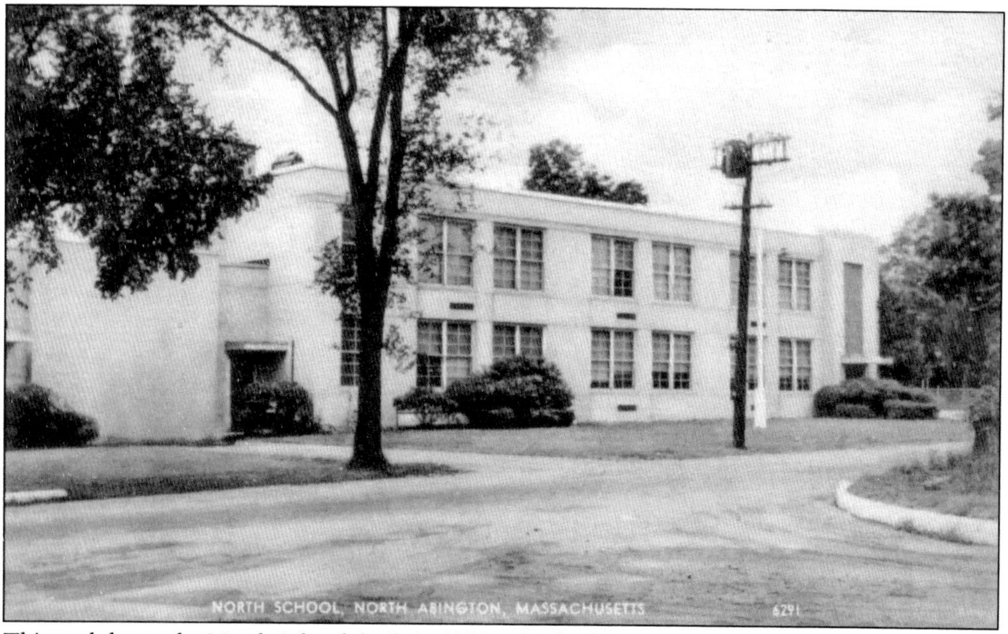

This card shows the North School, built in 1939. This building replaced the Adams Street School. It has a straightforward, practical design that was popular in the late 1930s for commercial and public buildings. Whereas schools built before the 1930s reflected an architectural style of the past, this school does not. It has a flat roof, the windows are well spaced, and the overall effect is of balance and strength, which gives an impression of an efficient and functional building.

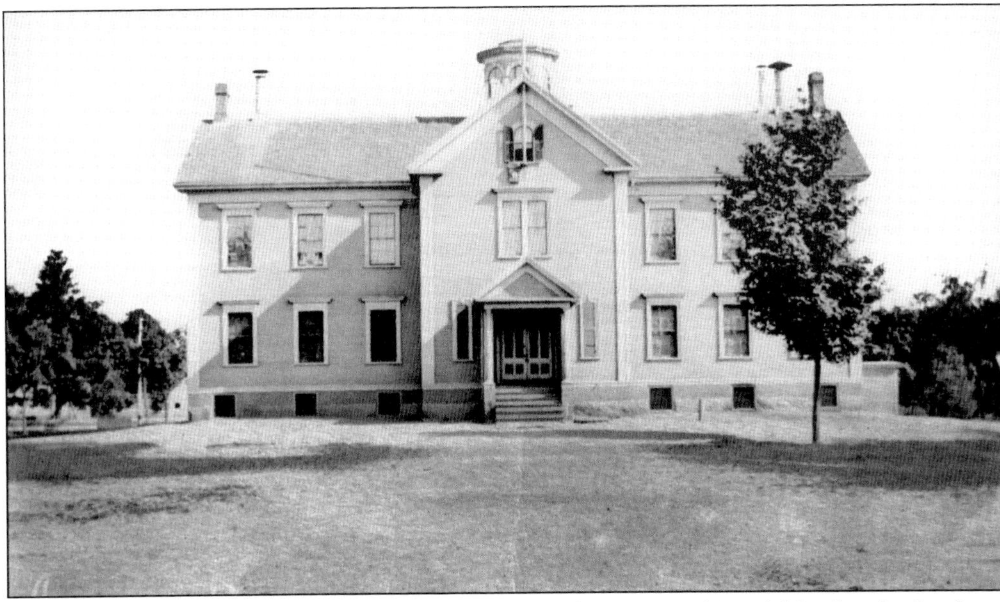

The Adams Street School was built in 1867 and razed in 1939. This neighborhood school was identical to the Church Street School in East Abington. Both had a cupola above the center axis. Although this school was built near the end of the popularity of the Greek Revival style, it is still considered within this style, with little hints of a change in tastes seen in the arches above some of the windows.

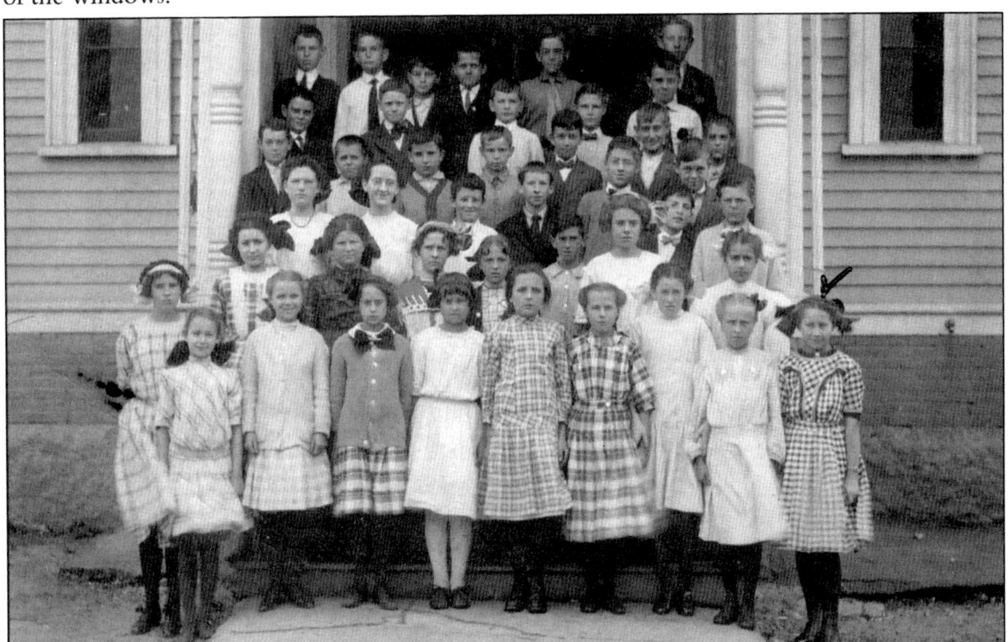

The students and teachers are unidentified in this 1911 photograph of the Adams Street School's seventh-grade class. The check mark certainly indicates the particular girl that the owner of the postcard wanted to point out. One of the results of publishing a book like this is that readers often add to a town's history by providing information that the authors were unable to find, in this case hopefully the names of the students in this postcard.

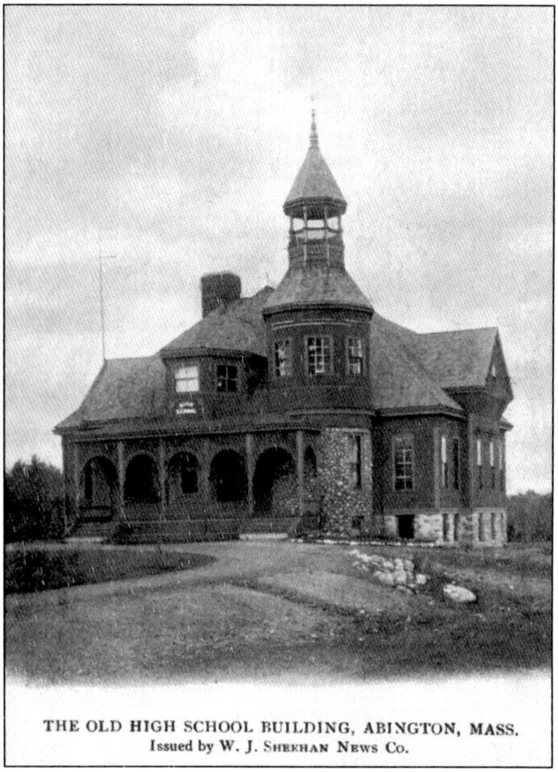

Abington built its first high school, located at 1027 Washington Street, in 1890. Before the existence of this building, the high school students were located in various other schools, having, in most cases, a floor of their own. This school opened with five classrooms and 61 students. By 1902, the high school students had to move again to a new larger building. The town rented this building as a residence. Later, it became known as the Memorial Building and the headquarters for the Lewis V. Dorsey Post No. 112 of the American Legion.

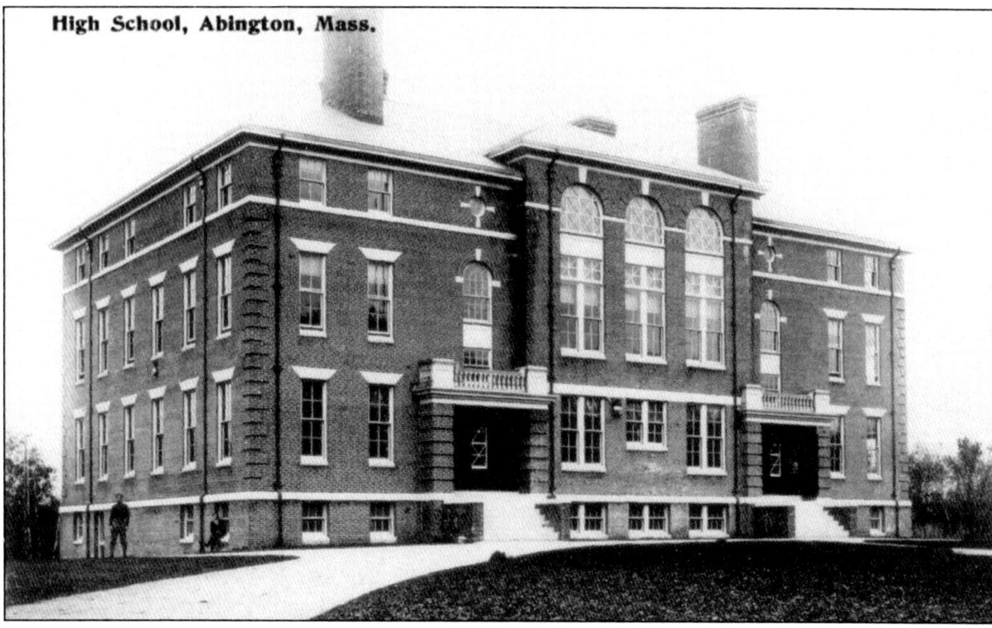

In 1903, Abington opened a high school built just south of the first school on Washington Street. The building was constructed of brick and was in the Georgian Revival style, popular for schools at the turn of the 19th century and into the 20th century. On December 18, 1934, fire destroyed this building. The fire started in the chemistry lab and there was not enough water in the standpipe to give proper water pressure to extinguish the fire, resulting in a total loss.

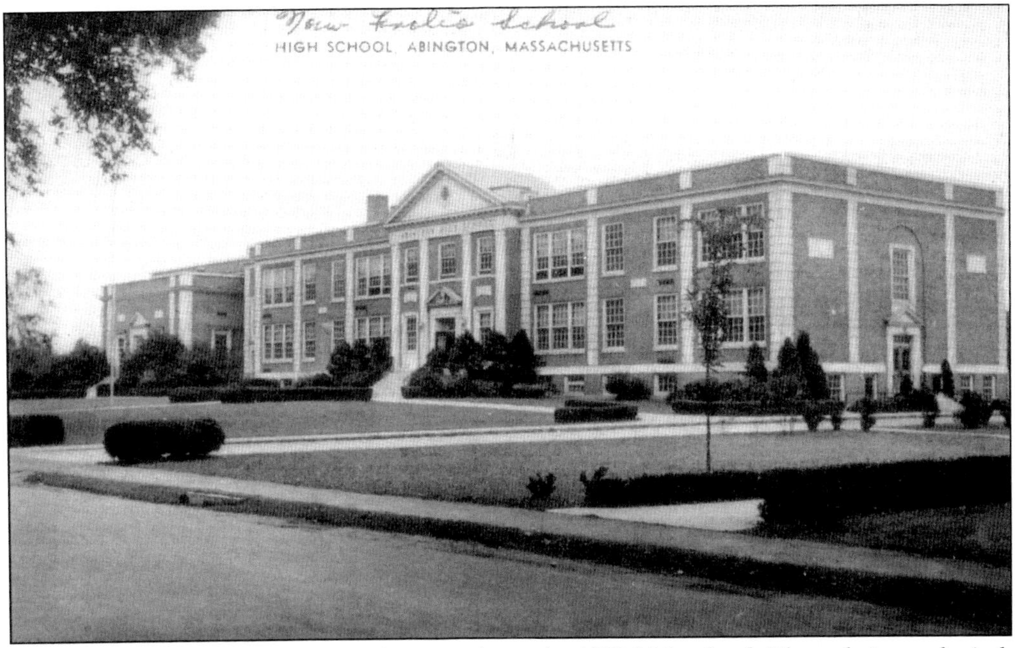

This building was built in 1937 on the same site as the 1903 high school. The style is neoclassical. Between the loss of the old building and the construction of this one, high school students had their classes in the administration building of the Crossett Shoe Company on Birch Street. In 1962, this building became a junior high, named after its beloved principal Charles M. Frolio.

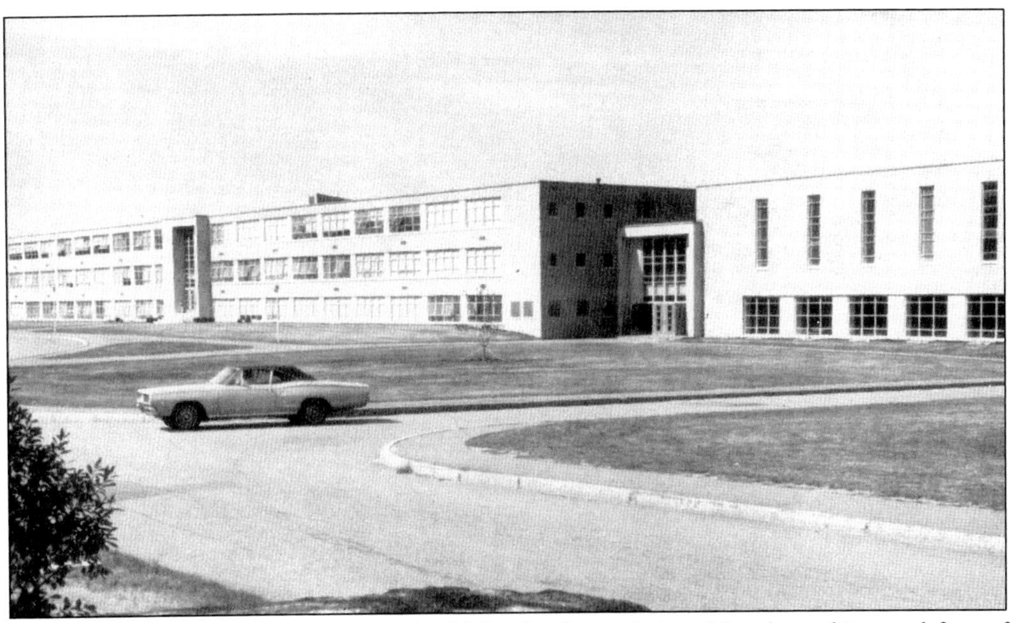

Dedicated to the youth of Abington, this high school was designed by the architectural firm of Aisner and Atwood in 1962 in the International Style. Its efficient and functional designs appealed to school building committees in the 1950s and 1960s. The style was popular for commercial buildings and schools but generally not for houses. This was a time when the baby boomers were in the school systems and there was a need to expand resources to meet their needs.

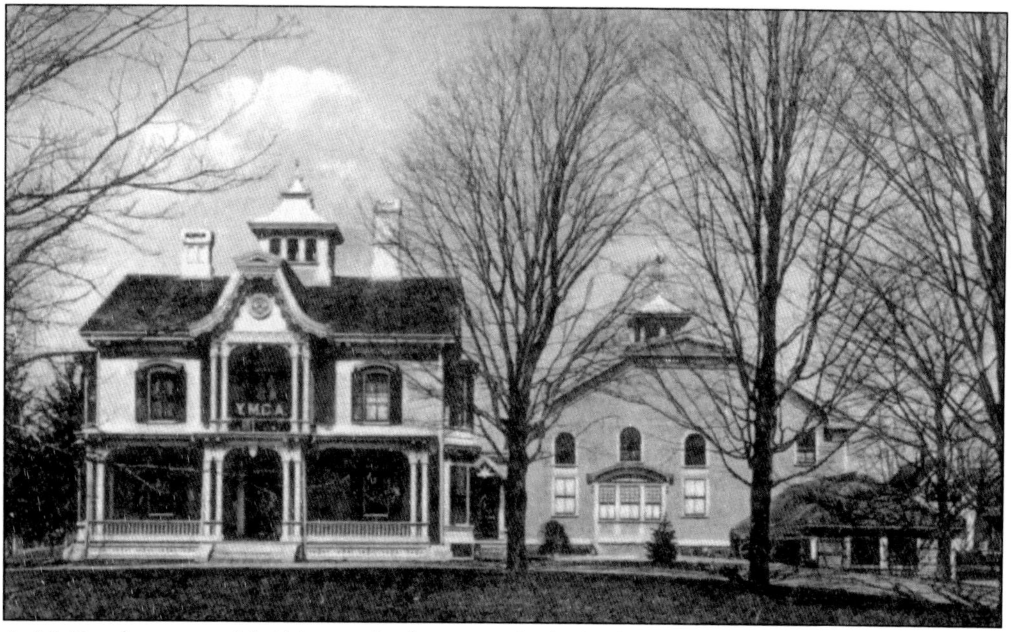

A. N. Reed, a successful Abington businessman, built this house *c.* 1870 at the north corner of Adams Street and North Avenue. It is a good example of the type of houses that were being built by business leaders following the Civil War. The house is, however, best known as the site of the YMCA. It was taken down in 1964. A gas station replaced it.

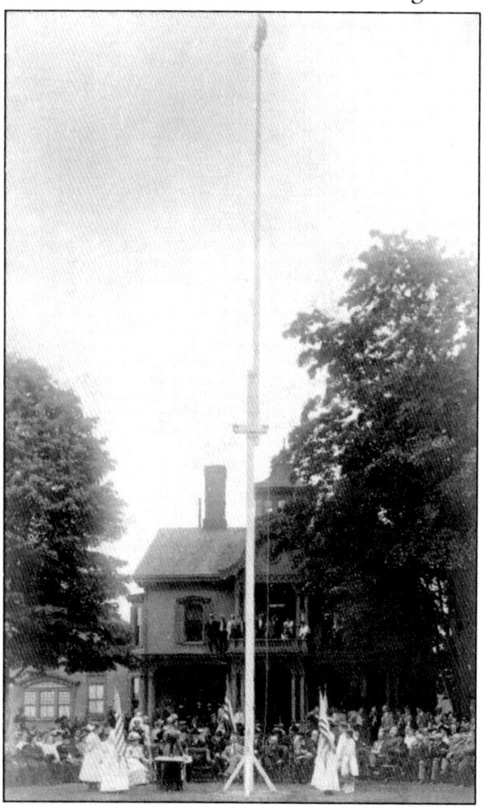

This is the dedication of the flagpole at the YMCA during the bicentennial celebration in 1912. This was most likely Tuesday, July 11, for that was children's day in the week-long celebration. This is no doubt in the morning, as the days turned out to be very hot and humid. According to the newspaper, by the afternoon the young and old were sweltering with heat and sunstroke.

This is the fire station that was built at Dunbar and Bank Streets in 1883. There were two stations built at the same time. The other one was at Brighton Street in North Abington. The tower at the rear was used to dry hoses after a fire.

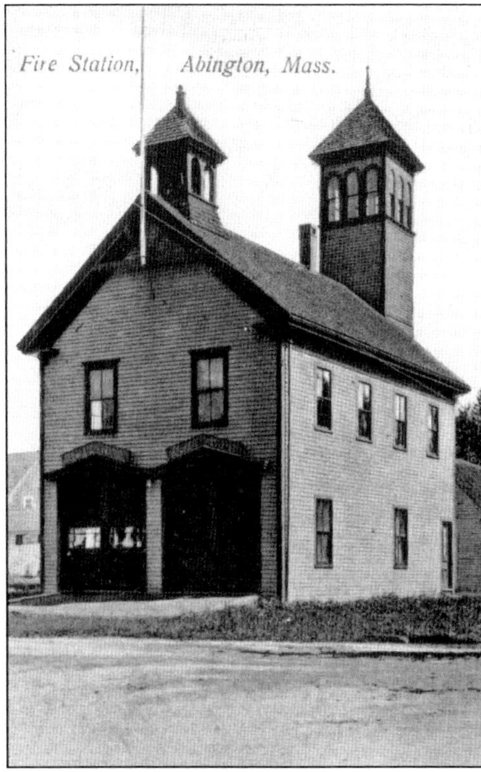

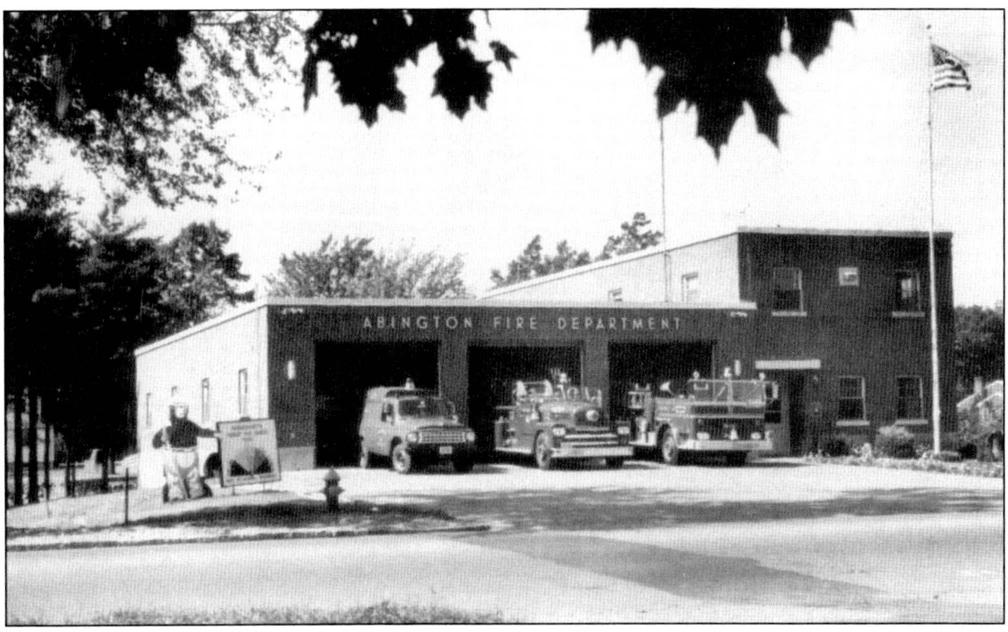

This postcard was made shortly after the Bedford Street fire station was opened in 1964. In the late 1950s, the need to modernize and relocate the fire station was apparent. Architect Frederick H. Gagnon of Worcester was selected based on his reputation of designing efficient and economical fire stations. Showing a Smokey the Bear sign on the lawn, this view gives the impression that Abington was a rural place in the 1960s.

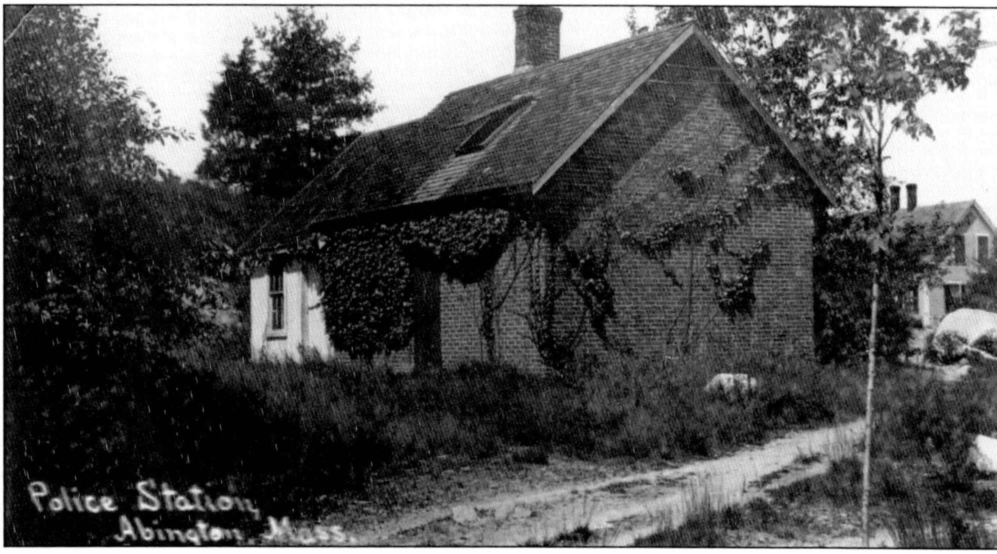

In the 1910 town report, Chief John F. Hollis complained that the two police stations, one in Center Abington and one in North Abington, were unfit. He suggested that the lockup in North Abington be enlarged and "fitted up in a proper manner." The one in Center Abington on Lake Street was in such decay he suggested it be abandoned and "a room in the bank block fitted up with four modern steel cells." One of the frequent guests, Bricky Welch, was sprung by his friends one night. With the help of a ladder and a sledgehammer, they smashed in the bars and got Bricky free, according to the reminiscences of Arthur W. Nash in 1962.

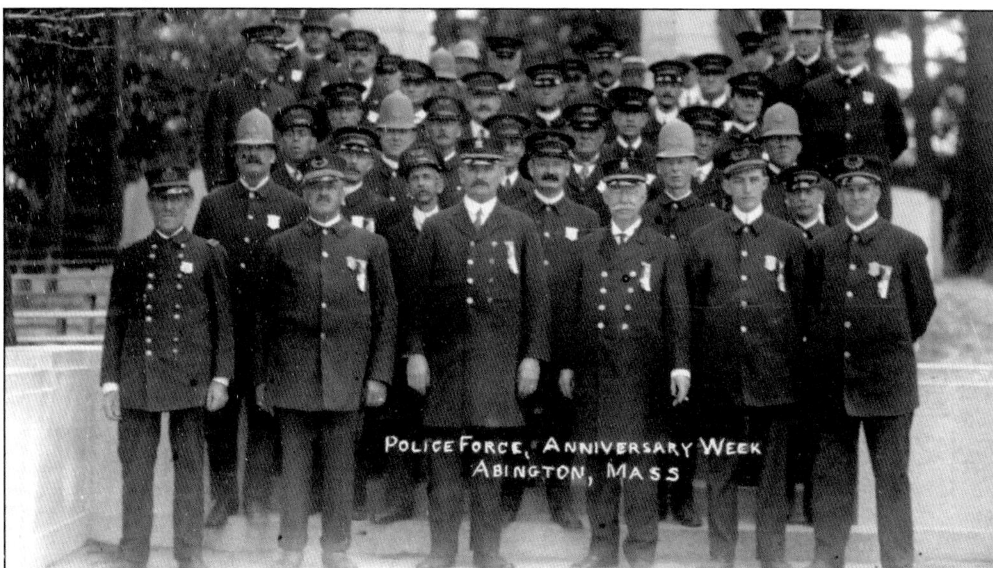

This is a good example of a postcard made at the time of the bicentennial celebration that was saved as a souvenir of the event. Police departments in the United States admired and modeled themselves on the London metropolitan police and adopted their style of uniform. Over time, a more American uniform for police was developed. The officers are posing in front of the memorial arch on the day it was dedicated, Monday, June 10, 1912, a beautiful day just before a hot spell. Chief John F. Hollis, who in 1909 advocated for uniforms for his department, is in the front row.

Six

PLACES OF WORSHIP

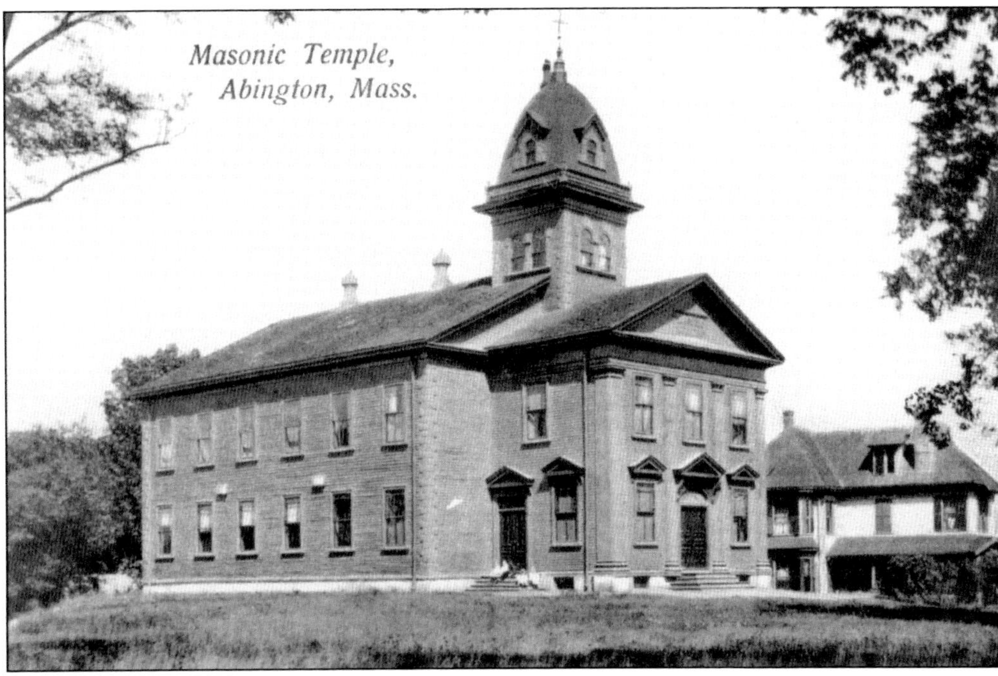

The center of village life in colonial Massachusetts was the church, and that church was of the Congregational denomination until just before the mid-19th century. In Abington, the first church was built upon Meetinghouse Hill in 1711. The second Congregational Church building, constructed in 1751, was known as the "blue church." Timbers of this old church were salvaged when it was torn down and were used in the third building at 416 Washington Street. The Masonic temple building was originally the third structure of the Congregational Church. There is evidence that curved planks of white oak, originally destined for the USS *Constitution,* were used in the construction of this building, which was the location of abolitionist meetings in the decade before the Civil War. The most notable of these meetings took place when George Thompson, an English abolitionist, came on October 15, 1859. A hostile crowd stoned the church, and he escaped through a back window in fear of his life. The district court of Plymouth County met here to conduct the North Abington Riot trial on August 23, 1893.

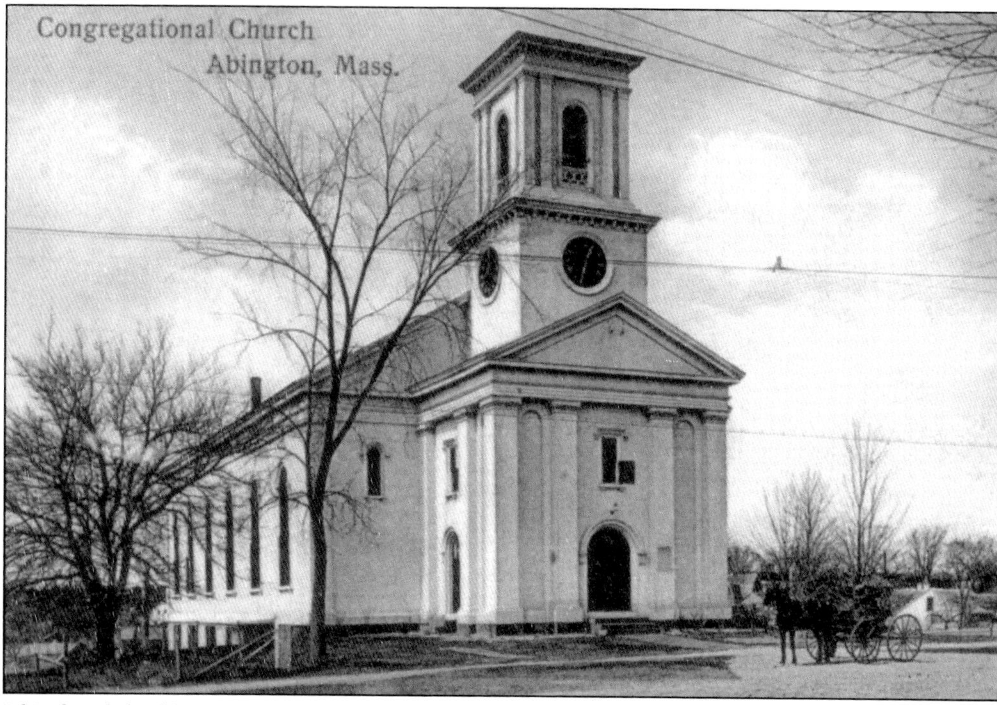

This fourth building of the First Congregational Church, located at 400 Washington Street, was built in 1849 in the Greek Revival style. It replaced the building that came to be known as the Masonic temple. All four churches were known as the First Congregational Church of Abington. In 1960, this church, like many New England Congregational churches, joined the Evangelical and Reformed Churches to become the Abington United Church of Christ.

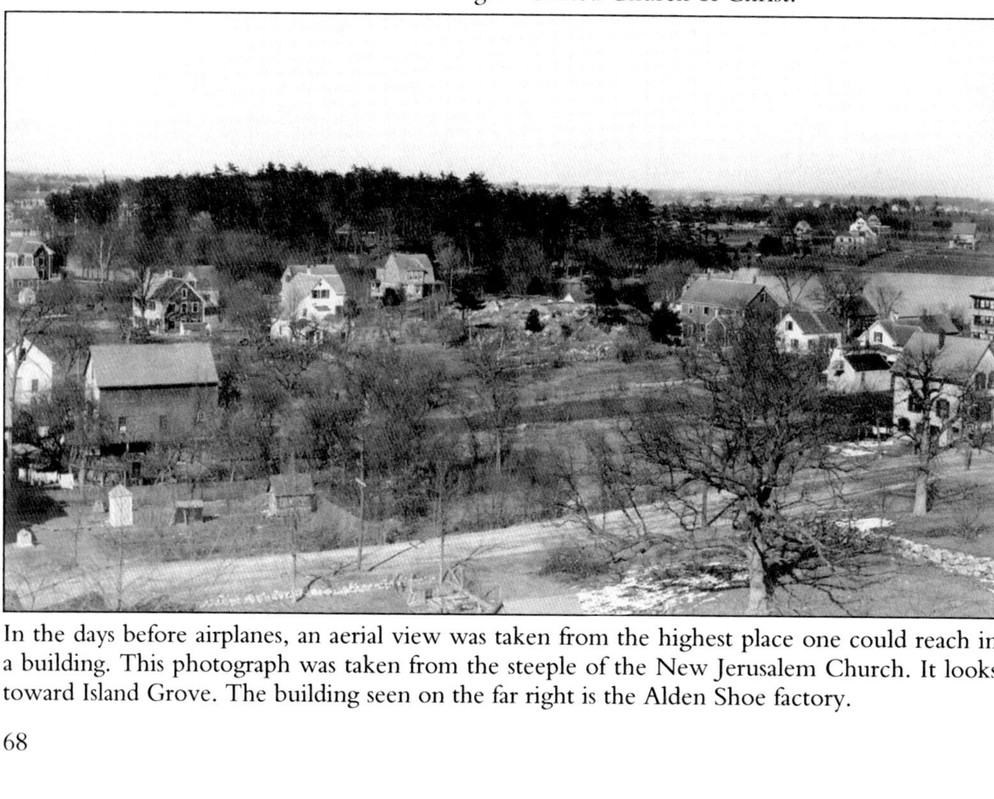

In the days before airplanes, an aerial view was taken from the highest place one could reach in a building. This photograph was taken from the steeple of the New Jerusalem Church. It looks toward Island Grove. The building seen on the far right is the Alden Shoe factory.

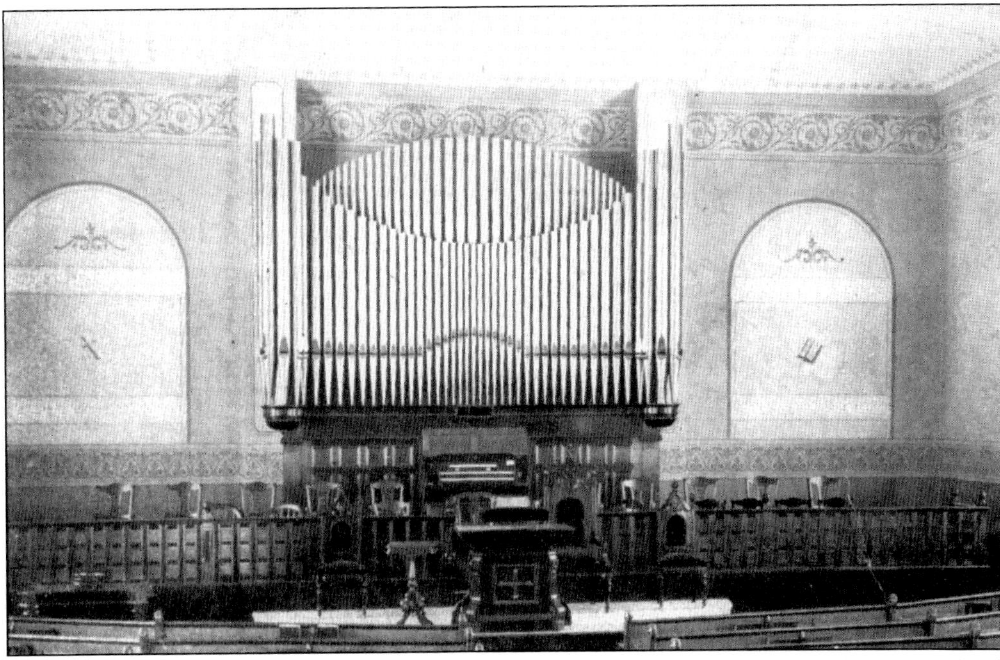

This is an interior view of the North Congregational Church, which was located at 33 Randolph Street. Postcard views of the interiors of churches are scarce. The organ is an Estey pipe organ manufactured in Brattleboro, Vermont, by the Estey Organ Company.

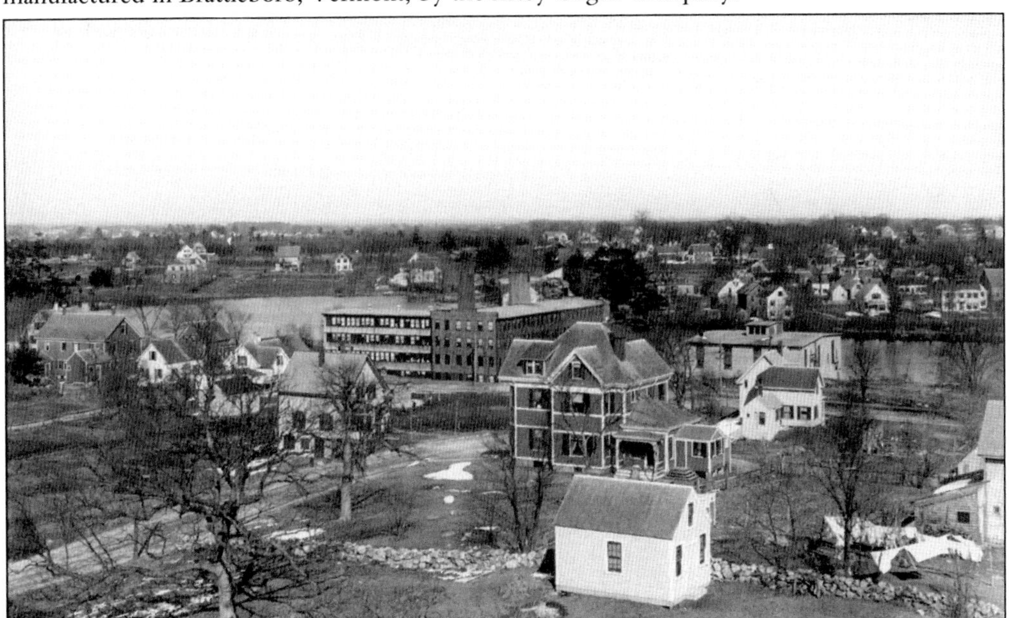

This postcard is the second in a set of two. Seen are the Alden Shoe Company and the power plant used for the street railway system, both on Lake Street. The house in the center is 35 Cliff Street. This was the home of John Coughlan and his wife, Kathaleen. John was an attorney and served as town clerk for 20 years, and upon his death in 1943, Kathaleen served as town clerk for another 20 years. She also started the Coughlan Country Day School in her home. It was the forerunner of Abington's kindergarten.

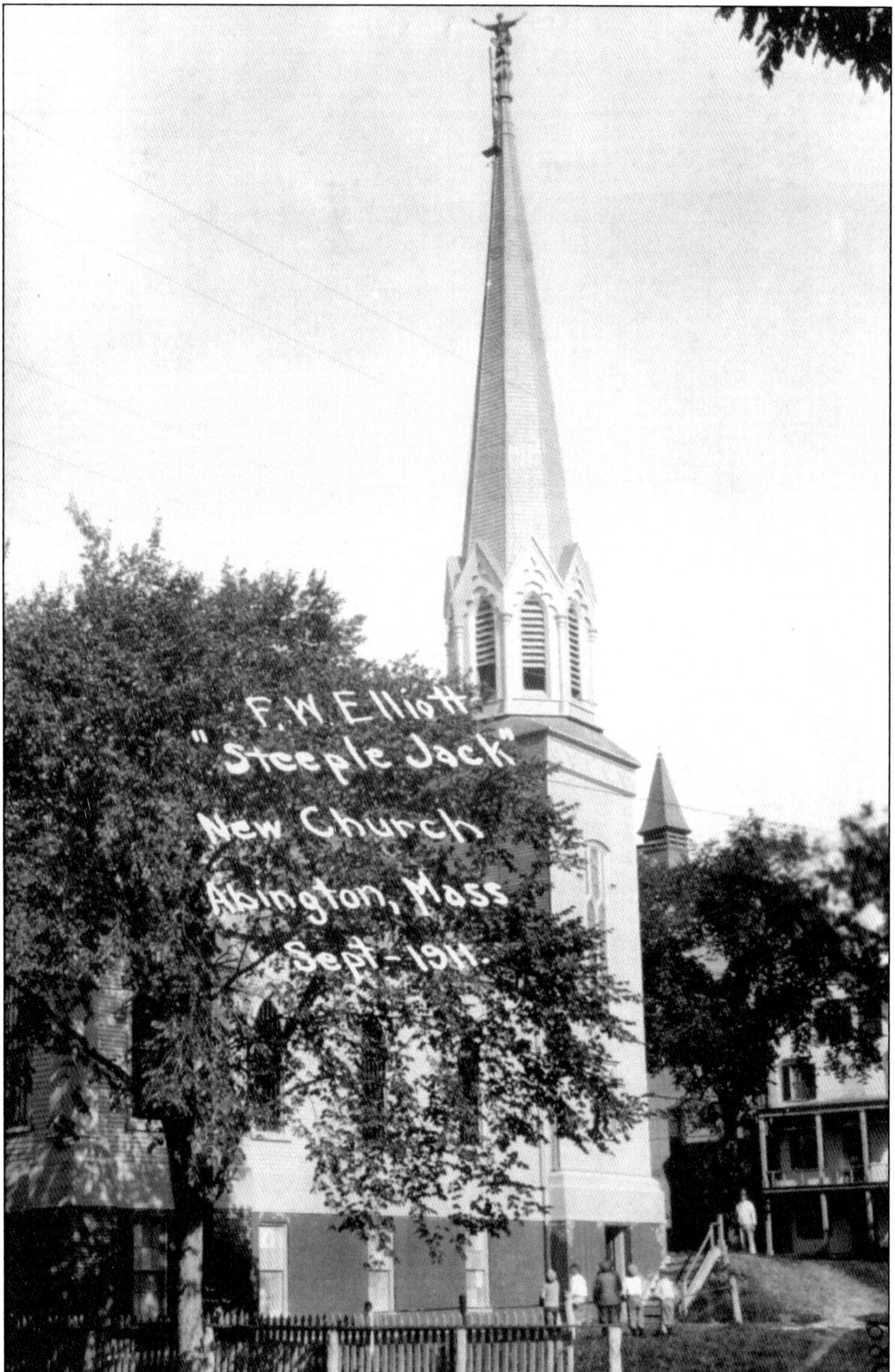

This unusual postcard shows off F. W. Elliot, the steeplejack at the very top of the Swedenborgian Church.

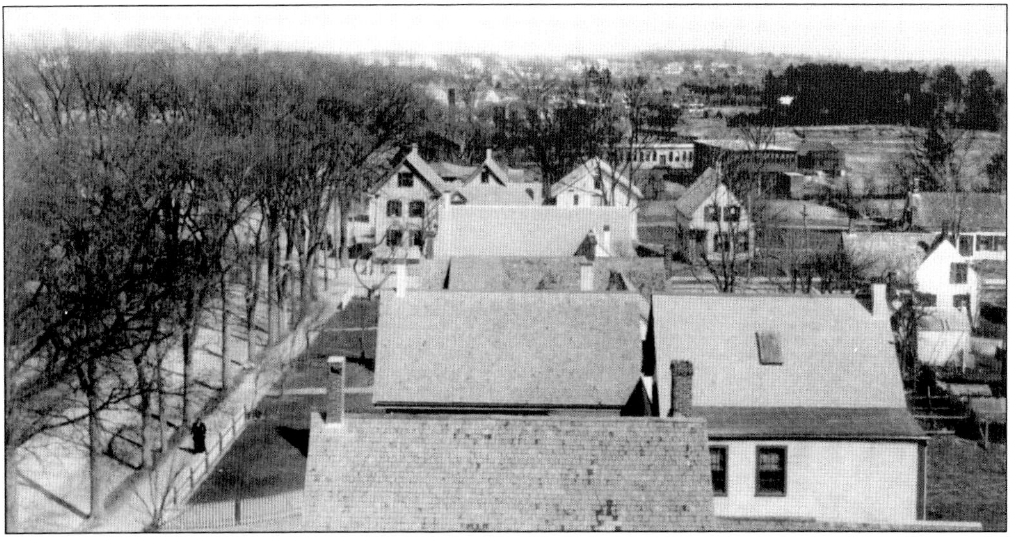

This photograph was taken from the steeple of the Swedenborgian Church on Centre Avenue. The building was sold and became the Glad Tidings Assembly of God Church. The view looks toward Rockland, where the standpipes on Beech Hill are visible on the horizon. The photograph was taken no earlier than 1912, for it was in that year the second standpipe was constructed.

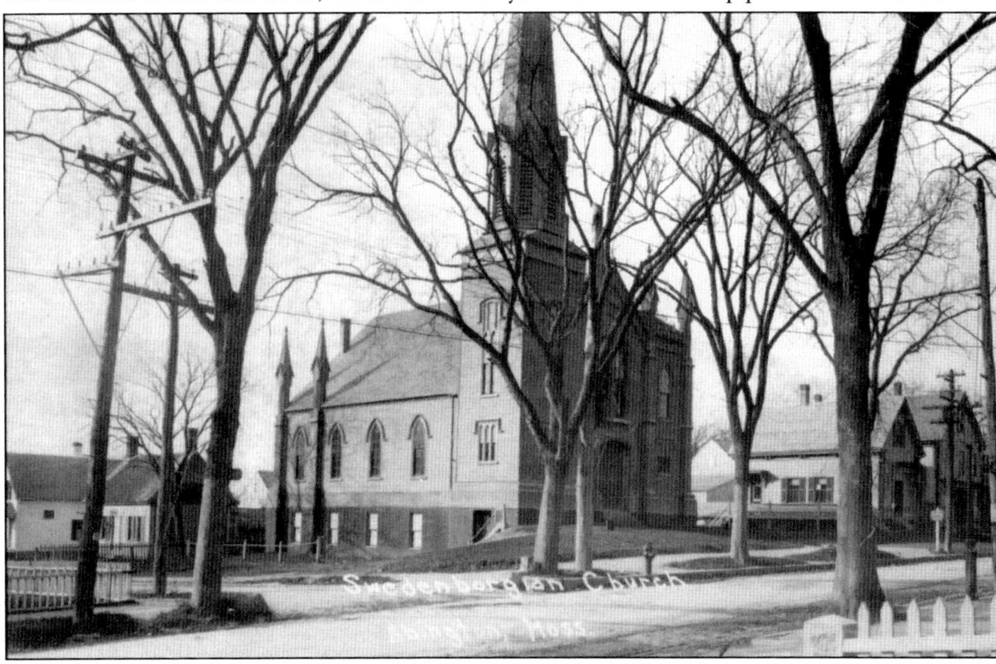

The Swedenborgian Church, also known as the Church of the New Jerusalem, was built in 1834 in early Gothic Revival style. It stood at 19 Centre Avenue and was taken down in 1998 to make way for the Abington Savings Bank drive-through window facility. The Swedenborgian denomination started in England in 1787, and its beliefs were based on the writings of Emmanuel Swedenborg (1688–1772). The church was brought to North America by an Englishman named James Glen. John Chapman, also known as Johnny Appleseed, was a missionary of the church. Ralph Waldo Emerson, as well as other transcendentalists, was influenced by Swedenborg's work. Helen Keller belonged to the denomination.

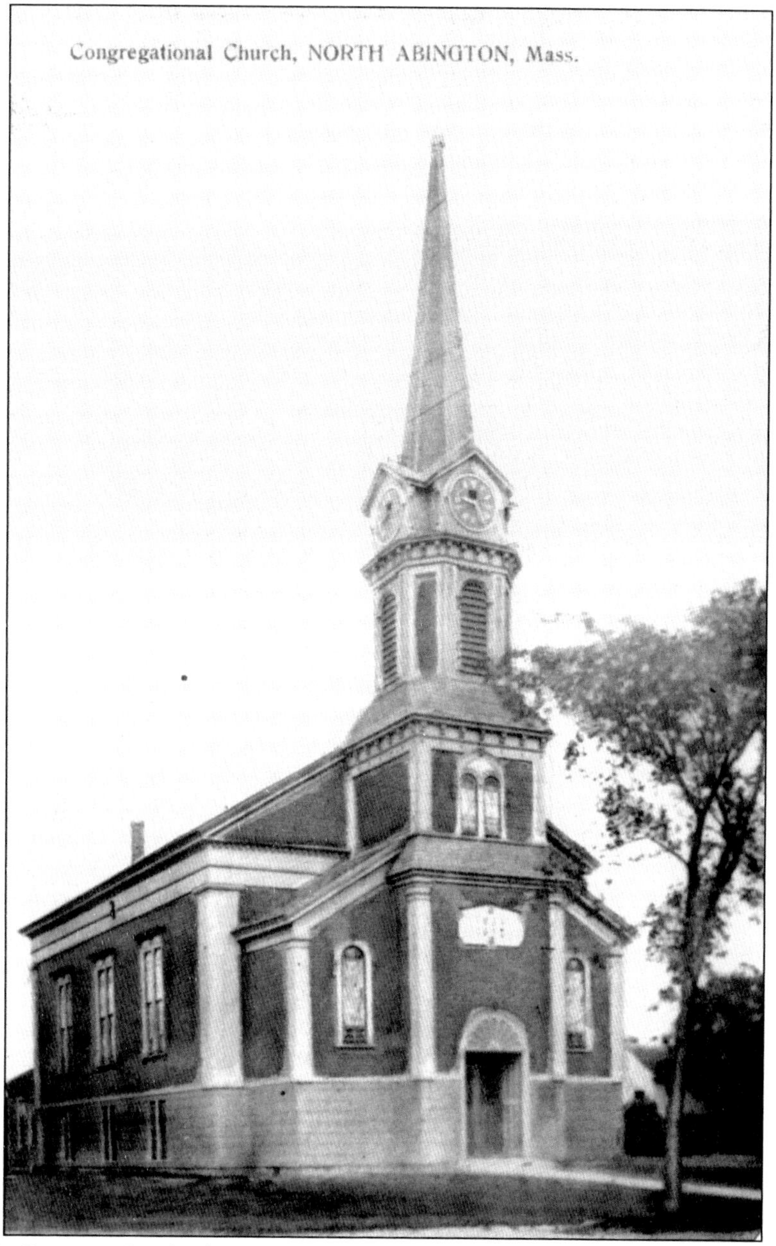

The North Congregational Church, at 33 Randolph Street, was built in 1833 in the Greek Revival style. In the postcard, the church looks as if it has been jacked up to allow a full basement. The pilasters on the corners do not go to the ground, and the foundation seems to allow for a ground floor. This congregation broke from the first parish in 1839 and rejoined it in 1970. The empty building became the town hall until 1998, when the town offices moved to new quarters. The building was sold and converted into apartments. Rev. Jesse H. Jones, a longtime minister of this church, was well known for escaping death at the battle of Gettysburg by wearing a breastplate that absorbed the impact of a bullet. He was also active in the labor movement, supported voting rights for women, wrote books and newspaper columns, and served in the Massachusetts legislature.

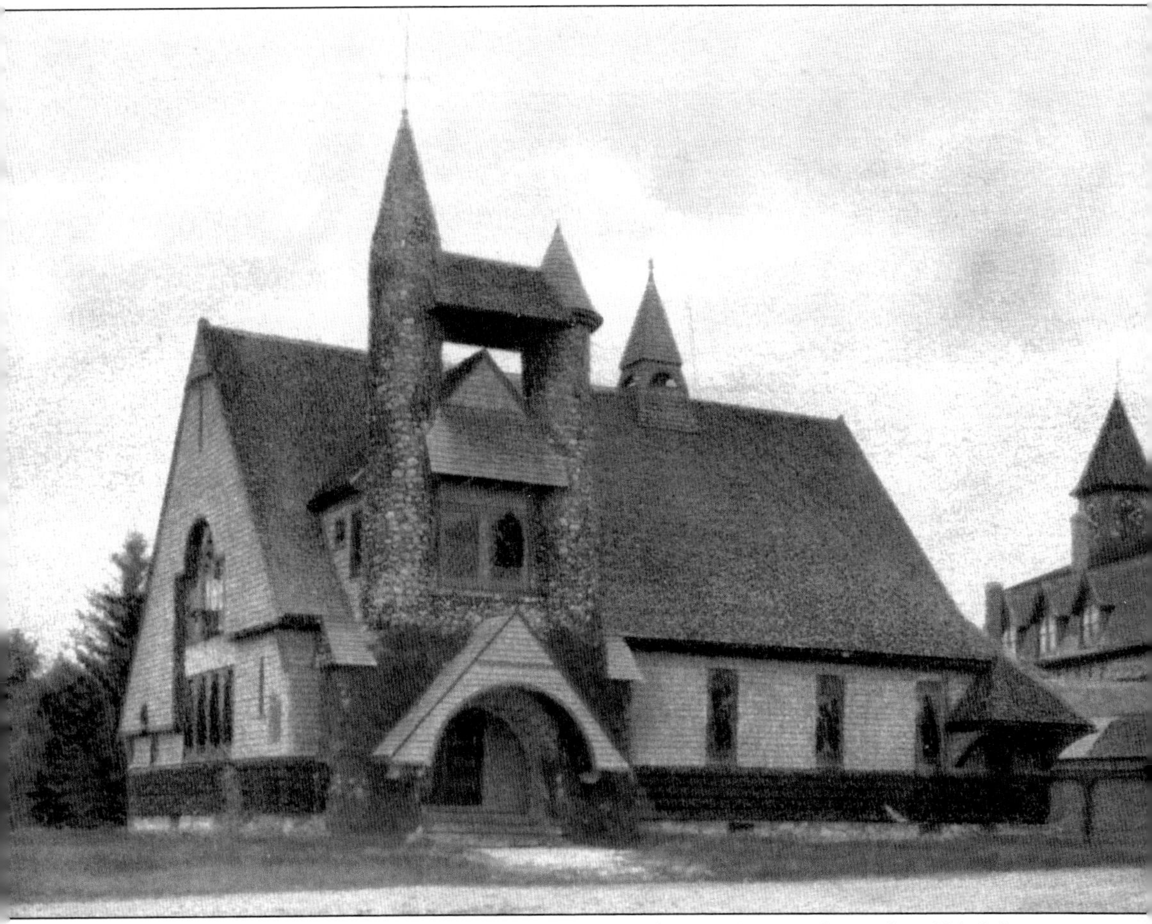

The First Baptist Church was built in the Queen Anne style in 1887. It is located at 231 Adams Street. The Baptists organized in 1886 under the leadership of the high school principal, George E. Wales. The stonework in this church makes it one of the most interesting buildings in Abington and an excellent subject for a postcard.

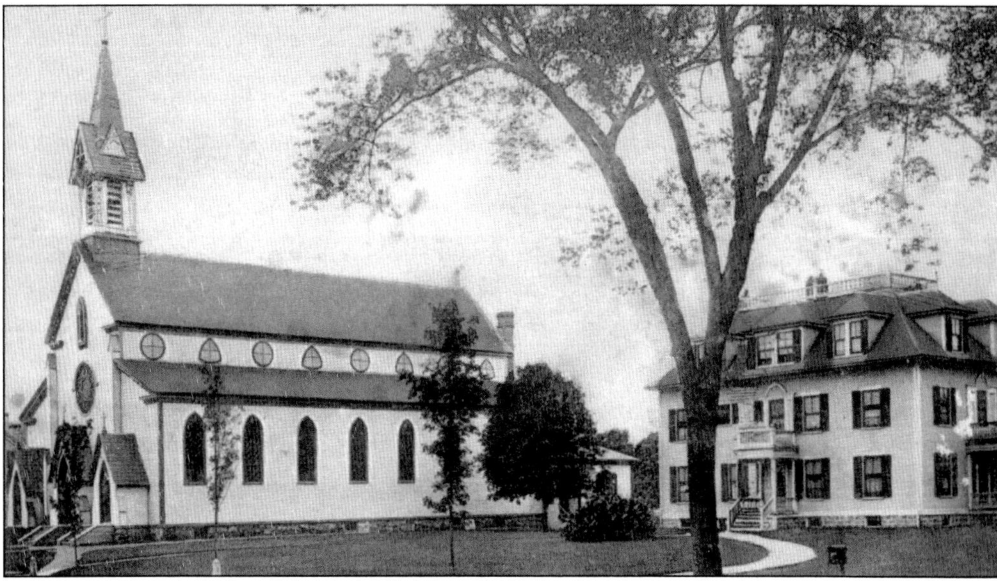

St. Bridget's Roman Catholic Church is at 135 Central Street and was built in 1863 in the Gothic style. St. Bridget's parish was established when Fr. Aron L. Roche bought the lot at the corner of Central and Plymouth Streets from Jess Dunham. Until that time, Abington was a mission of St. Mary's in Randolph. St. Bridget's, in turn, became the mother parish for churches in the towns of Rockland, Whitman, Hanson, Hanover, and others. In this postcard is the rectory that was built in 1905 in the Colonial Revival style.

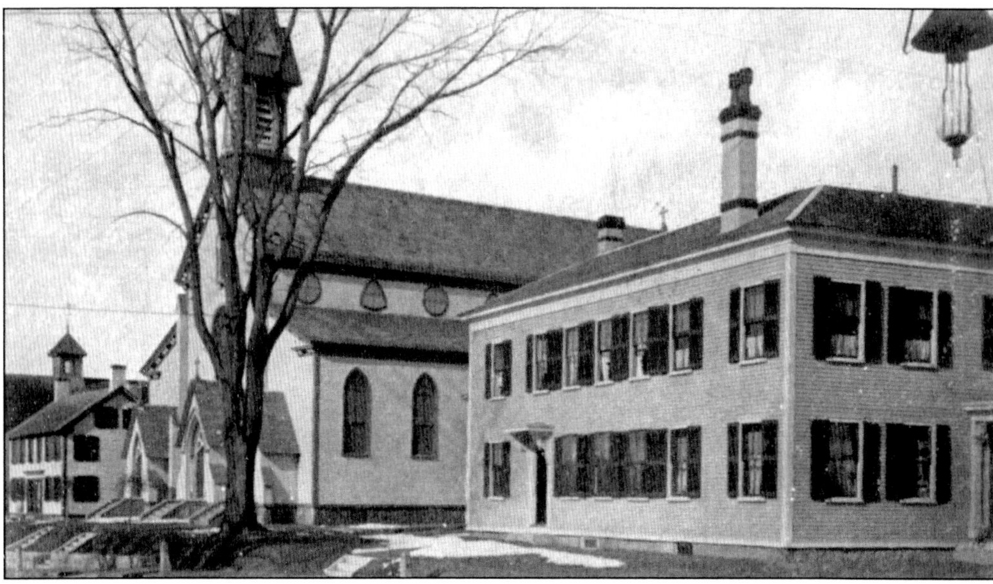

This postcard shows the Federal-style home of Jess Dunham, the bankrupted shoe manufacturer who sold his property to the church in 1862. The house was used as the rectory until the new one was built in 1905. This house was moved in 1905 and again in 1965. The spire has been removed. The building on the left with the cupola is Lyceum Hall, constructed with surplus federal money in 1835. It was the sight of abolitionist meetings when it was too rainy to go to Island Grove. Abington town meetings were also held here. The meeting in which the people of East Abington voted to separate from Abington and form a new town was also held here.

Seven

FUN AT ISLAND GROVE

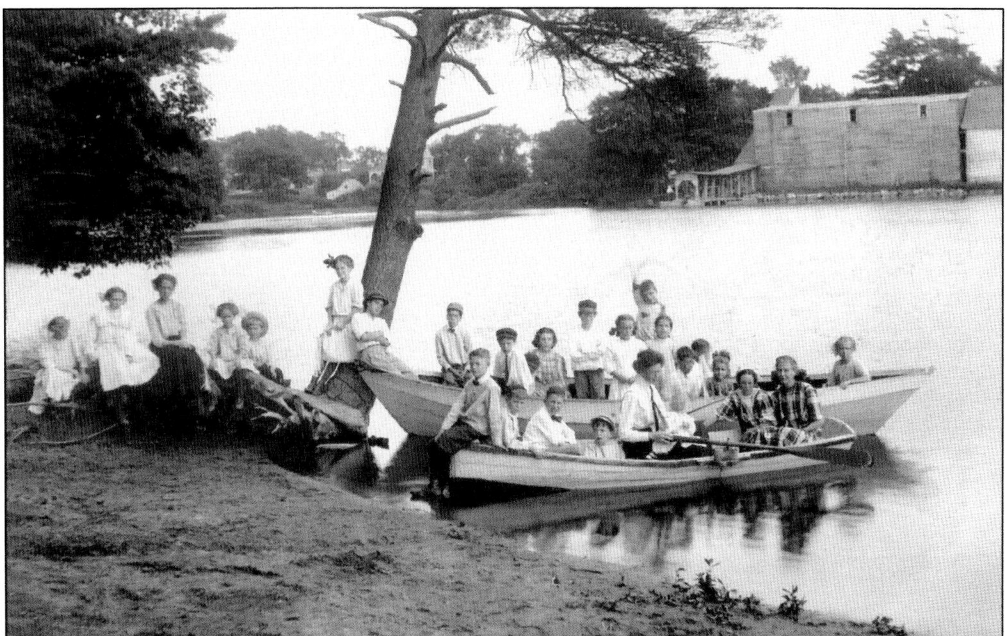

In the late 1800s, as the country shifted from a predominantly agrarian to an industrial society, thanks to the accelerating forces of the Industrial Revolution, Americans found that the old adage about idle hands and the Devil's work was not necessarily always true. Suddenly, with new forms of communication and transportation allowing people to interact more than ever, like-minded individuals sought each other out to share their passions. Relaxation became an important piece of everyday American culture, and there was nowhere better in Abington to relax during this time than at Island Grove.

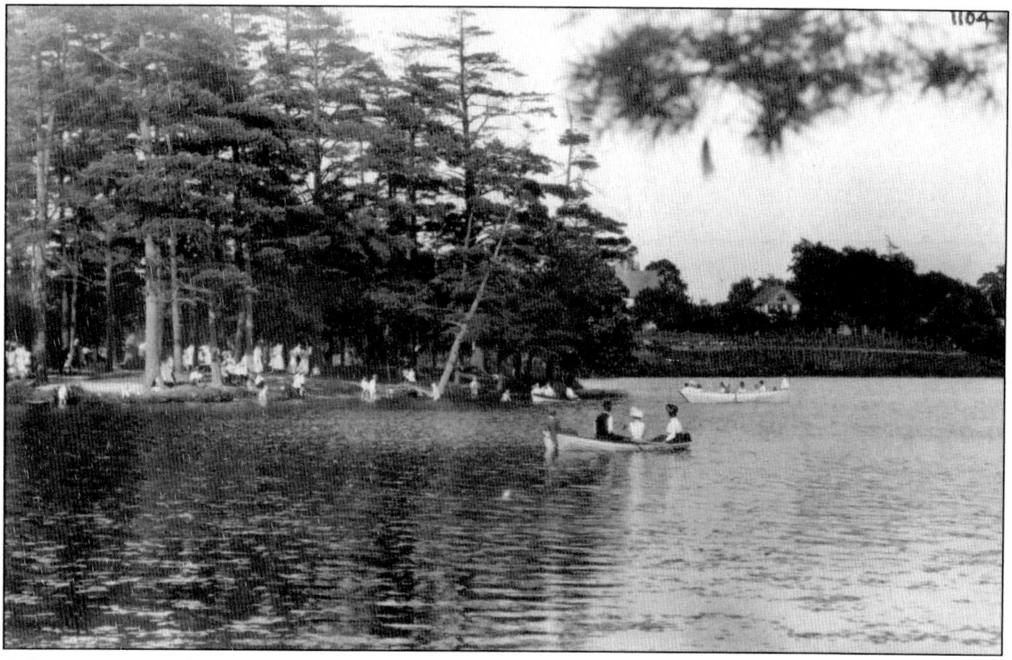

Of course, more than one person had the idea of relaxing at Island Grove at one time. A summer Sunday could see a dozen small boats on the pond and maybe a church picnic taking place on the grounds of Island Grove Park. Until the arrival of streetcars and easy access to Nantasket Beach, the people of Abington could always find their way out to the grove for a chance to stick their toes in the water.

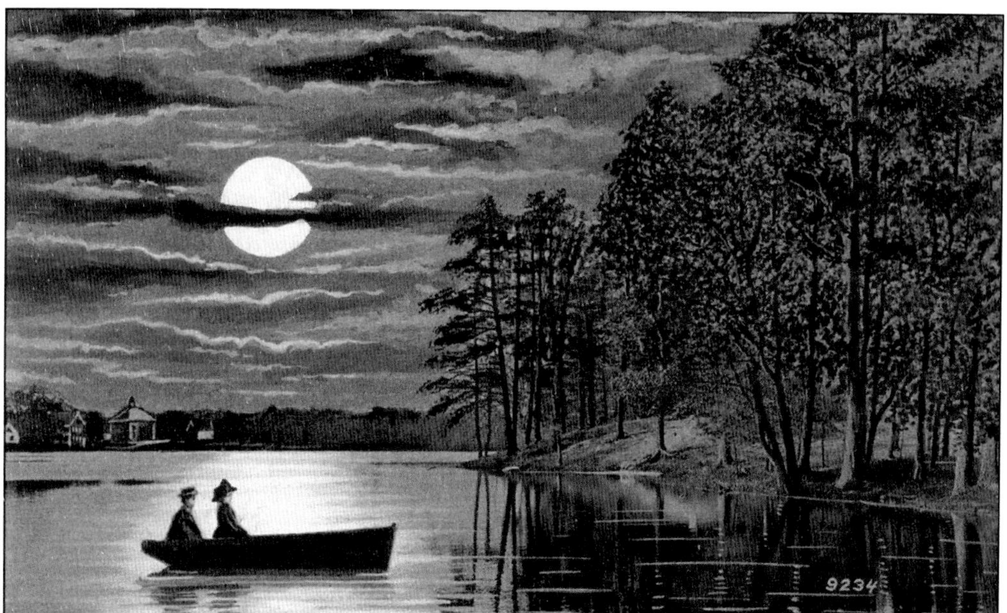

Not everybody sought crowds, though, when they set out for Island Grove Pond. A slow row under the silvery moon could do as much for the soul as the revelry of a church or school outing. And postcard dealers knew how to pull at the heartstrings of their patrons with cards like this one.

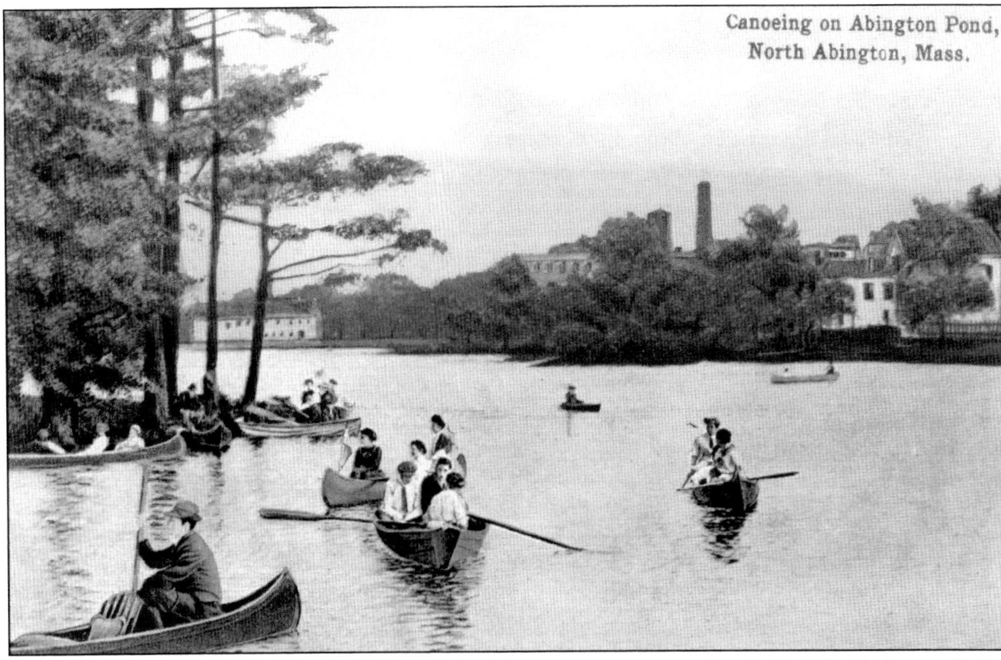

Before the construction of the memorial bridge and monument in 1912, Island Grove Pond afforded a wide-open run around the point of the park for rowboats, canoes, and anything else that floated.

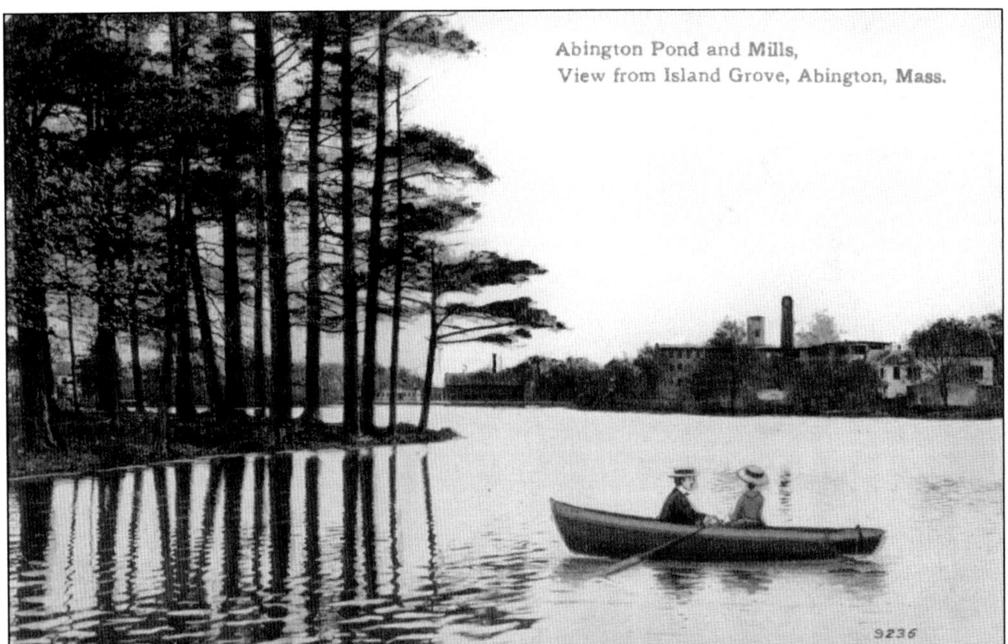

By far, Abington produced more postcards of Island Grove and its surroundings than of any other location in town, save for the Abington Savings Bank building, which comes in second. The postcard begs the question: is that the same couple that was rowing on the previous page, and if so, have they been rowing all night?

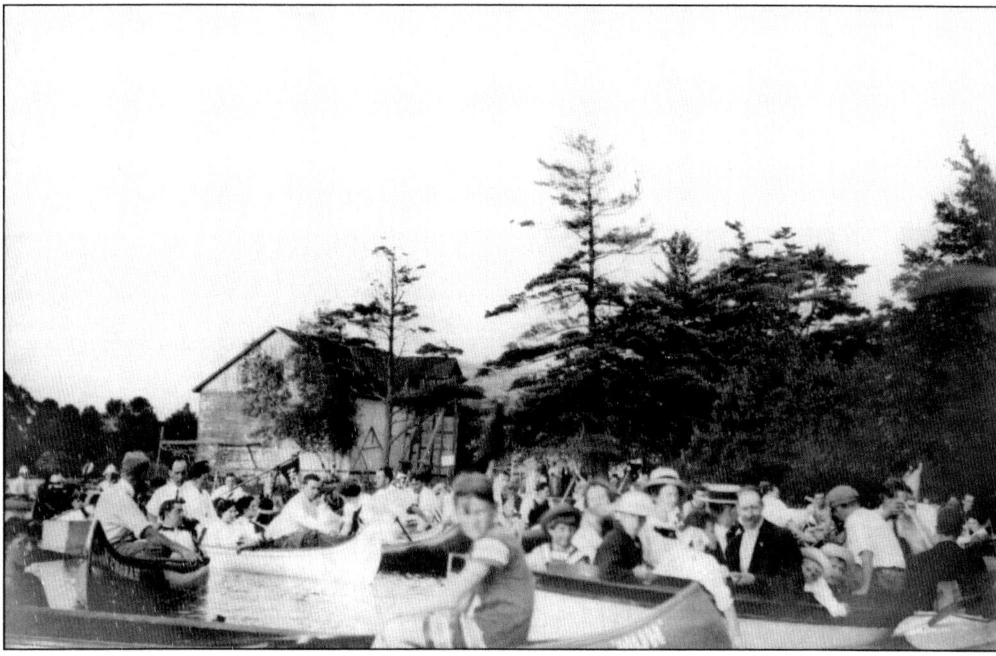

As Americans enjoyed acceptable leisure time (previously, a person could only get away from work for health or spiritual regeneration), some interesting imagery was produced. Here, the Island Grove Boat Club meets in front of an icehouse, the former symbolizing escapism and collective fun times and the latter symbolizing the hard manual labor of the working world.

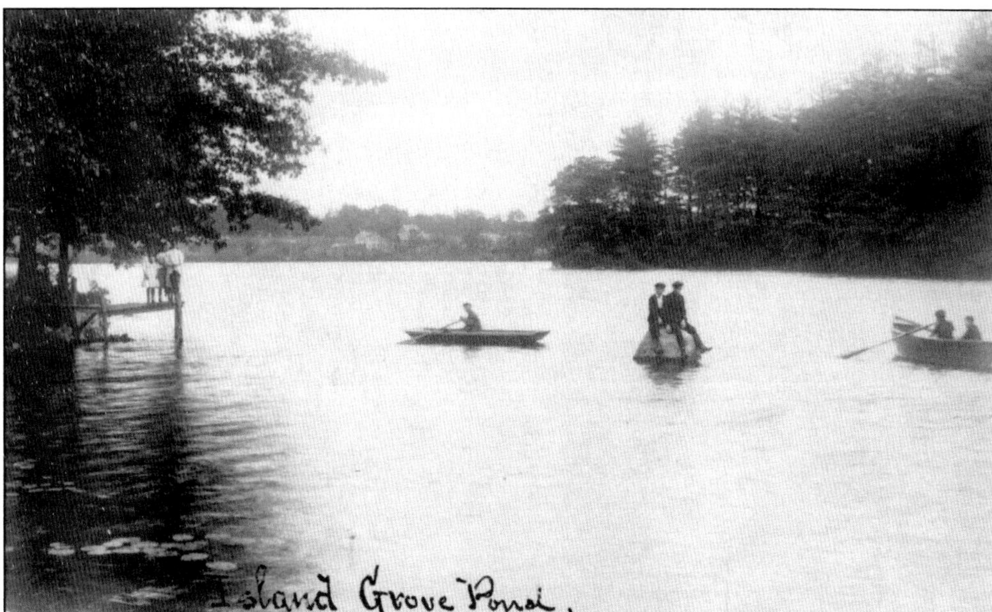

Island Grove Bridge today runs right past Lighthouse Rock, where two boys are seated in this image. How they planned to get home without getting wet nobody knows.

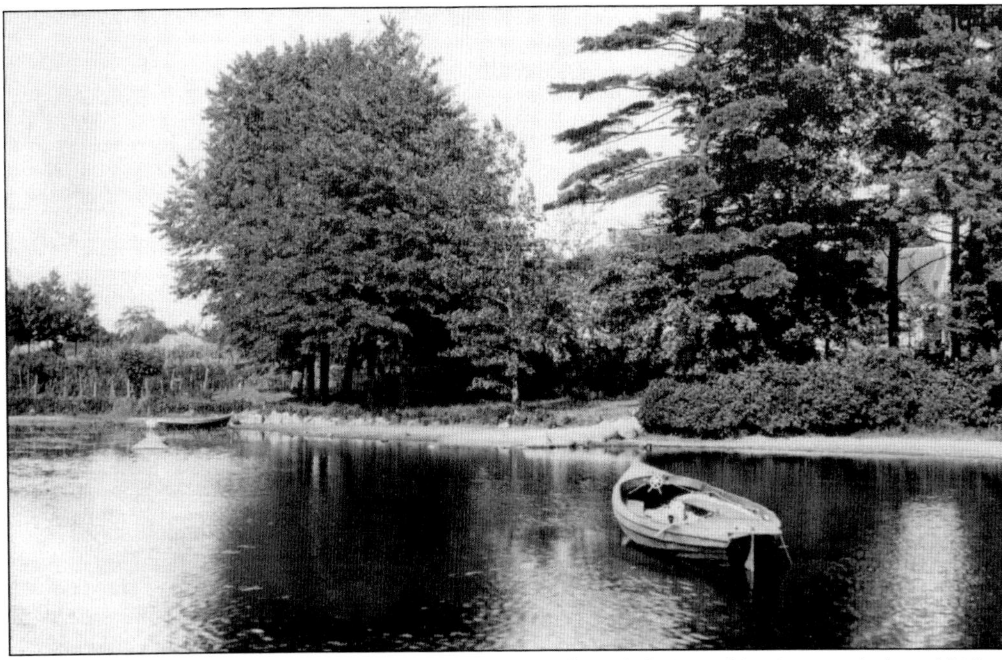

Postcard photographers loved to capture the unusual, and during this time period, *c.* 1905, a motorboat was a curious thing to see. This one, moored off the grove, belonged to Fred Meserve, according to a note on the back of the card.

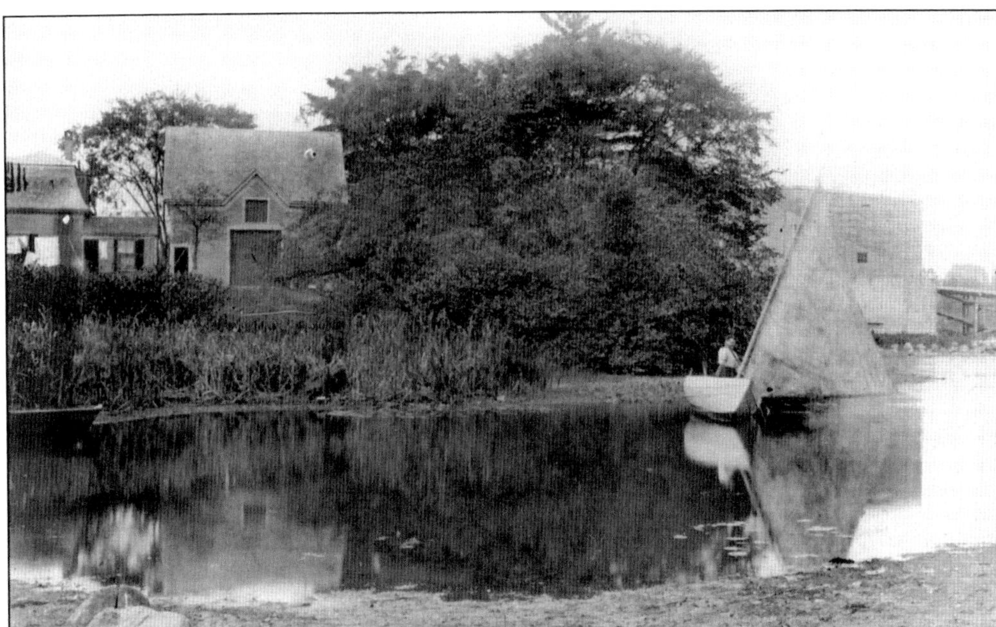

More common would have been the traditional sailing yacht, although it would have to be pretty small to safely carry its helmsman around the pond. This scene shows the icehouse on the right and a home on Granite Street on the left.

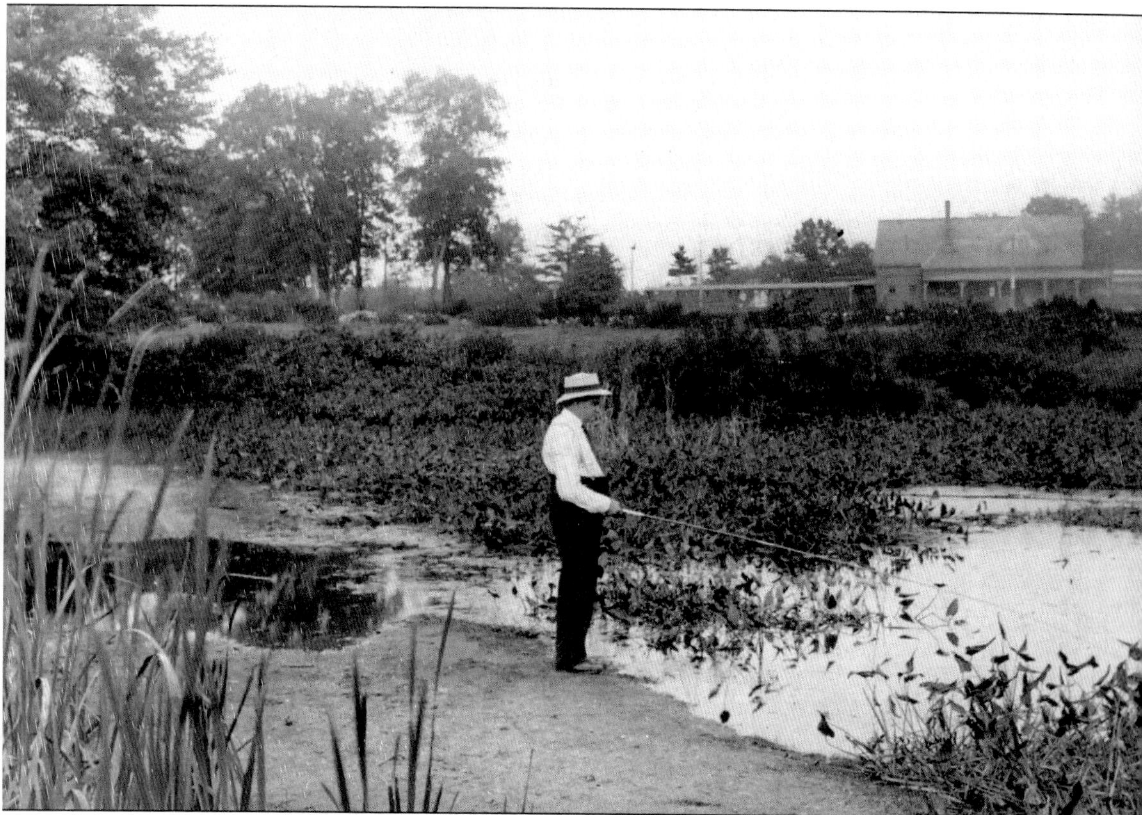

Fishing was one of the mainstays of the Massachusetts economy from the beginning. Just visit the statehouse to see the sacred cod in the house of representatives and the holy mackerel high above the state senate's chamber. In fact, according to a letter found in England recently, addressed to Christopher Columbus from Bristol fishermen of the 1490s, America had been discovered years before the master navigator had arrived. The fishing was so good, they said, that they did not want to tell anybody where they had been going. Fishing as a pastime, though, came with the rest of the late 19th century's amusements and quickly became the sport of presidents. Even before George H. Bush and Dwight Eisenhower dropped their first lines in the water, Grover Cleveland was known to visit the South Shore to "drown a few worms." The Adams men, John and John Quincy, were known to fish the region as well. But the best way to immortalize yourself as a fisherman was to have your photograph taken, like Henry Claflin did. As a postcard publisher, he could then market himself to the world.

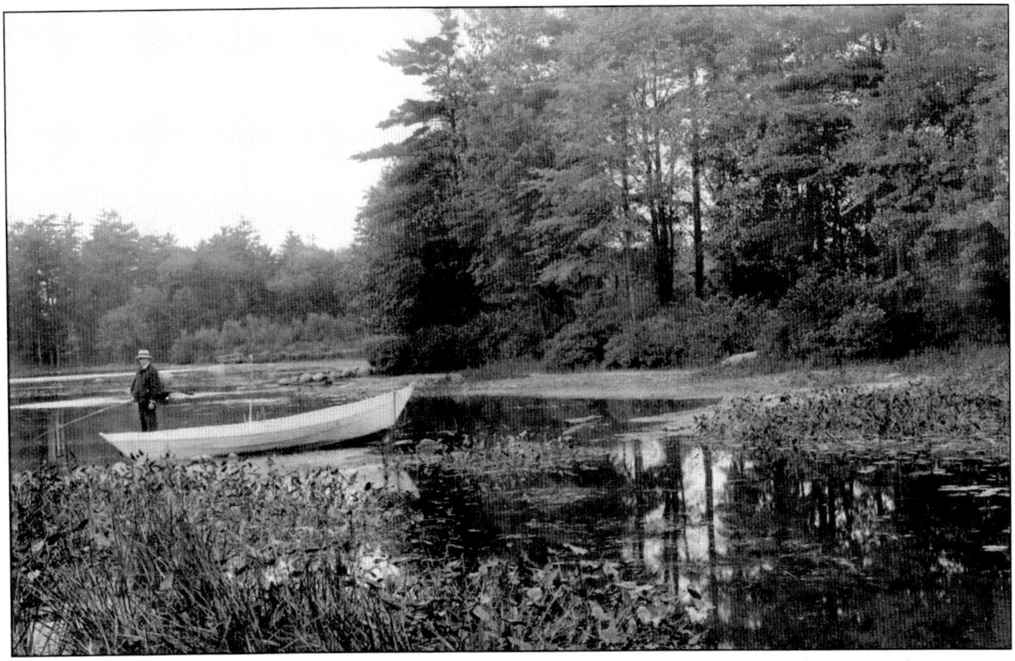

Depending on what a fisherman was looking for, shallow water could be as productive as deep water.

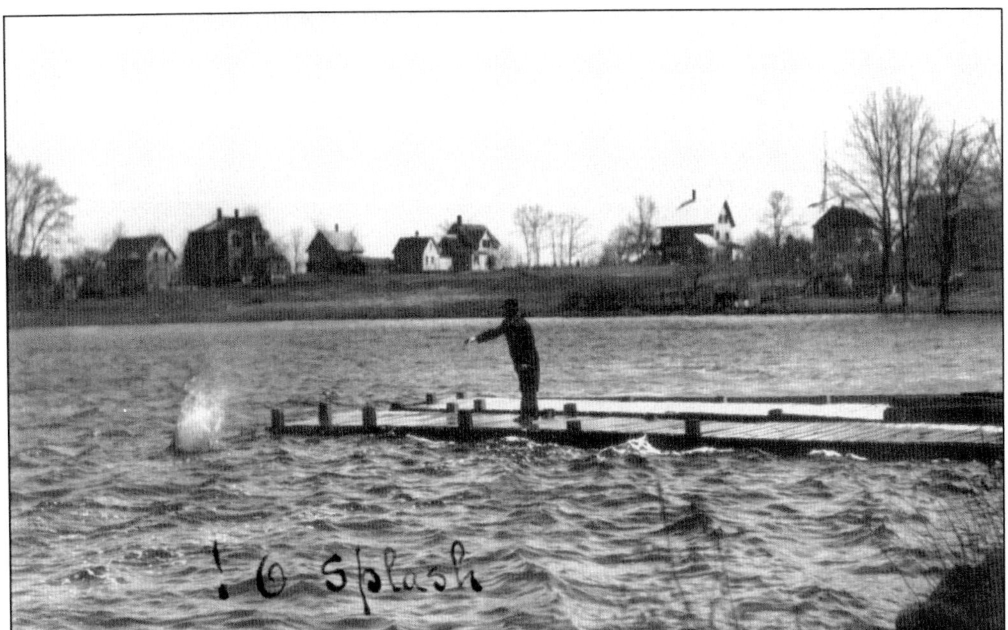

The value to anglers of the icehouse run, the runway on which the ice moved to the top of the icehouse after cutting, could not be overstated in spring and summer. In the background are houses on Park Avenue and Pond Street.

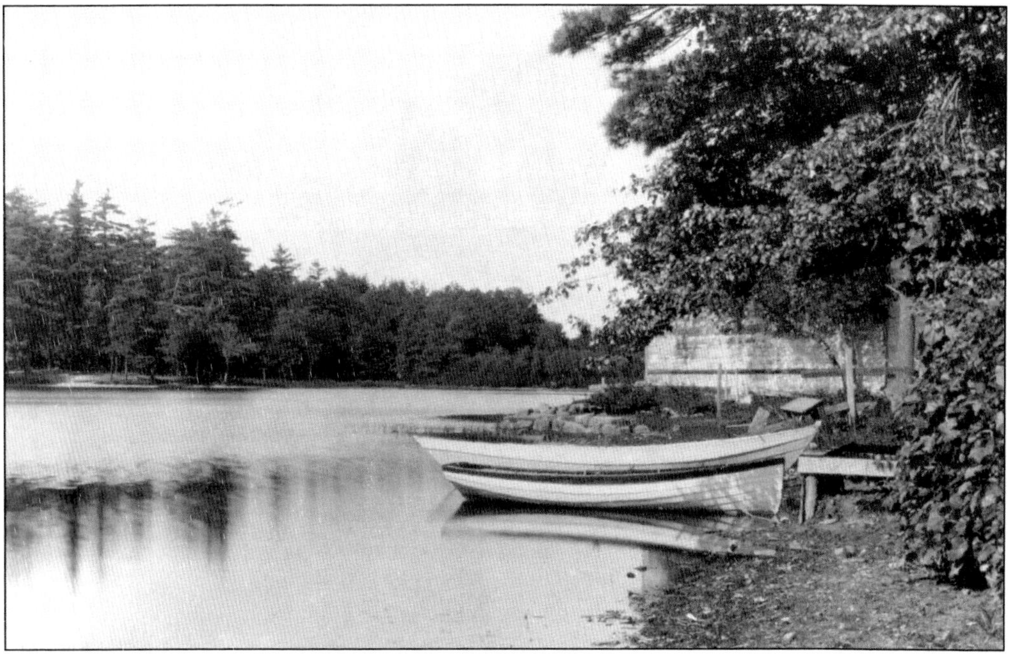

Island Grove was nothing if not picturesque. The natural beauty of the pond and trees, combined with the summer sun and the classic, sleek lines of handmade wooden boats, made for some dramatic, romantic imagery.

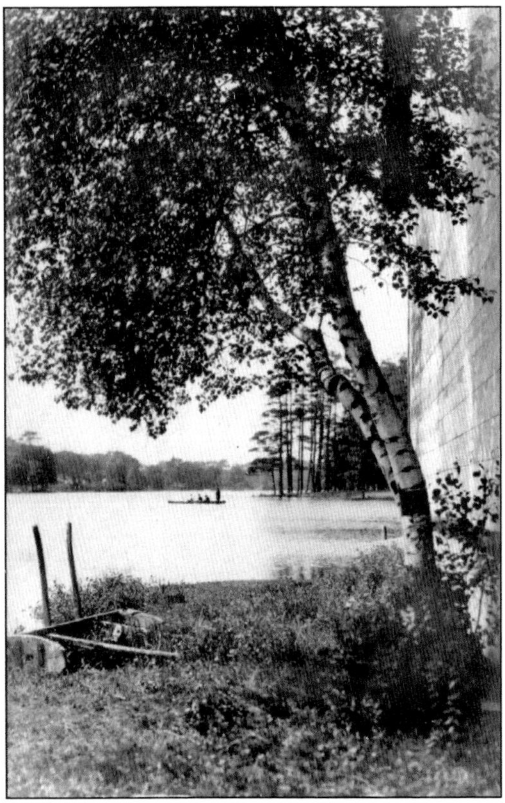

Seen are the discarded tools of the ice-cutting trade and a crew rowing across the pond in the distance.

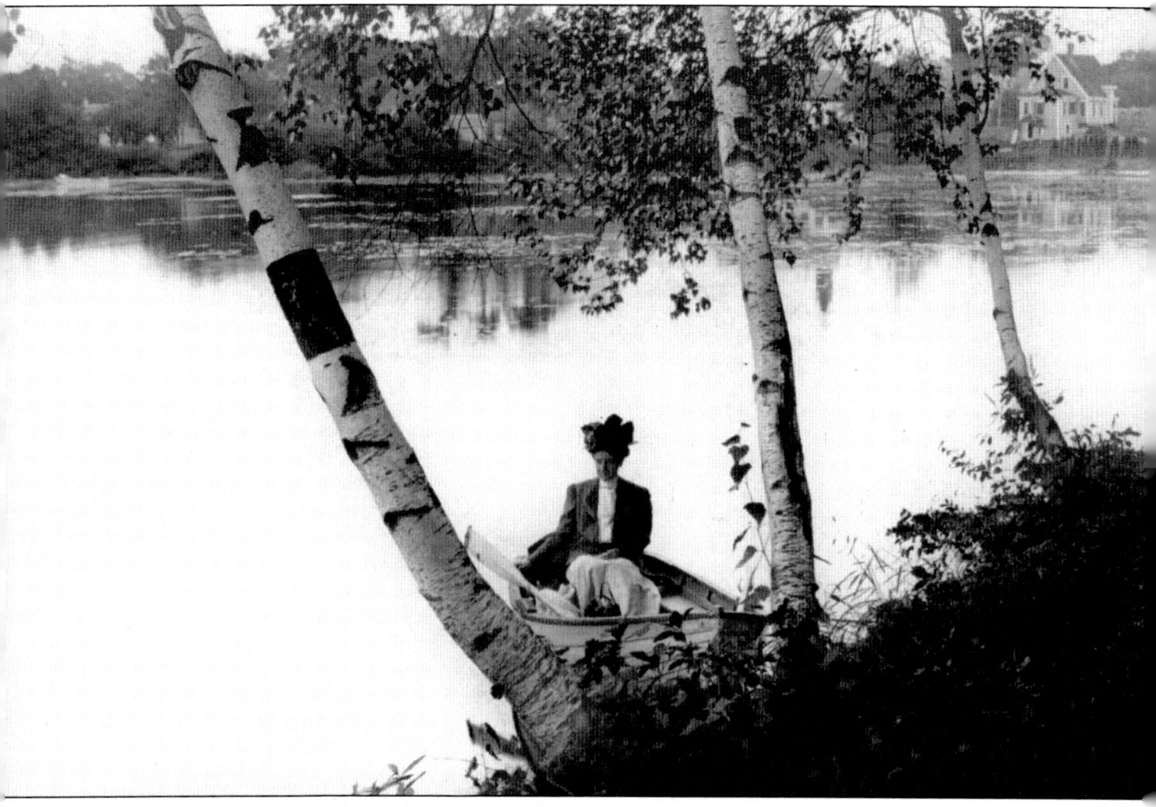

The romance of the grove and pond appealed to both sexes. But what has happened in this image? Did this young woman's date leave her stranded at the point, or is he the one holding the camera? We can only hope for the latter, but we can safely bank on the notion that she could row herself home either way. Female rowers were by no means uncommon in the 19th century. Two in particular, Grace Darling of England and Ida Lewis of Newport, Rhode Island, became famous as lifesavers, rowing out from lighthouses in their respective ports to save mariners in distress. Darling did so alongside her father, a lighthouse keeper, while Lewis rowed alone, rescuing approximately 25 people from drowning over the course of her life. Lewis would have been a hero to many young women of the early 1900s, as her story gained fame as she aged, inspiring other young women to take up the oar and give it a try.

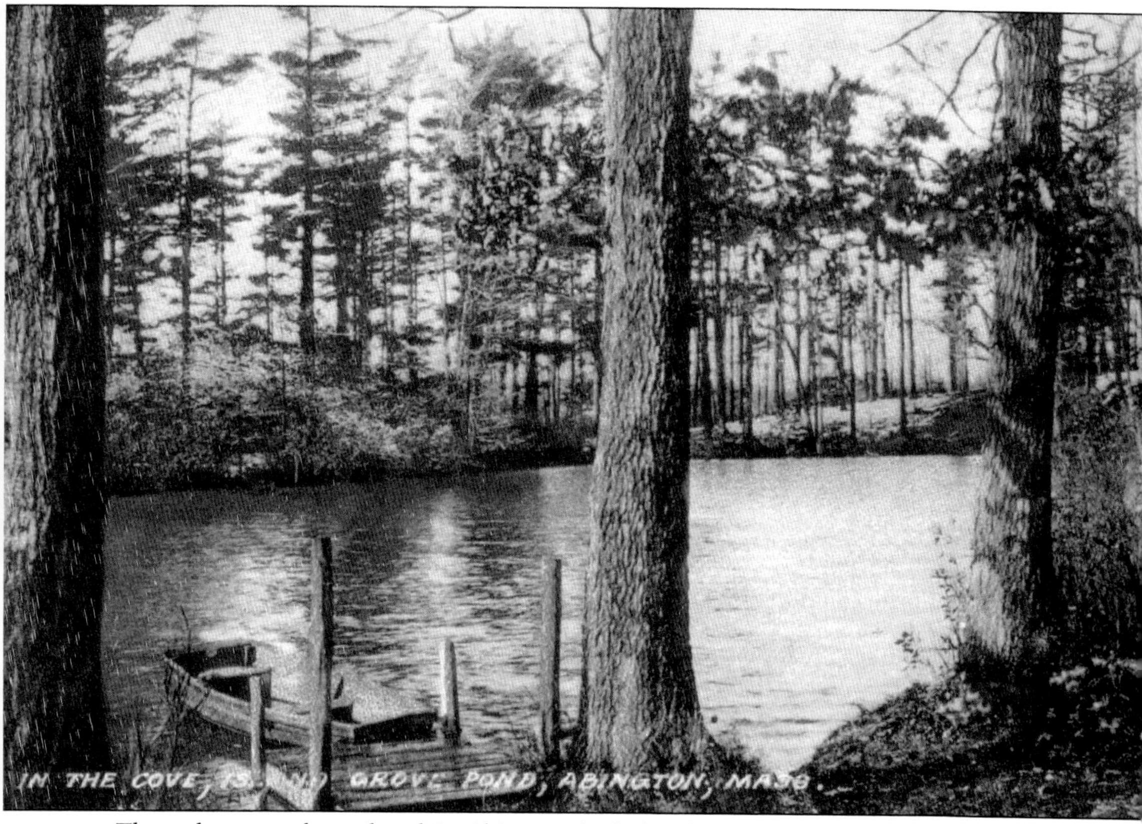

The early postcards produced in Abington (and elsewhere) fit into certain categories. For the most part, they had to represent recognizable landmarks. Few, if any, postcards in the collections of the Dyer Memorial Library and the Historical Society of Old Abington show side streets and lesser-traveled routes. The exclusion of these scenes from postcard history represents a gap in our knowledge of the people, places, and events of the town. Among the images in these collections are numerous shots of Island Grove, taken from every possible angle, like here in the cove. This card shows that even in a time of huge factories pushing out thousands of pairs of shoes a day within view of the grove, some vestiges of nature still remained in town, open space to be enjoyed and not absorbed by the modern culture of industrialism.

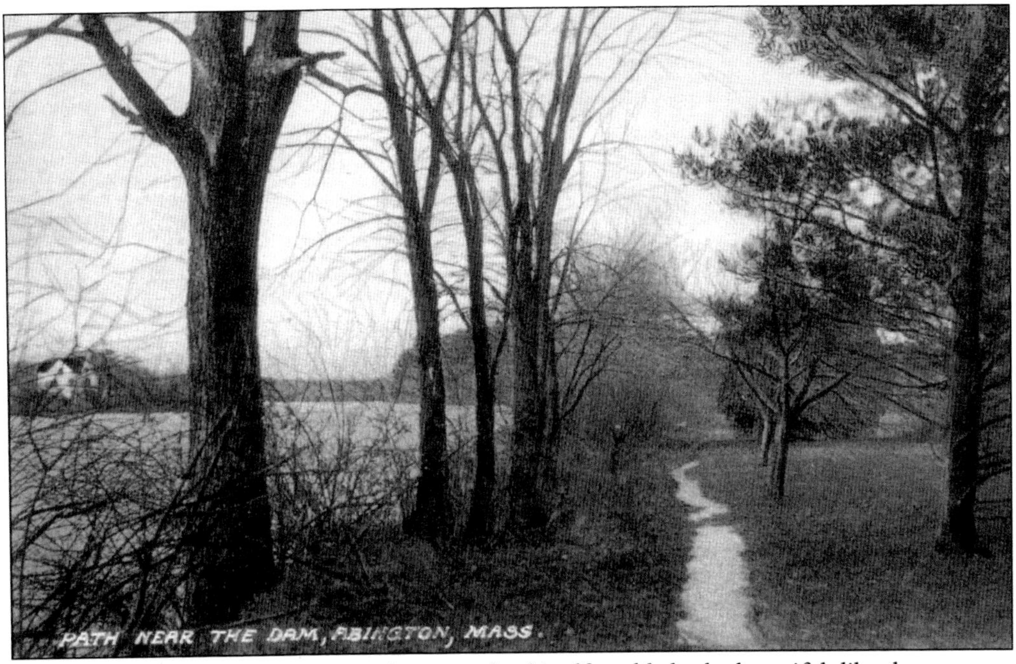

Postcards showing the pathways on the grove land itself could also be beautiful, like the one seen here, showing the path near the dam.

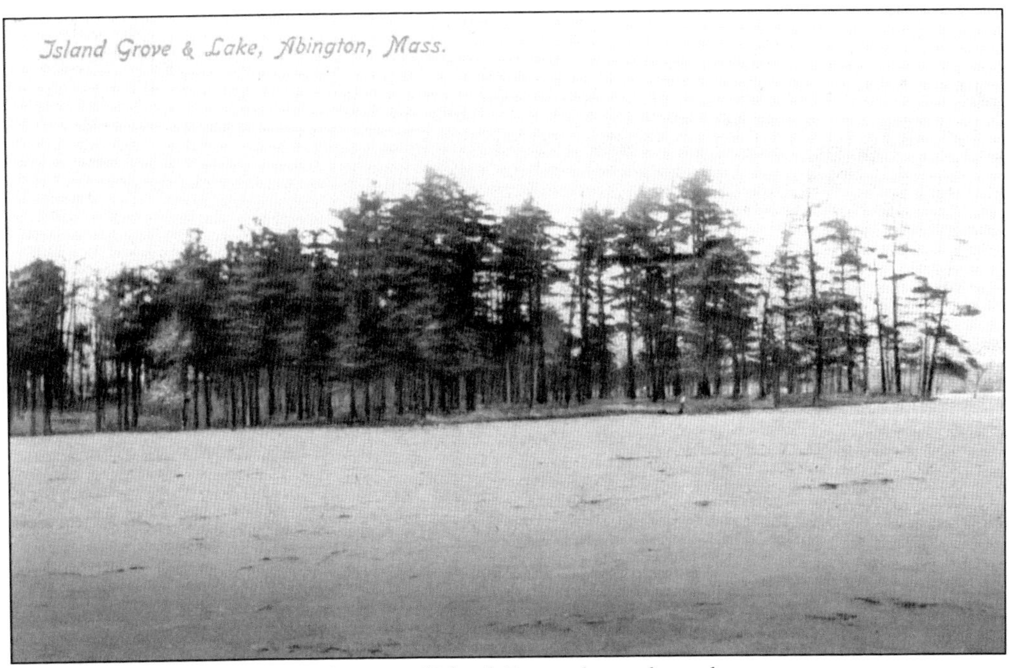

When seen from afar, the true beauty of Island Grove shone through.

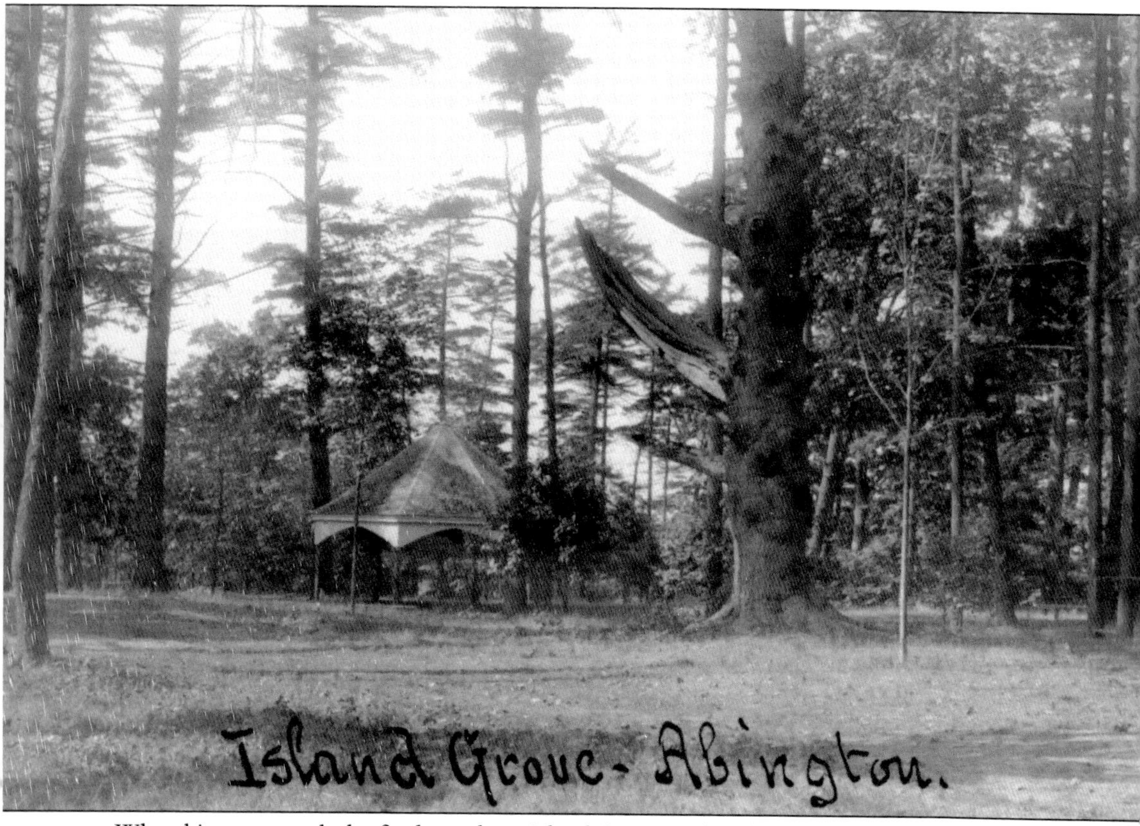

When history records the final words on Island Grove Park, what story will it ultimately tell? Will it be the story of the enjoyable times spent there by groups of young people in the years prior to 1912, when baseball gloves and butterflies captured the attention of the youths for a day? Or will one of William Lloyd Garrison's abolitionist speeches ring through the trees with the venom of a man possessed by his cause? Perhaps the dedication of the soldiers and sailors memorial and the memorial bridge will be the defining moment for Island Grove. Or maybe, as each passing generation defines its own sense of place, new understandings of Island Grove will be formed. Whatever the case, we can safely say that Island Grove will continue to be an important place in the hearts of the people of Abington.

Eight

Remembering the Past

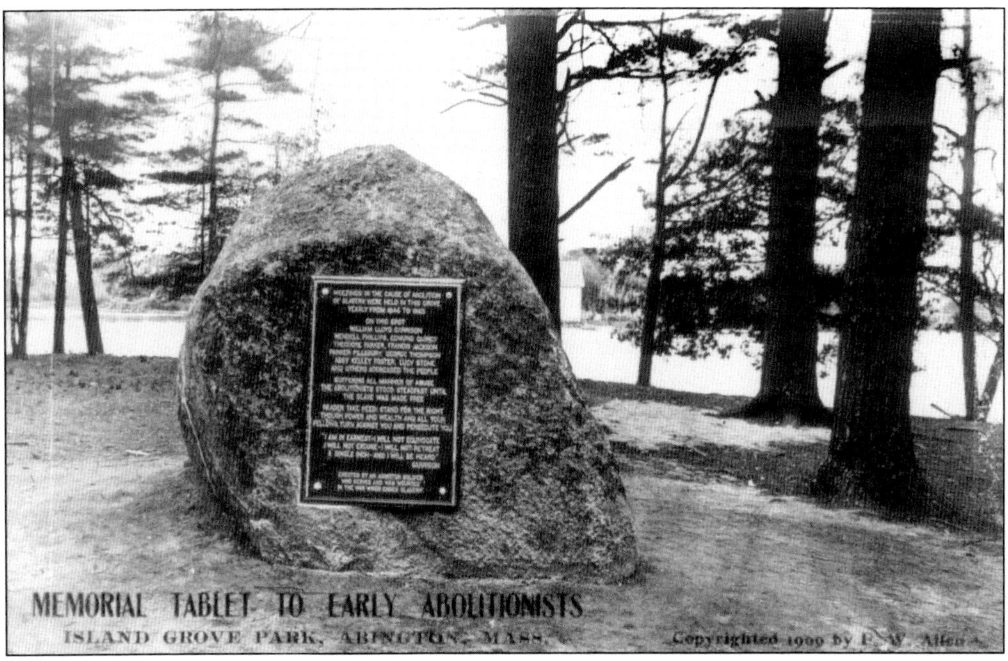

When Abington consisted of all three Old Abington towns, 1,266 men were sent to fight in the Civil War, including 954 infantrymen, 122 sailors, 106 artillerymen, and 5 cavalrymen, all of whom ranged between 15 and 60 years of age. One of those men, Moses N. Arnold, a captain with the 12th Massachusetts Volunteer Infantry, returned from the war with a wounded neck, pierced by a Minié ball at the Battle of Antietam in 1862. But Arnold felt so strongly about the war and the abolition of slavery that he erected a monument at Island Grove in 1909 in memory of the famed antislavery orators who used the grove as an oasis before the war. The people of Abington had thanked their returning soldiers with a reception on those same grounds 44 years earlier.

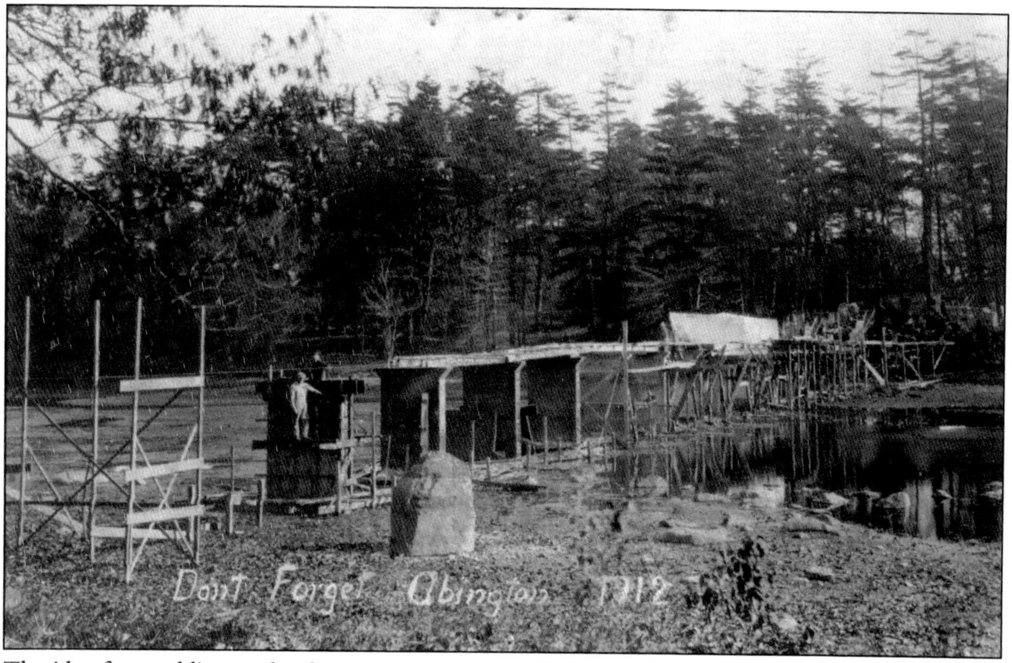

The idea for a soldiers and sailors memorial grew from Arnold's actions. The town of Abington accepted his monument on Memorial Day 1909 and began plans for an even larger project. At the March 1910 meeting of the town, it was voted "that a committee of twelve to consist of the park commissioners, the moderator and eight other members be appointed . . . to investigate the matter of a soldiers' memorial bridge or soldiers' monument."

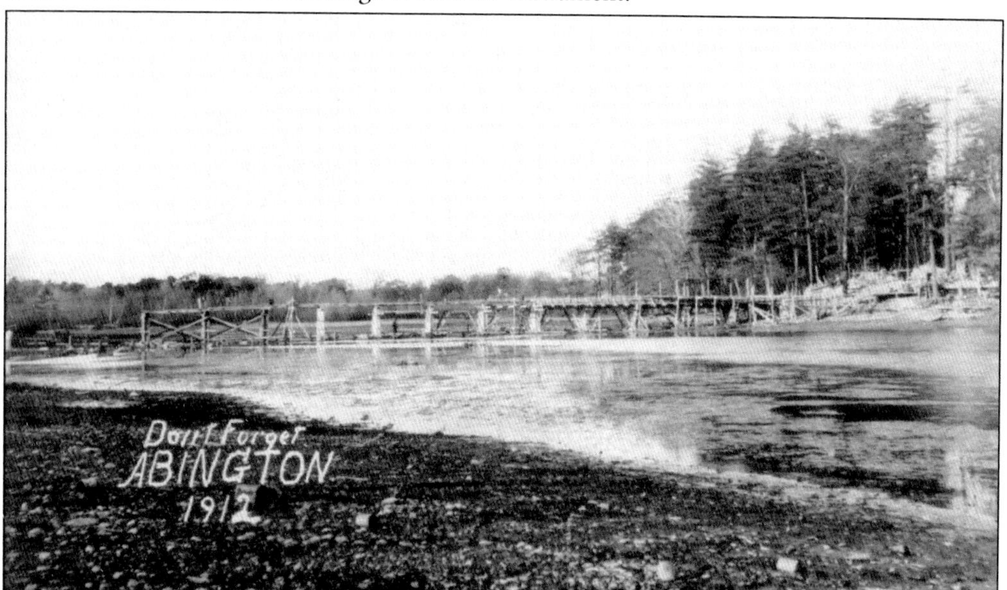

The following year, the committee recommended that both a bridge and a monument be designed to stand as memorials, and fund-raising began. The men of the Grand Army, though few were still around, spearheaded that cause, while architect J. Williams Beal, the landscape architecture firm of the Olmsted brothers, and sculptor Bela Pratt began their plans and specifications for the appropriate designs.

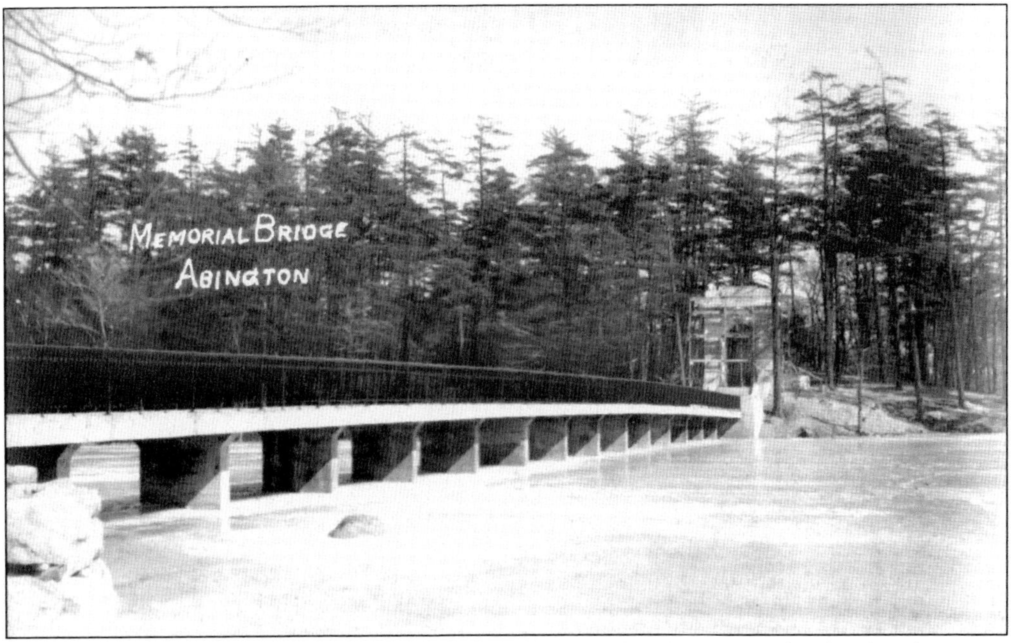

The bridge, 300 feet from buttress to buttress, was to stand 6 feet above water level and 12 feet wide. It was of cement construction with iron railings. To facilitate access to the site, superintendent of streets E. J. Rourke and his crew completed grading and stonework on Lake Street. The Boston firm of Wilson & Tomlinson outbid all others and secured the contract to build the bridge.

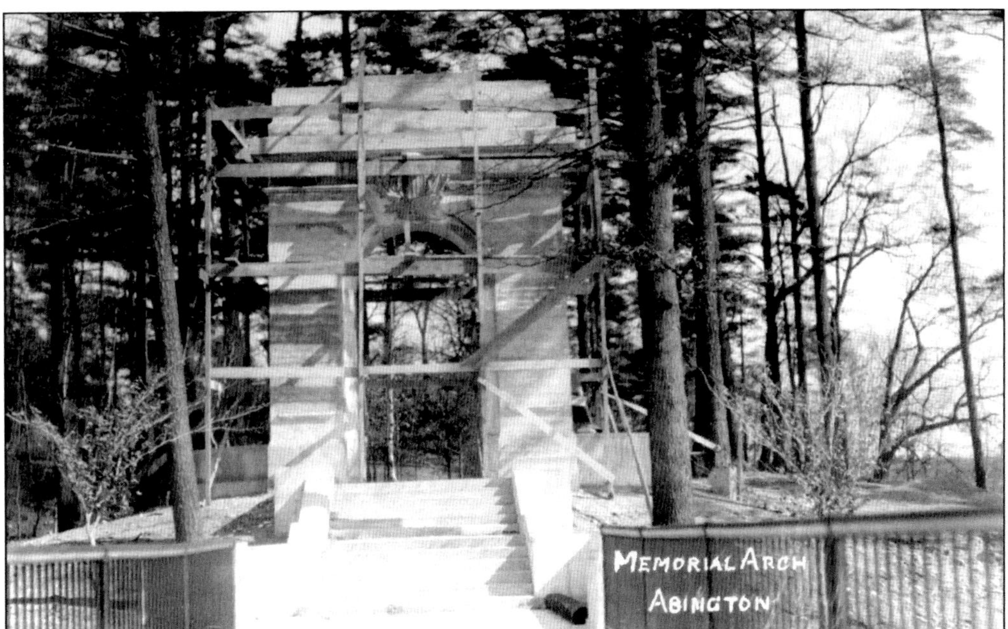

Once the bridge had been completed, work on the monument could begin. The Boston firm of Emerson & Norris secured that contract. The specifications called for an arched platform 12 feet above water level and 33 feet wide at the base, including the parapet walls. The arch itself was to stand 25 feet high and 19 feet wide.

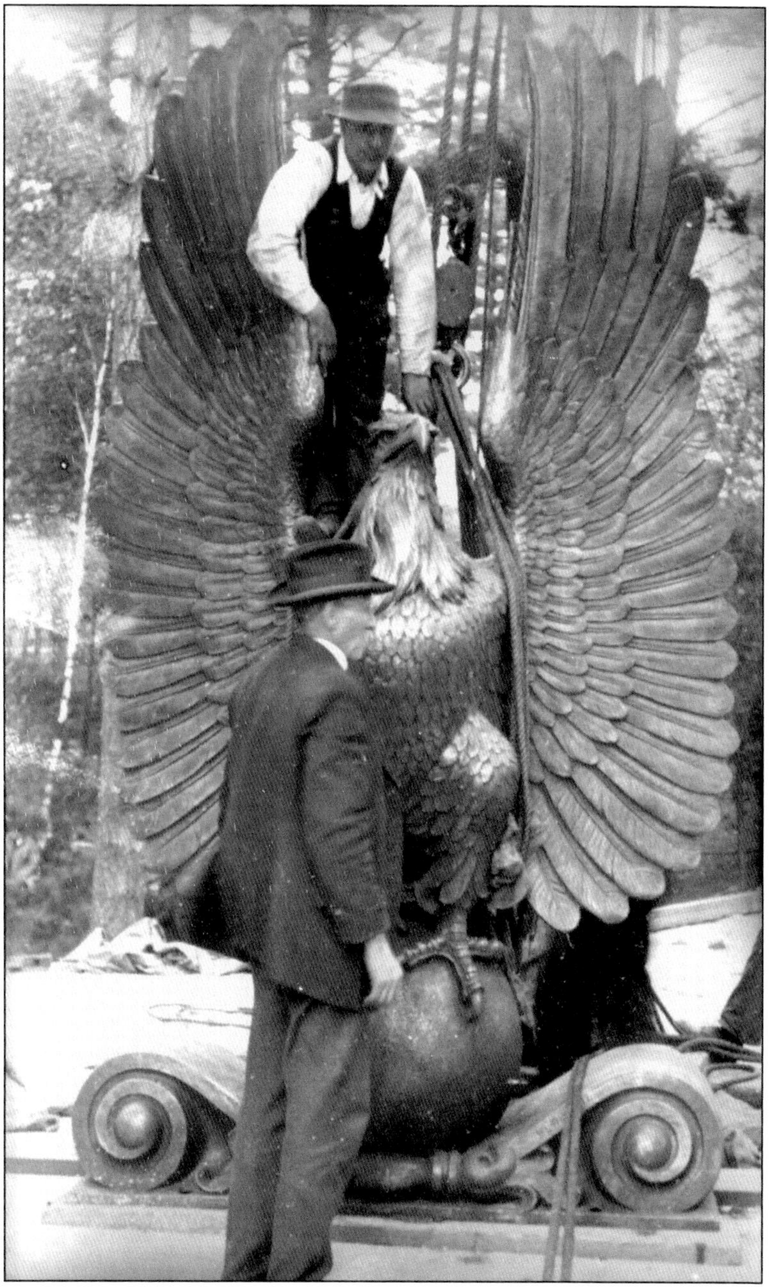

The most striking aspect of the monument is the sculpted eagle perched atop it. The people of Abington spared no expense when they selected the man for the job, sculptor Bela Pratt. Pratt, born in Connecticut, studied under Augustine Saint-Gaudens and was widely known for the designs of both the $5 and $2.50 American coins, as well as numerous statues around Boston and elsewhere. The grand eagle atop the monument was to be 11 feet high and made of bronze. In all, it stood 50 feet above the line of the water, the eagle's wings raised in triumph. The sculptor completed his work well in advance of the celebration of the 200th anniversary of Old Abington, delivering it on May 24, 1912. Andrew Gale of Brockton, standing in this image, was the mover who got the eagle to its final destination at the grove.

Bas-relief military figures, one representing a sailor and the other a foot soldier, flanked the opening of the arch's west side. The base of the arch was separated 50 feet from the buttress of the bridge.

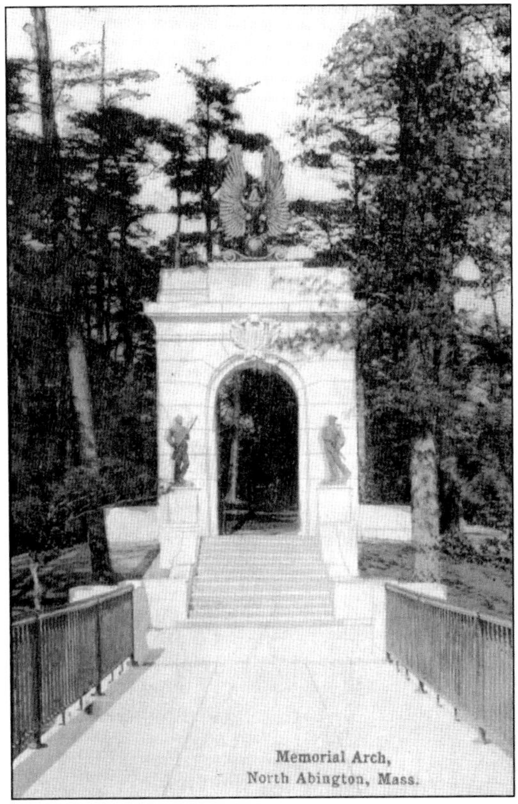

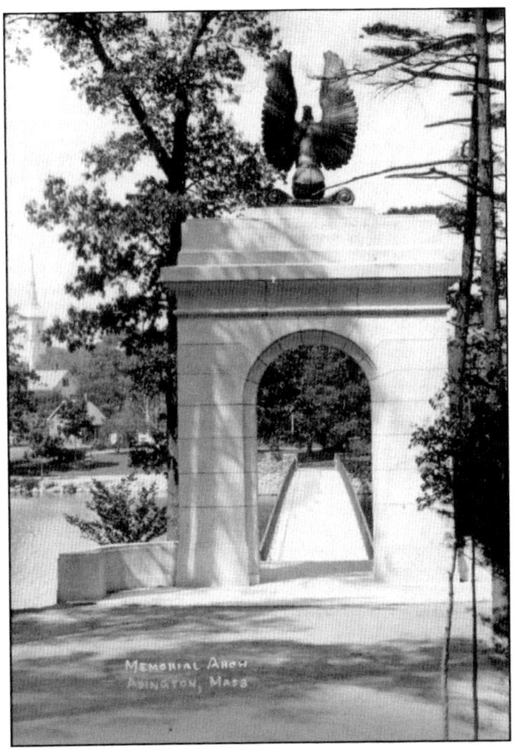

The view from the grove was equally as impressive. Postcard printers understood the impact these images would have on the people of Abington and quickly sought to get them out to the public.

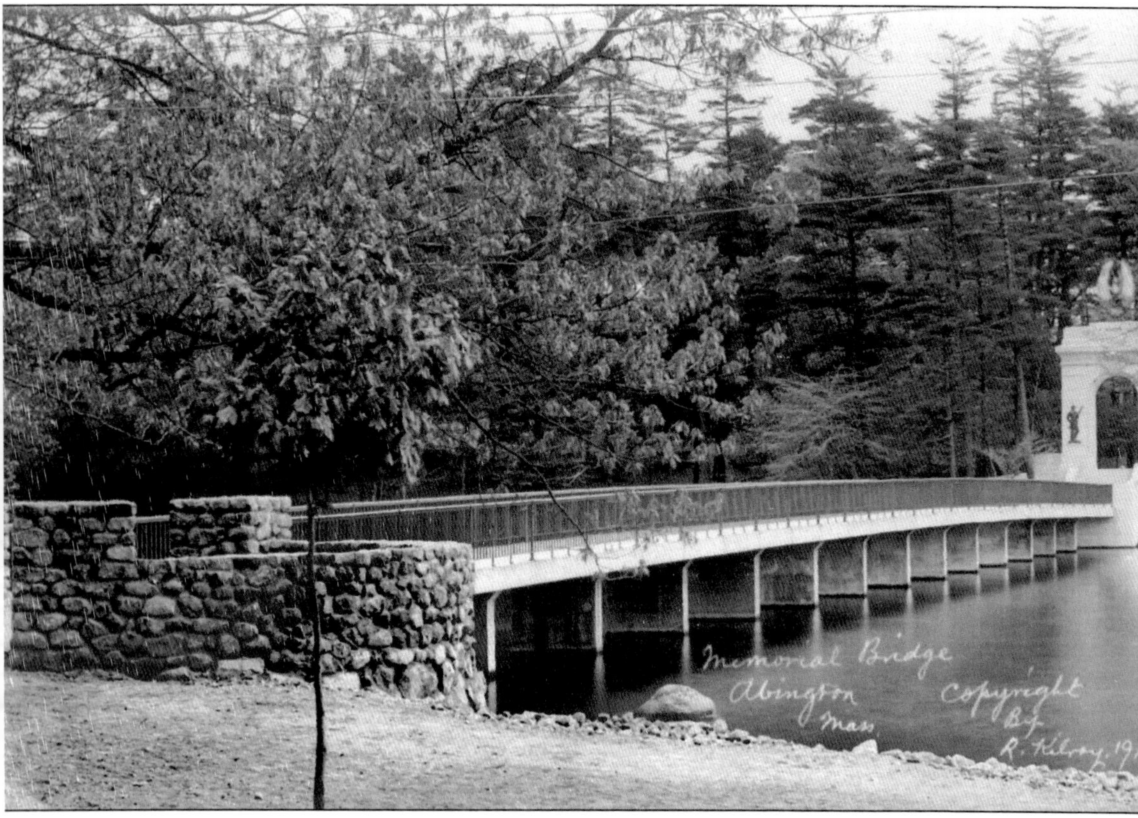

The quietude of the grove at that time could only be broken by the echoes of the abolitionist meetings of the past. The members of the Massachusetts Anti-Slavery Society regularly met at the grove; the first meeting was held on the Fourth of July in 1846. Later, meetings were held annually on August 1, the date that 800,000 slaves were released in the West Indies in 1834. Problems arose in 1851, according to a report of the Fourth of July at Abington in the July 11 edition of *The Liberator.* The report stated, "On arriving at the Grove, our ears were saluted with the sound of cannon, discharged from the opposite shore, placed there purposely to annoy us, but failing entirely in producing the effect intended. Some Webster Whigs had raised about forty dollars, it is said, for the purchase of powder, and had employed men to load and fire all day. . . . But it will take more gunpowder, with shot added, than was ever yet made, to silence the voice of truth, and more than forty dollars' worth of gunpowder to blow Daniel Webster into the White House at Washington."

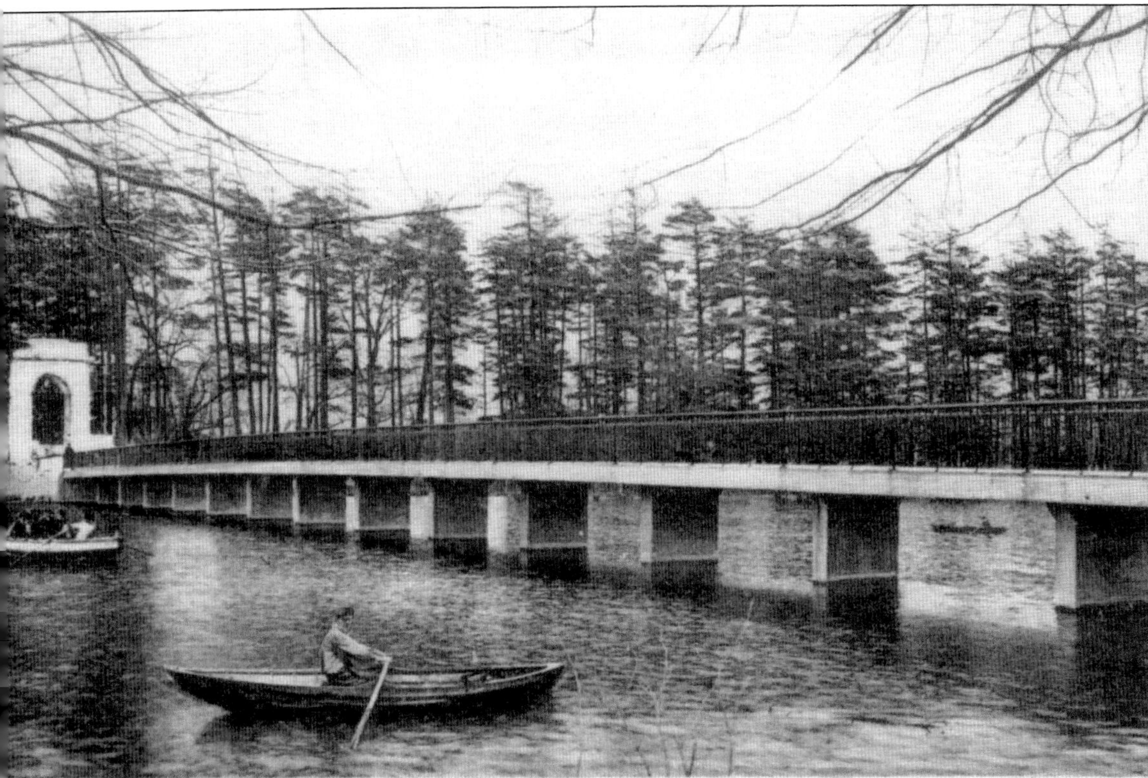

2428. ISLAND GROVE POND, MEMORIAL BRIDGE, ABINGTON, MASS.

Perhaps to others, the echoes of Island Grove recall the words of Joshua S. Gray, who spoke during the 200th anniversary. Gray said, "When the full history of the [Civil] war shall have been written, side by side will appear on its front pages the names of its daughters as well as its sons. To the soldier fell the weary march, the lonely picket duty, the fierce excitement of the battle's fray, the lingering existence of the hospital or prison-pen, and, perhaps, an honorable death on the battlefield; but, to wife and mother, sister or sweet-heart, came the dreary home-turning after bidding goodbye and Godspeed to loved ones. The anxious waiting for tidings of sanguinary battle, and the sudden shock, when they came, that husband, son, or brother had fallen. Every bullet that found its victim on bloody field of carnage rested not there, but, speeding over hill and dale found its lifelong resting place in the heart of some patriotic woman at her fireside."

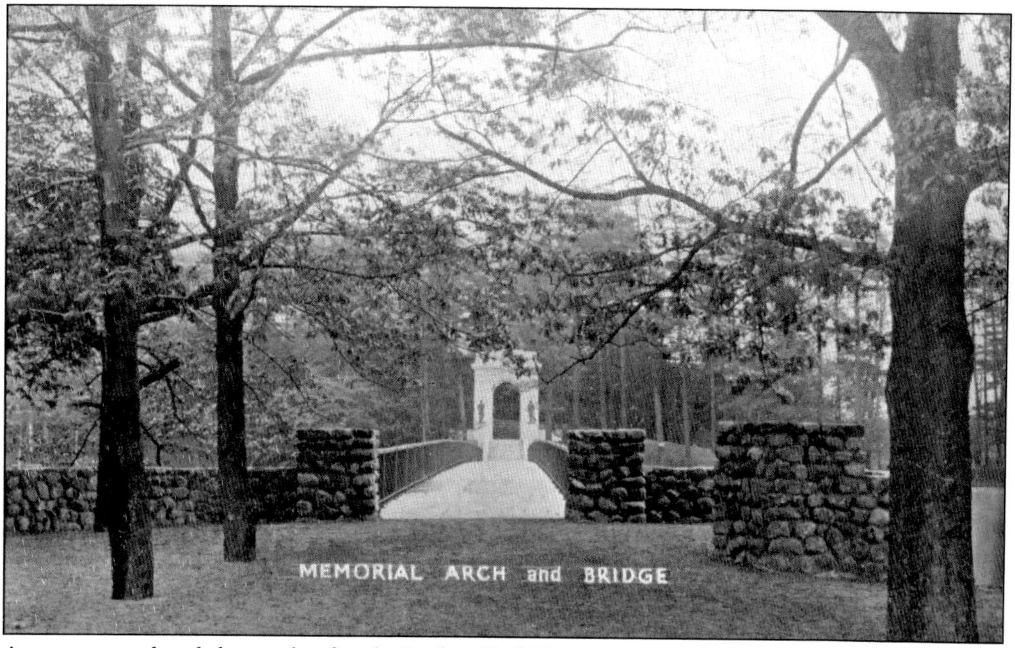

As years passed and those who fought in the Civil War or against the institution of slavery died off, memories of blood on battlefields and sweat rolling off the backs of slaves on the plantations of the South faded away. The bridge and monument at Island Grove mean far less today to the average Abington citizen than they did to those who knew people who had lived through the trying times of the mid-19th century.

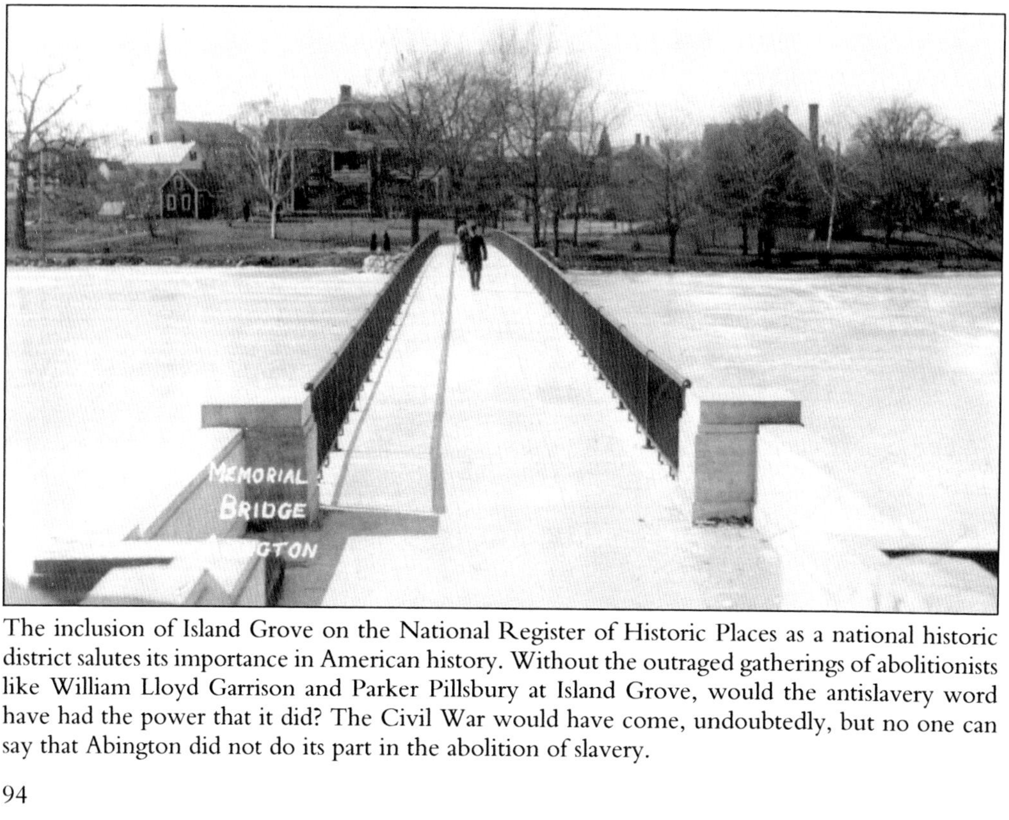

The inclusion of Island Grove on the National Register of Historic Places as a national historic district salutes its importance in American history. Without the outraged gatherings of abolitionists like William Lloyd Garrison and Parker Pillsbury at Island Grove, would the antislavery word have had the power that it did? The Civil War would have come, undoubtedly, but no one can say that Abington did not do its part in the abolition of slavery.

Nine

Abington Happenings

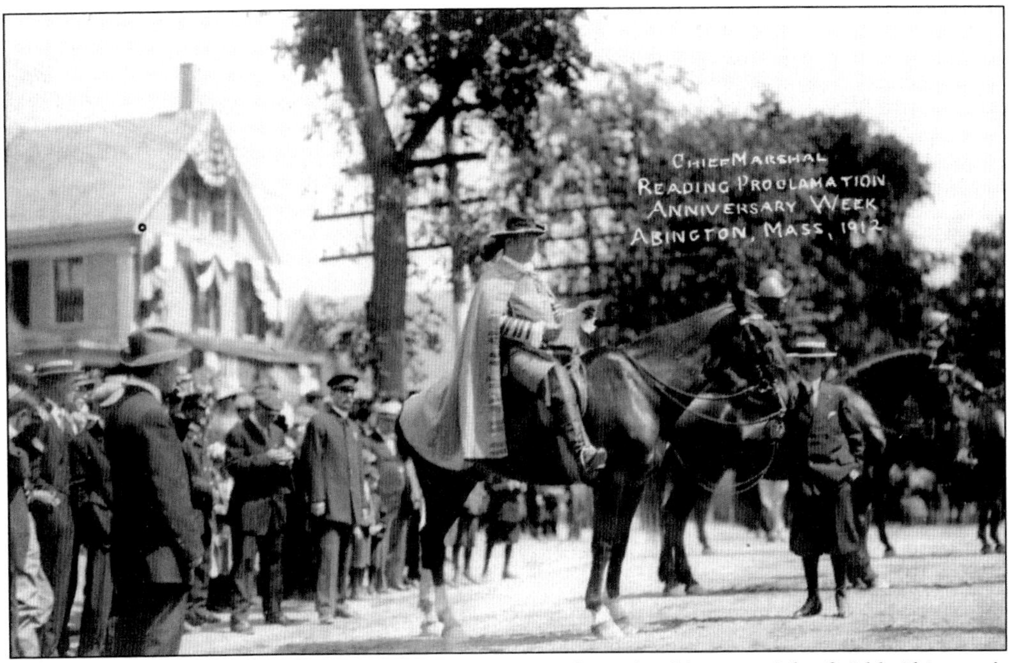

The pageantry that marked the celebration surrounding the bicentennial of Old Abington's incorporation—a week-long outdoor party that spanned three towns—will probably never be seen in Abington, Rockland (East Abington), or Whitman (South Abington) again. According to the official program, to properly open the celebration, Rockland's Alfred W. Donovan, "accompanied by his mounted marshals and aids, in the costumes of ancient heralds," proclaimed from horseback, "Ye week beginning ye ninth day of ye June in ye year of ye Lord one thousand nine hundred and twelve, one grand holiday; and ye General committee further commend all ye people—ye men, ye women, ye children—mindful of ye benefits, to give thanks to ye God for ye many blessings vouchsafed; forgetful of ye sordid cares, to rejoice and be glad . . . God save ye old town of Abington." Photographers found plenty to capture during the next seven days, leaving behind a solid record of the grandest social event ever thrown in town.

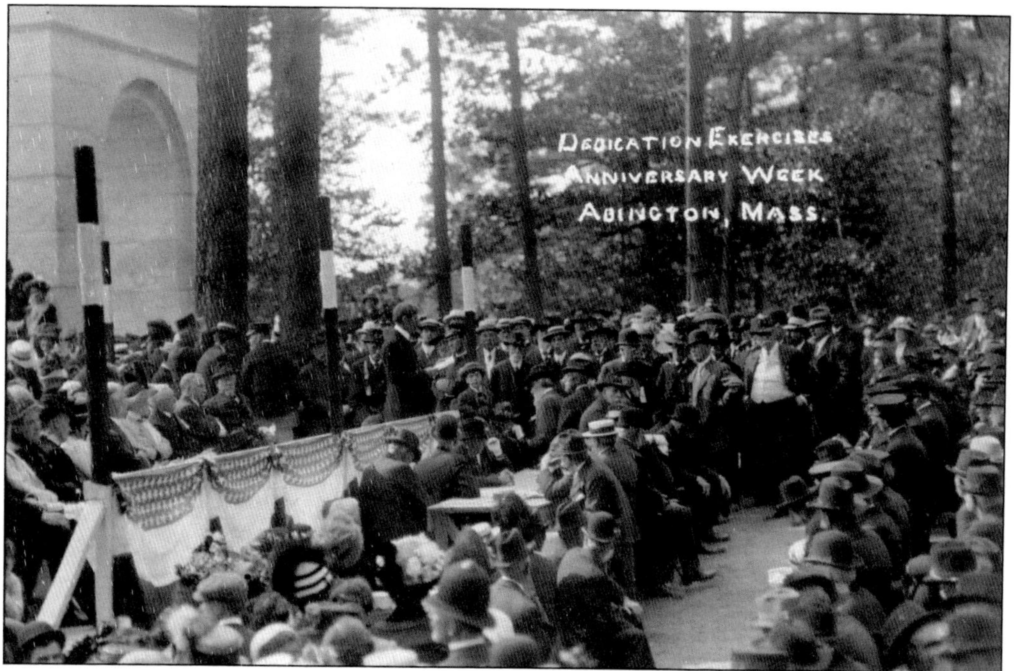

The town wrapped the dedication of the Island Grove Soldiers and Sailors Memorial into the week's events, reserving the entire first full day, June 10, 1912, exclusively for that purpose. Although the town had invited Pres. William Taft to speak at the dedication, he politely declined at the last possible moment, citing concerns in Washington, D.C., that would keep him away.

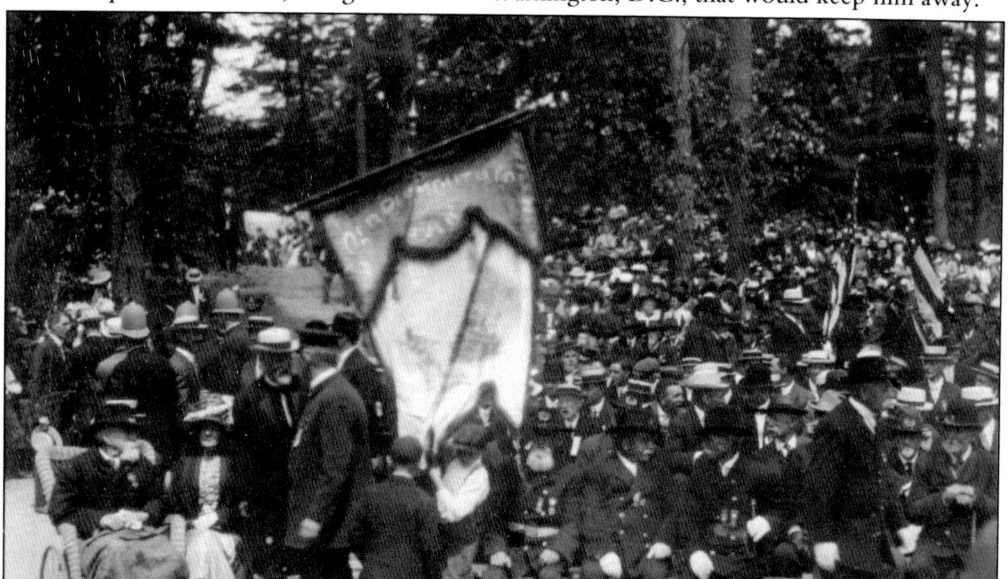

The faces that stared back at the day's speakers showed the ravages of age and of war, as the men of the various Plymouth County posts of the Grand Army of the Republic, all Civil War veterans, flooded the scene. A sea of dark blue uniforms bearing polished medals and faded ribbons, contrasted by bright white gloves and similarly white mustaches and punctuated by the occasional proudly displayed American flag, swelled and receded with the words of their own deeds and misfortunes.

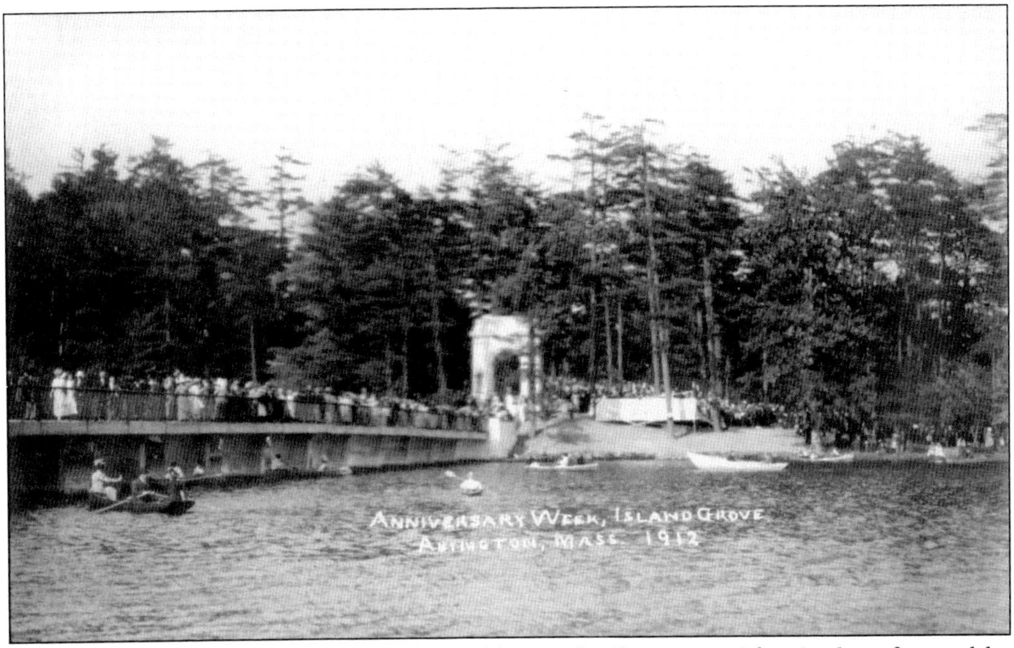

Folks attending the dedication of the new soldiers and sailors memorial arrived on foot and by boat. The bridge passed its first stress test that day with ease, while rowers darted back and forth underneath the new connector, which was the first manmade obstruction to be built on the pond.

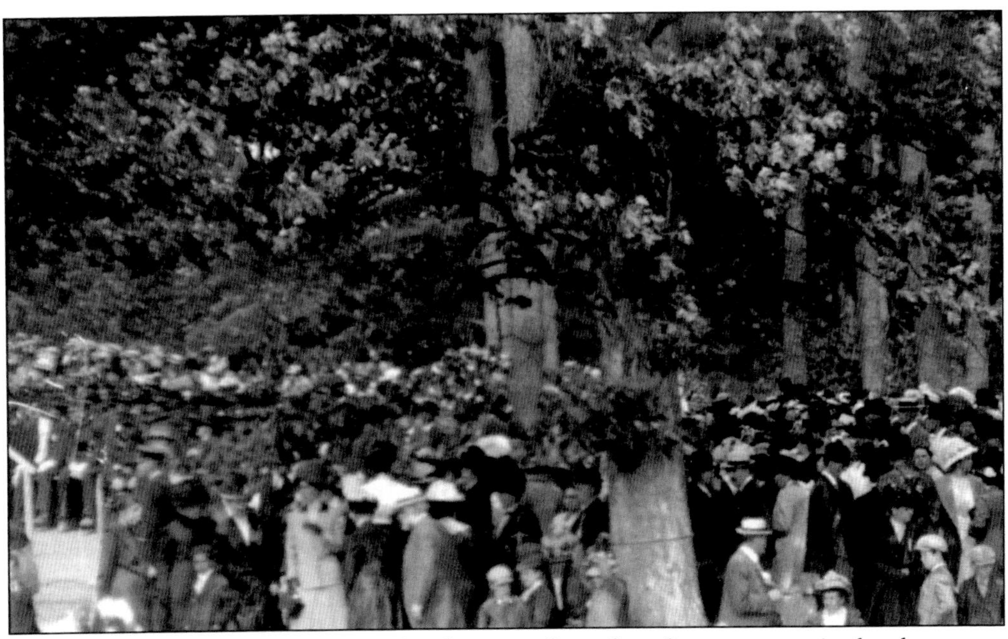

By the time the ceremony had started, barely a spare foot of standing space remained at the grove.

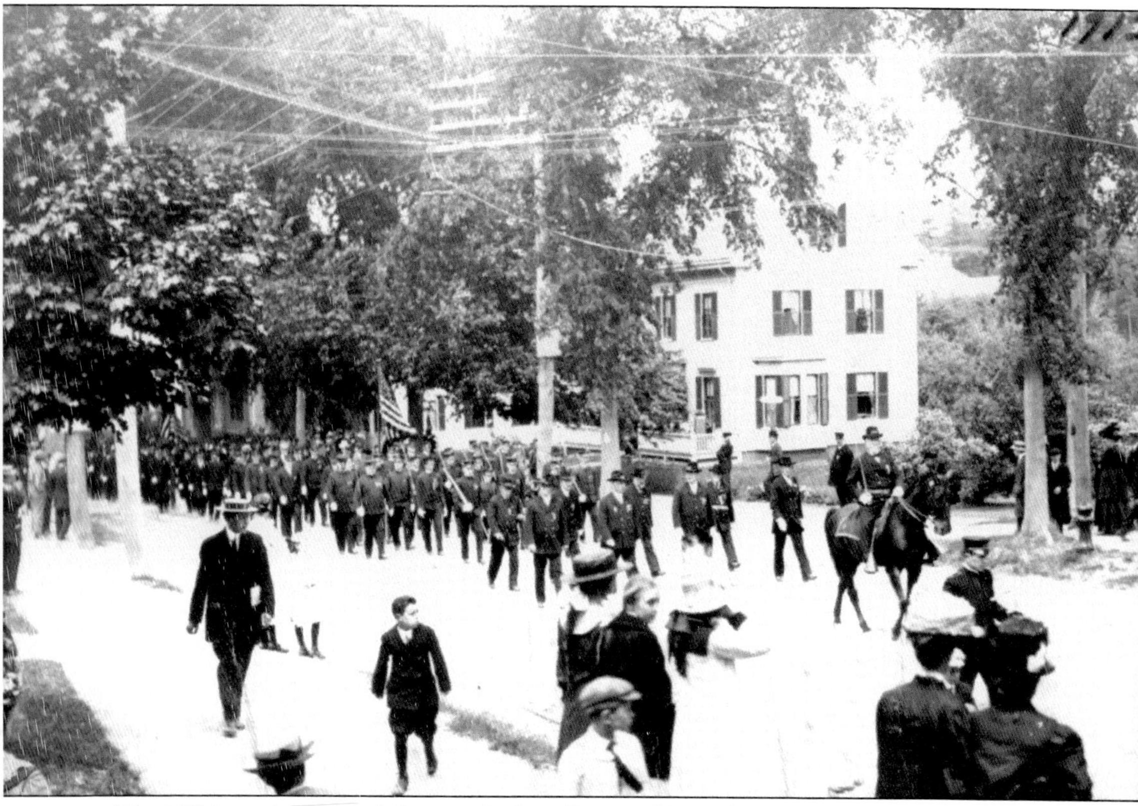

The 200th anniversary of the town's founding could not have passed without a parade. Here, the men of the Grand Army of the Republic, McPherson Post No. 73, pass in front of the home of M. Ferdinand Nash at Washington and Chapel Streets. Formed on December 23, 1868, the McPherson post (named for Maj. Gen. James Birdseye McPherson, killed in action at the Battle of Atlanta) over the years boasted a membership of 217 veterans. By 1884, that number had dropped to about 100. By 1912, nearly 50 years after the end of the Civil War, only a handful of members remained. At its height, the McPherson post had members representing 67 different infantry, cavalry, and artillery units and 12 different naval ships. The Grand Army held sway over the political arena as one of the most influential lobbying organizations in the United States.

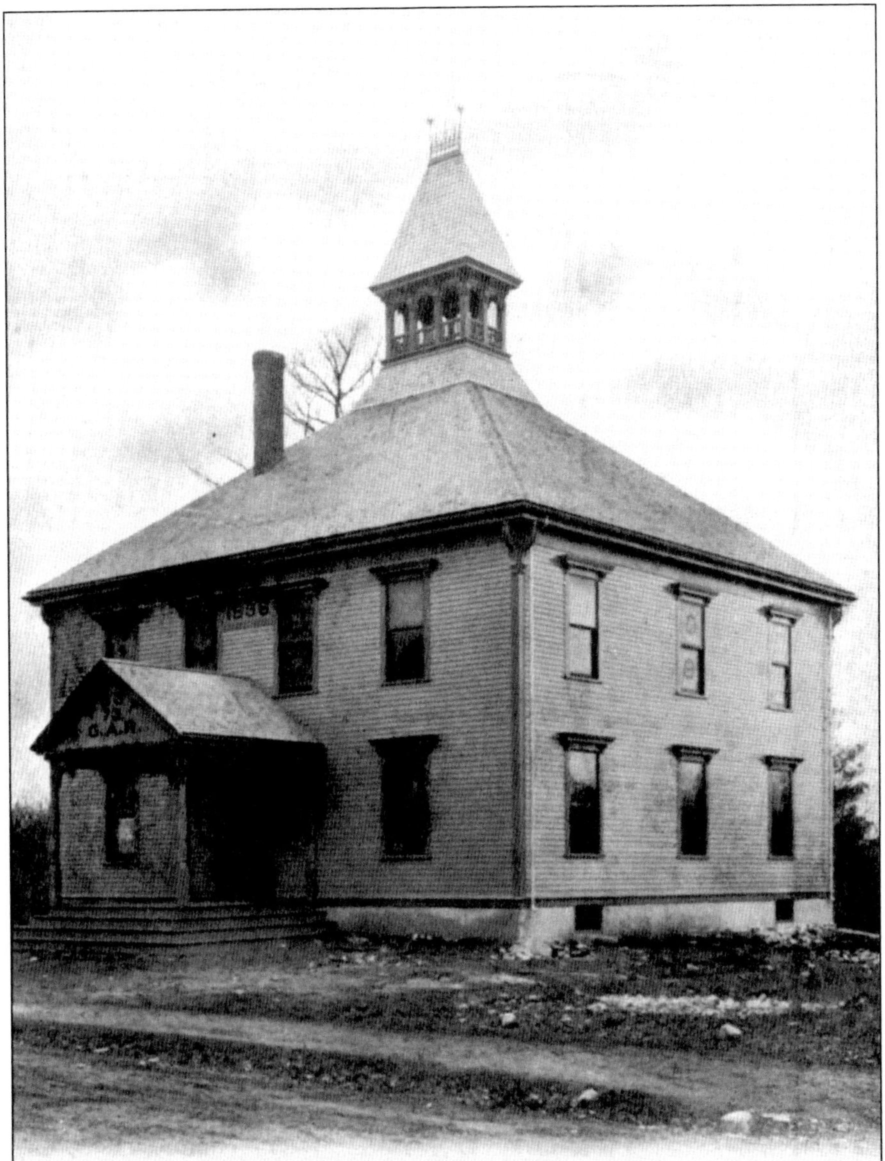

G. A. R. HALL, ABINGTON, MASS.
Issued by W. J. SHEEHAN NEWS CO.

The men of the McPherson post met every Wednesday throughout the year (except in June, July, and August, when they met every other Wednesday) at the Grand Army Hall at 833 Washington Street at the corner of Central Street. Built in 1896 after fire destroyed their meeting place, the hall became the home of the Grand Army men, the Gen. George G. Meade Camp No. 67 of the Sons of Union Veterans, and the Women's Relief Corps. The nomadic Grand Army men first convened in a hall over a shoe shop, then moved to Hatherly Hall, back to the original site, over to the hall above Blanchard's Market, and finally to a shoe shop they purchased on the site of the present building. That burned in 1895, making way for the current structure. The building is noticeable for its pyramidal roof and the stained-glass windows on the upper floor, many of which still bear the names of their donors.

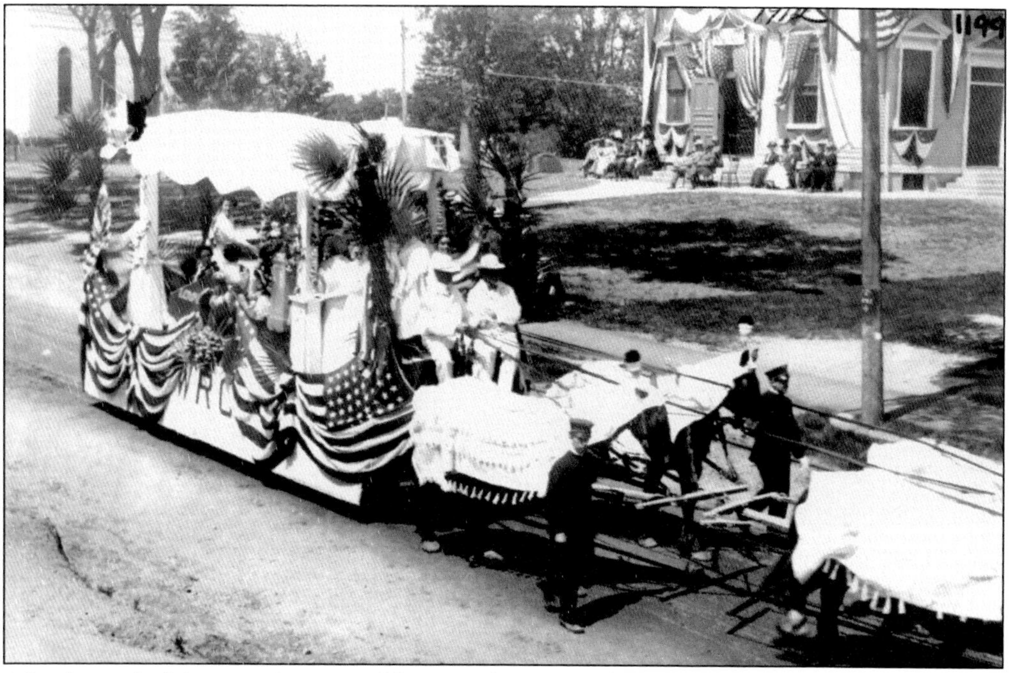

After the end of the war, the men of the Grand Army could comfortably know that they would never march alone again, in any sense of the phrase. The Women's Relief Corps, McPherson corps No. 108, stood by them, helping to raise funds for wounded veterans, providing communal meals for them, and generally aiding the men who had sacrificed their youths in service to the causes of the Union.

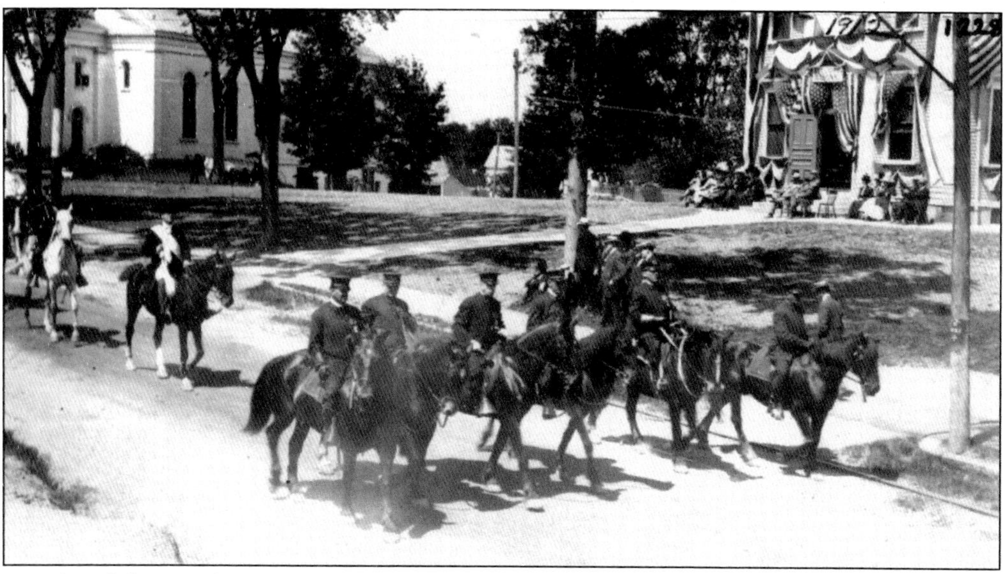

Proud to follow in their fathers' footsteps, the Sons of Union Veterans also took up the cause. Splitting time at the Grand Army Hall with their fathers' organization and the Women's Relief Corps, who met there the first and third Tuesday evening each month, the Sons of Union Veterans met every second and fourth Tuesday evening. They also joined in parades and other events to honor their fathers' deeds.

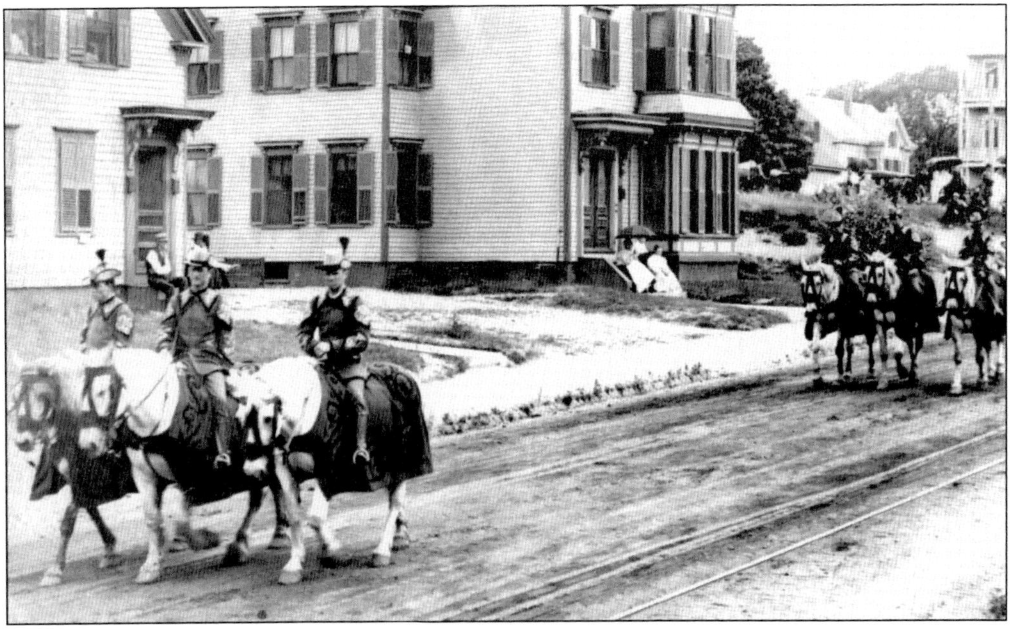

Alfred Donovan promised a spectacle when he opened the week's proceedings, and a spectacle the people of Old Abington received. Whether they are circus performers or are simply dressed as heralds for the week's events, these riders show the degree of splendor for which the parade's organizers strived.

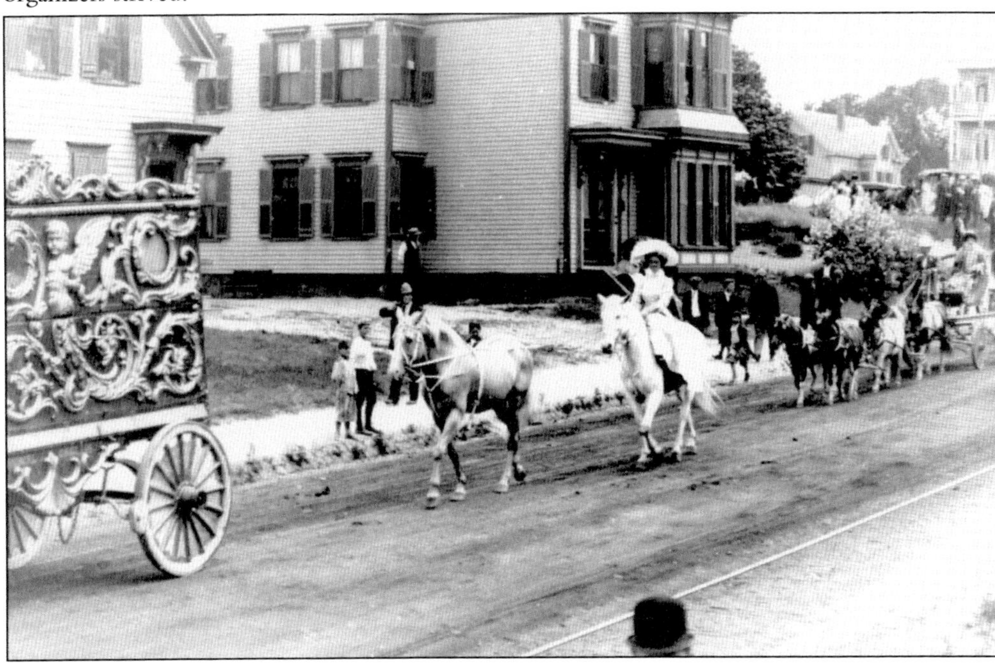

Various other parades took place during the week as well, including a children's parade, remembered 50 years after the fact by Whitman resident Doris M. Penniman. Penniman says that when they learned they were going to march in a parade, "The girls all went into huddles with the question 'What will we wear?' " The most exciting news, though, was that every child was to receive ice cream at the end of the parade.

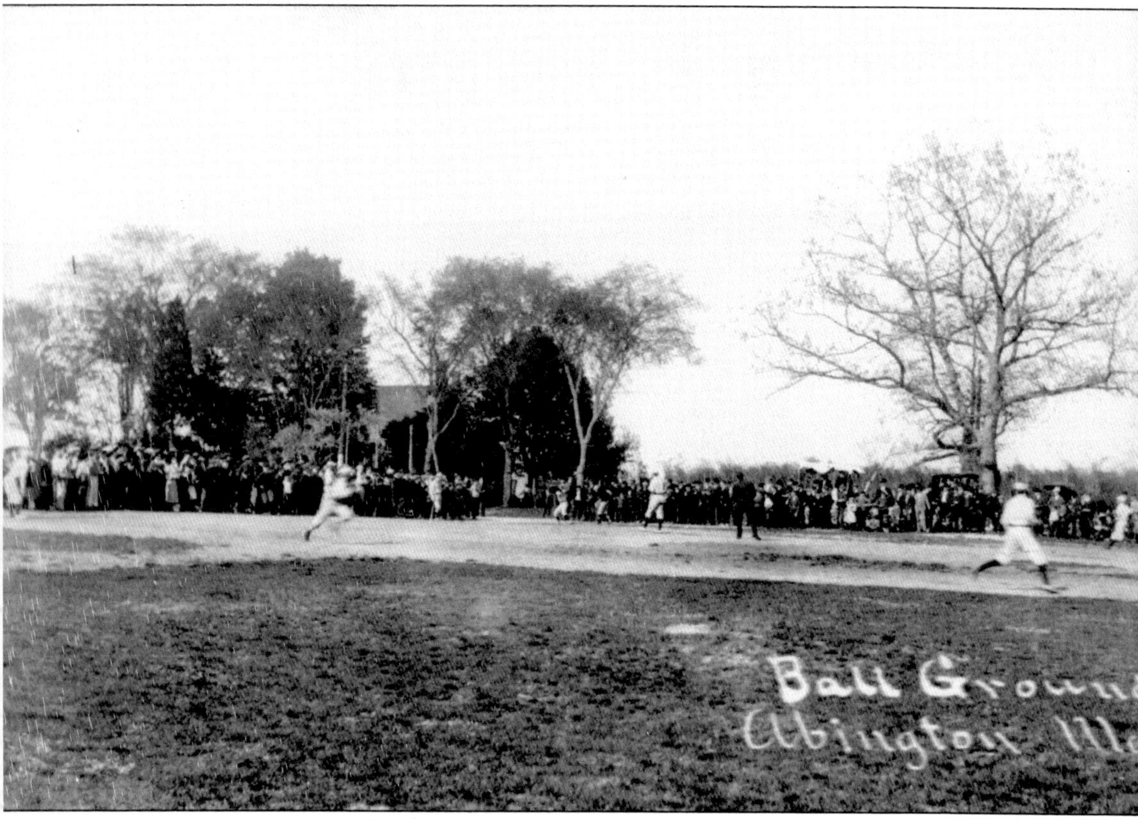

Before steroids, multimillion-dollar contracts, and big business took over the game, baseball was the national pastime. All summer long, in ballparks across the United States, young men dreamed of growing up to emulate men like Mike "King" Kelly, the first sports hero of American youth. Baseball particularly had a grip on the youth of the Boston area in the early years of the 20th century. In 1912, as the towns of Old Abington celebrated their 200th anniversary in the year that Fenway Park was built, the Boston Red Sox were on their way to winning their second World Series. In 1914, the National League Boston Braves won their first championship. Locally, the combination of two well-schooled amateur clubs could draw a crowd to rival that of any professional ballpark, as seen in this postcard of a ball ground in Abington.

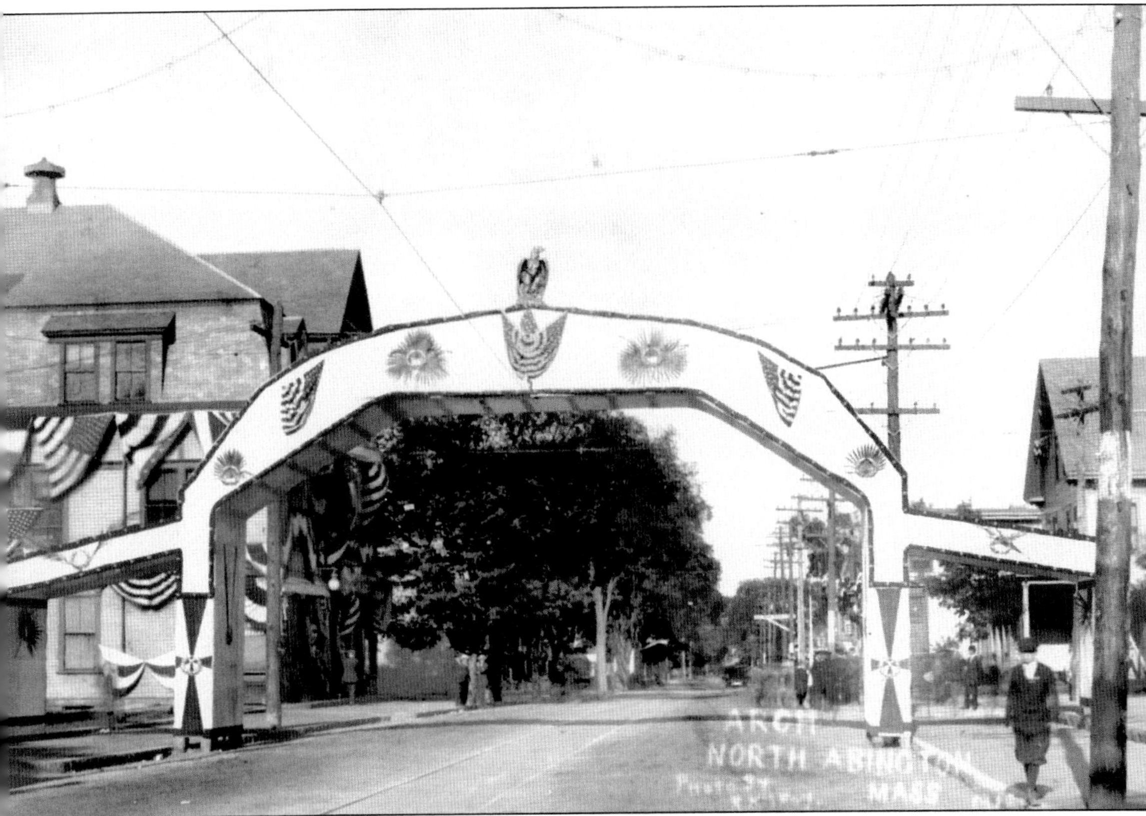

Grand celebrations of the past called for grand preparations. Although temporary in nature, parade arches symbolized a community's pride. Painstaking detail went into the design of an arch, with each adorning emblem, ensign, or other representative item—whether a noble eagle or a patriotic American flag—sending an appropriate message to the townsfolk turning out for the celebration. Parades usually kicked off under the arch. Once they passed underneath an arch, like this one at North Abington, participants knew they were underway.

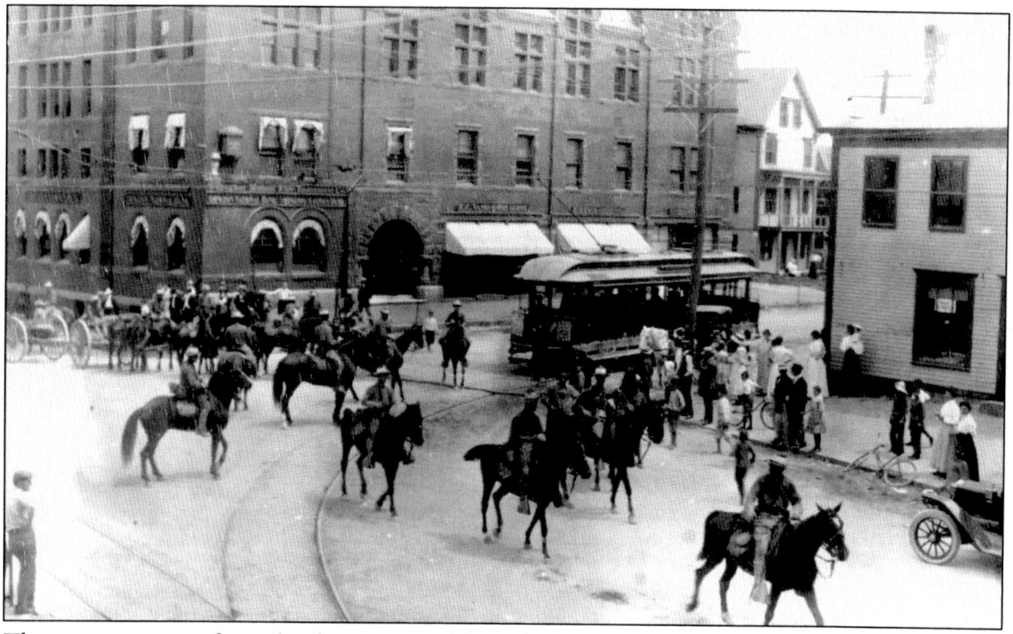

The news rang out from the front page of the July 16, 1909, edition of the *Rockland Standard:* "Troops May Invade Town: Selectmen Have Been Notified that Rockland may be Visited During the War Game—Rockland Maidens Preparing to Entertain." With the state militia participating in combat exercises with the militias of New York, Connecticut, Rhode Island, New Jersey, and the District of Columbia, the possibility of Old Abington being invaded suddenly existed.

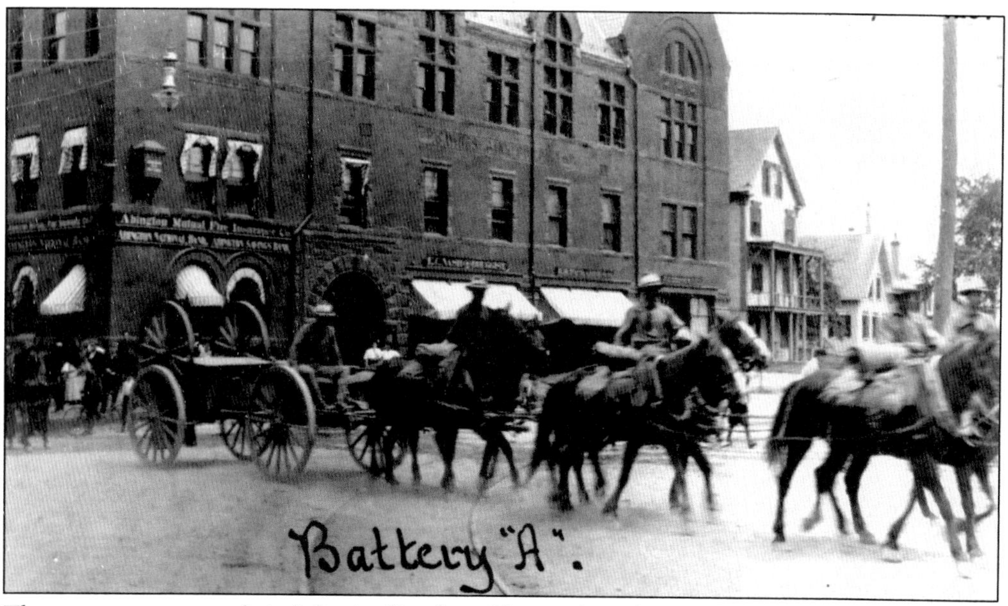

The state troops set up their defensive line from Plymouth to the Rhode Island border, ordered to prevent the invading enemy from reaching Boston. A brilliant feint by the invaders set them free on a course to the city, but the defenders caught them from behind and engaged them at Hanover Four Corners in a battle over the old North River bridge. When the invaders failed to take the bridge, they fell back, giving the field, and the war, to the boys from Massachusetts.

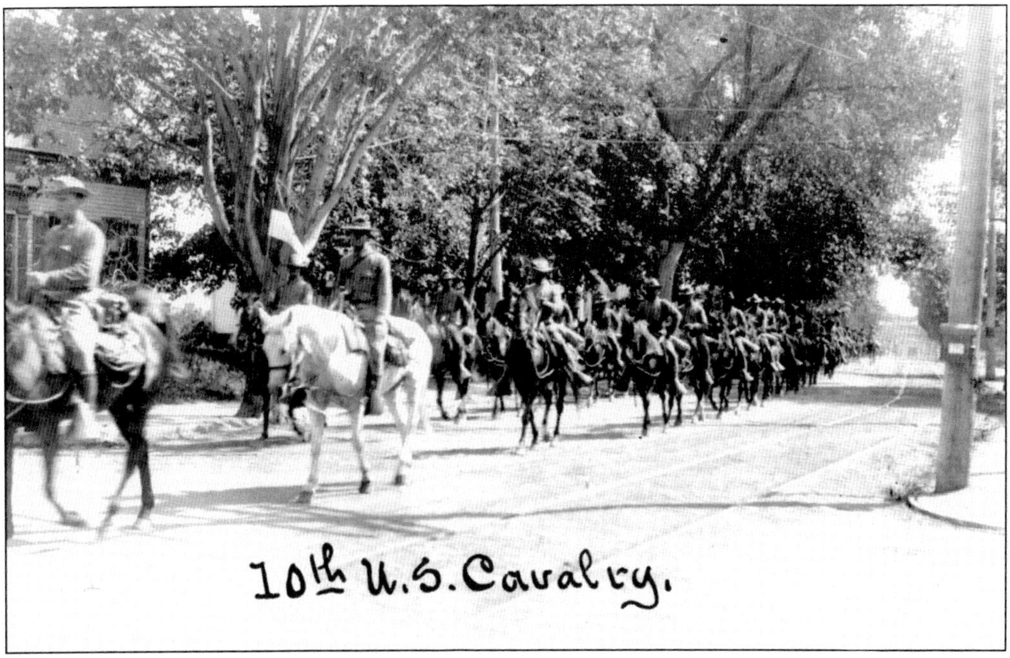

Over the next couple of days, the troops, including federal batteries and units, spared Rockland but marched through Abington, up Washington Street, and past the Abington Savings Bank building, the conquering heroes of a bloodless war. A magnificent painting of the passing of the army hangs in the Dyer Memorial Library on Centre Avenue.

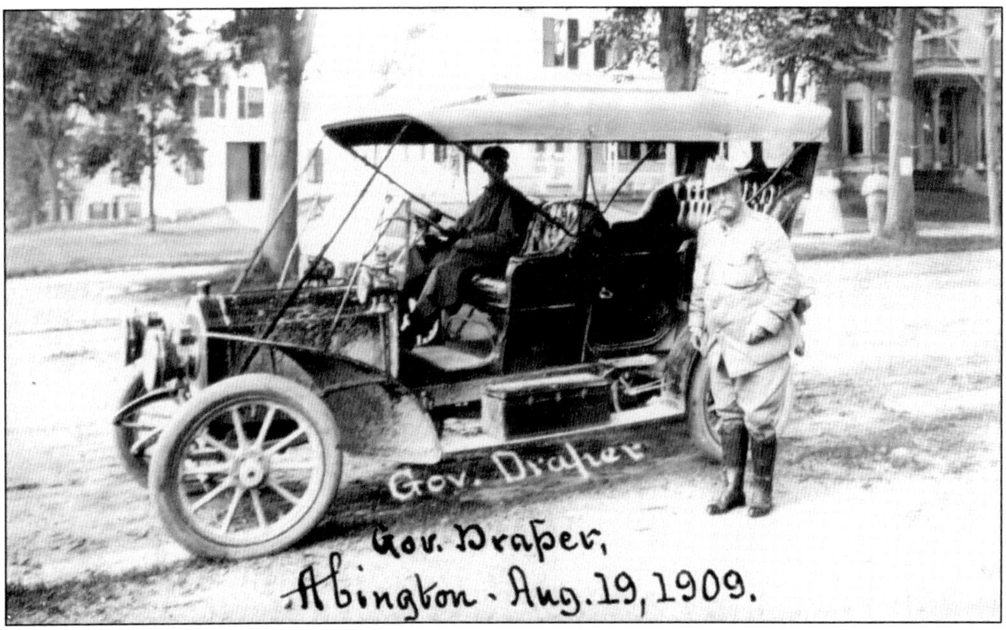

Always a politician, Massachusetts governor Eben S. Draper took his role of commander in chief of the state's troops seriously, even donning proper military trappings to reflect his stature. Unfortunately for Draper, 1909 marked his height in popularity with the state's residents, as his anti-labor stance would hinder his chances of gaining a third term in office two years later.

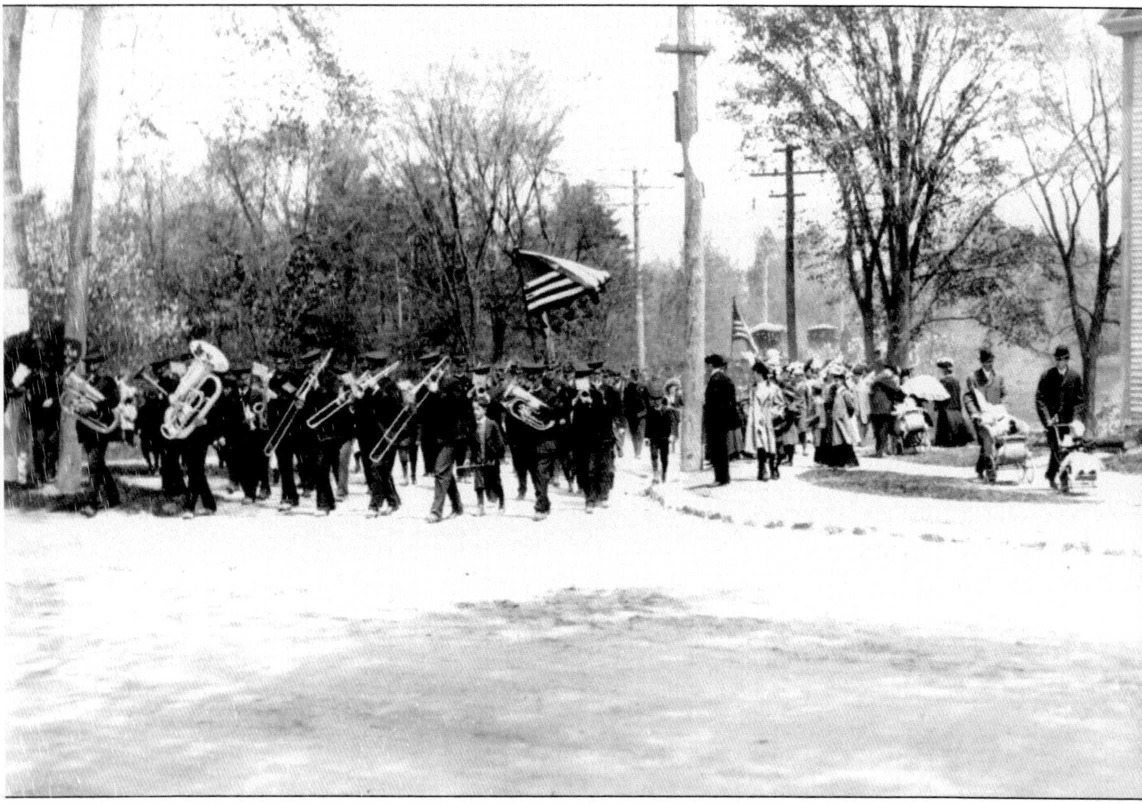

The people of Abington—be it old or new—never needed an excuse to gather. Although the disjointedness of modern American culture has separated many of the country's people from their ancestral roots, the tradition of Memorial Day parades in the north act as indicators that summer has arrived. It is a time to call friends and family back home for a refresher course on what Americans of the past went through to make Americans of today free. As shown in this May 30, 1907, Memorial Day parade in Abington, the collective spirit of the American people has never truly wavered since the Civil War. Take a snapshot of a parade today and compare it to this one to see the similarities. A postcard of a local parade sent to a loved one far away sent a message to never forget the town from which he or she came.

Ten

The Business of the Pond

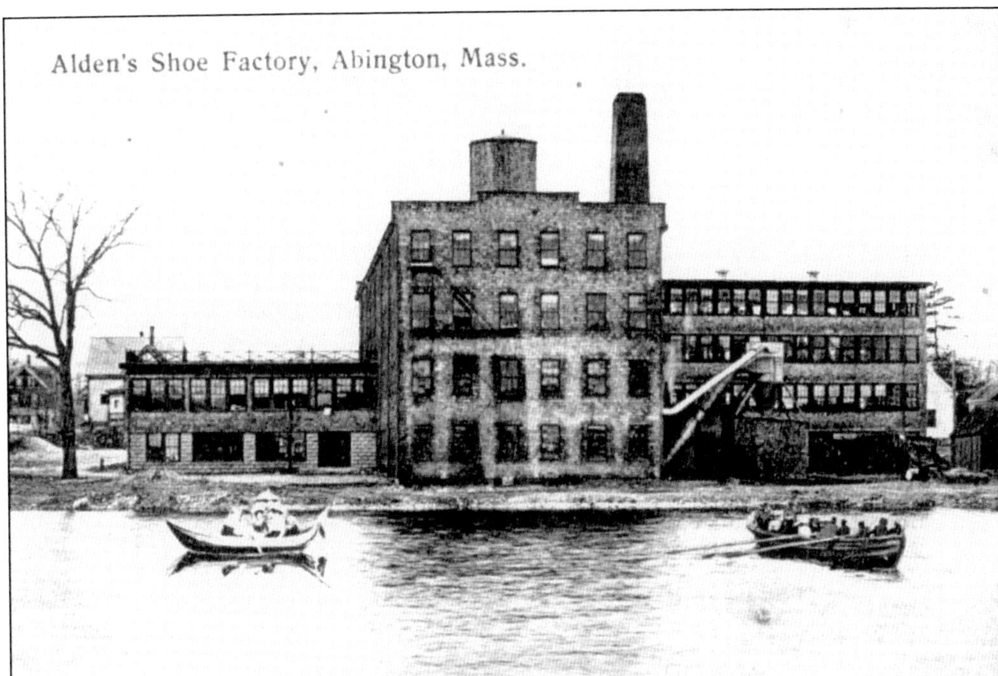

While many people in Abington, both today and in the early era of postcard production, saw Island Grove as a place of relaxation and repose, sunshine and sunsets, and moonlight and memories, many others were forever tied to the notion of the pond as a place of business, either directly on its surface or on its shorelines. Charles H. Alden purchased the Lake Street factory of Henry H. Dunham in 1896. The following year, upon the discovery of gold in Canada, he paid his workmen in that precious metal, forever earning the nickname "the Klondike" for his factory.

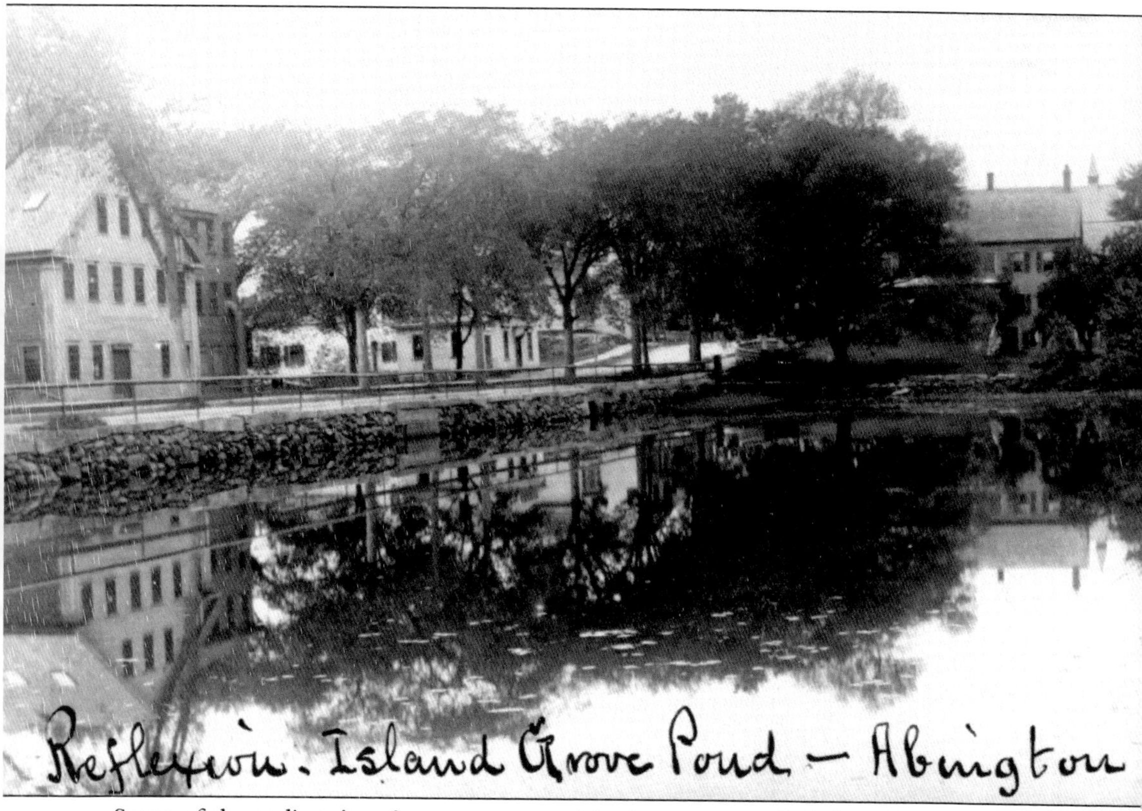

Some of the earliest American entrepreneurial adventures entailed damming small brooks and pooling water for later use in powering machinery. Many of the South Shore's ponds—from Straits Pond in Hingham and Hull to Old Oaken Bucket Pond in Scituate and others—were formed just this way, to power mills that ground corn, sawed wood, or performed a host of other needed tasks. Water also instantly became a necessary highway for the transportation of raw materials and finished goods to and from factories, retail outlets, and job sites. Of course, Island Grove Pond did not offer that particular advantage, but many businesses were constructed right along the water's edge nonetheless.

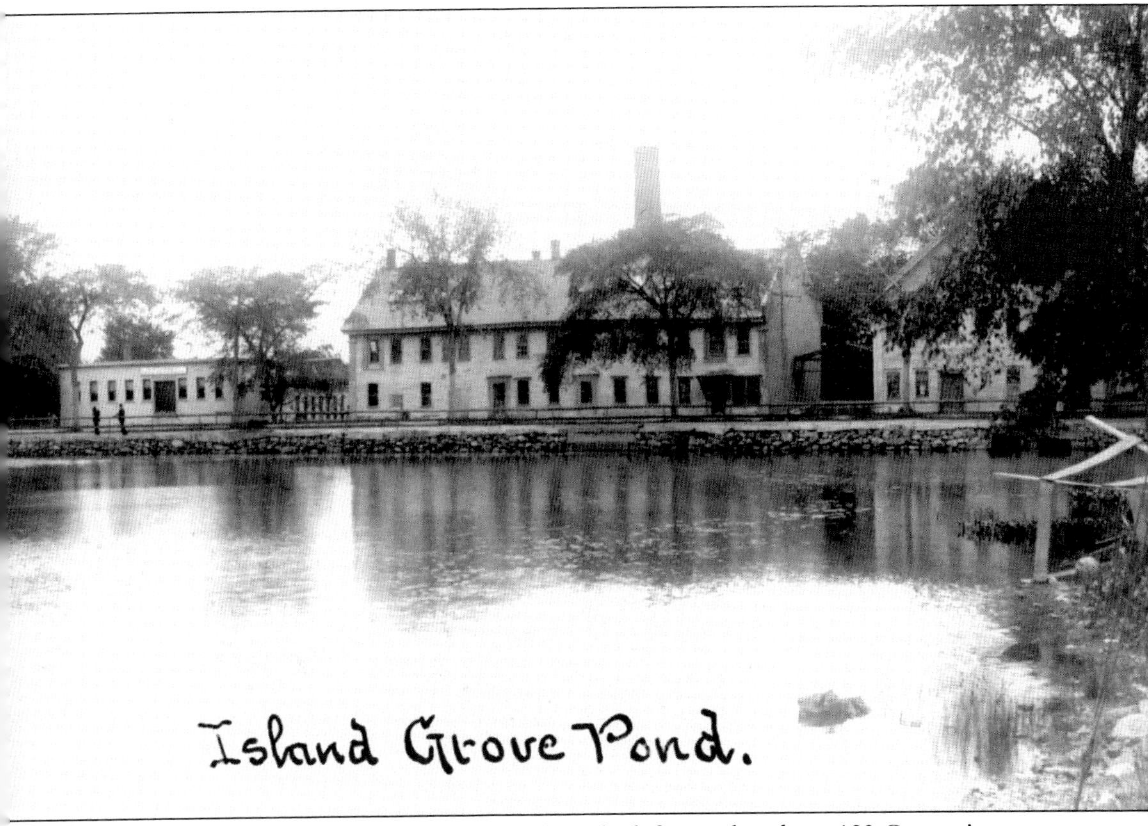

Herbert H. Buffum's factories, in the center and on the left, stood at about 123 Centre Avenue. Buffum, a true inventor if Abington ever had one, manufactured taffy-pulling machines that adorned the windows of shops on Nantasket Beach for years. He later diverted his attention to the manufacture of automobiles, developing his own four-cylinder chain-driven car in 1903. This car, unlike others that preceded it, utilized a steering wheel instead of a rudder for turning. Later, most likely after he moved to Brockton in 1908, Buffum developed plans for even larger cars, of 6 and 12 cylinders, although before building the latter he ran out of funding to do so. Buffum's large buildings also housed other businesses on rented space, including last makers for shoes and other attendant industries.

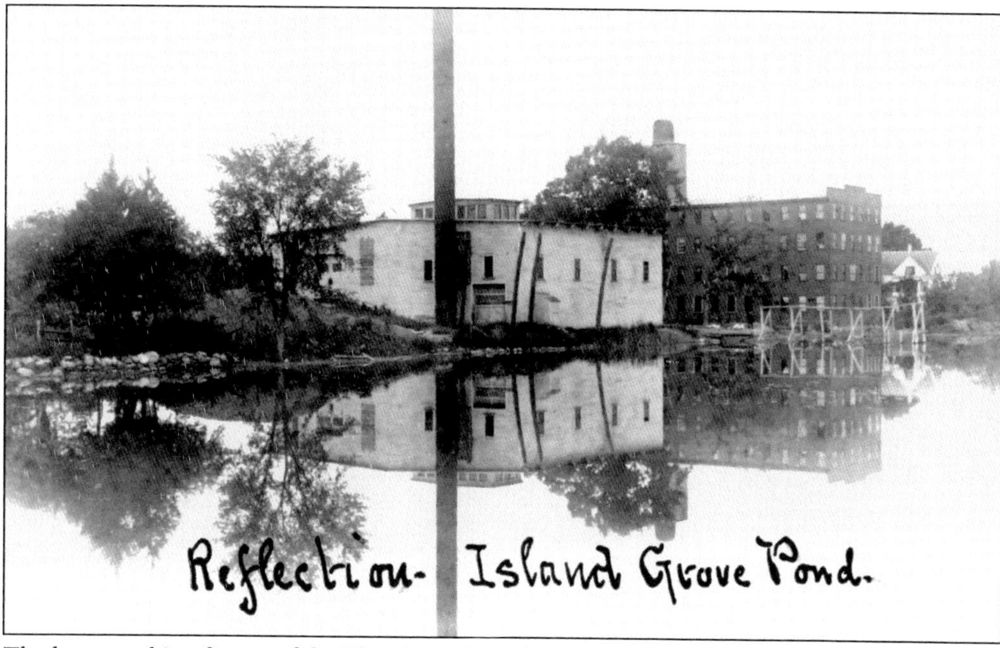

The long-reaching fingers of the Electric Light and Power Company of Abington and Rockland once touched homes as far away as Norwell, Scituate, and Cohasset. The old substation that generated the electricity to run the streetcars in town once sat on Island Grove Pond, next door to C. F. Alden's "Klondike" shoe factory. The company began operation in Abington in 1891, building a power station on Charles Street. After securing the contract to power the street railway in 1893, a five-year deal, they constructed the Lake Street substation.

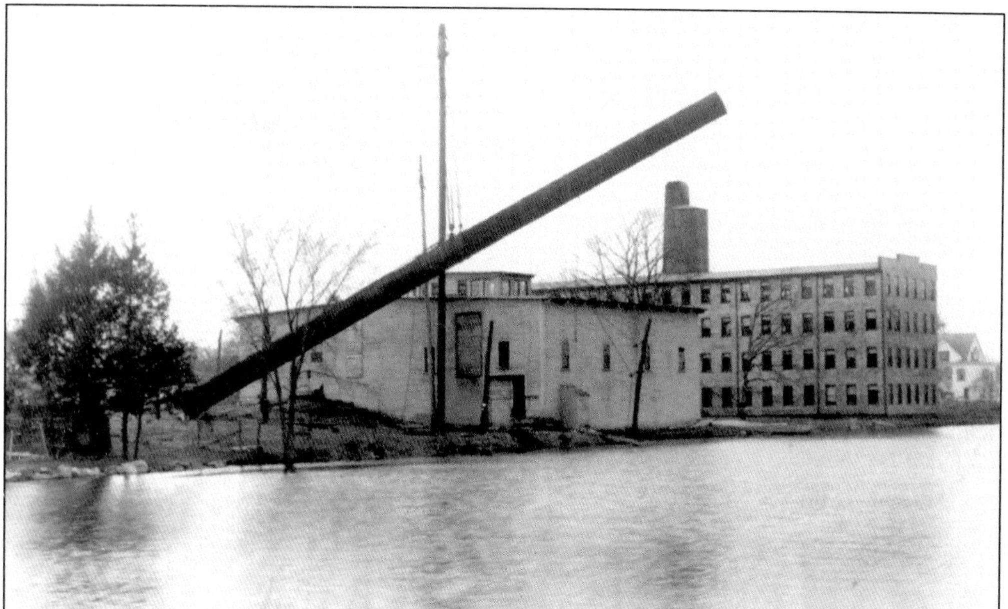

According to the power company's official history, "About 1896 it was found necessary, in order to take care of the exceedingly variable load of the Street Railway Company, to install a storage battery with necessary building. This battery at the time was an unusual feature, being of unusual size."

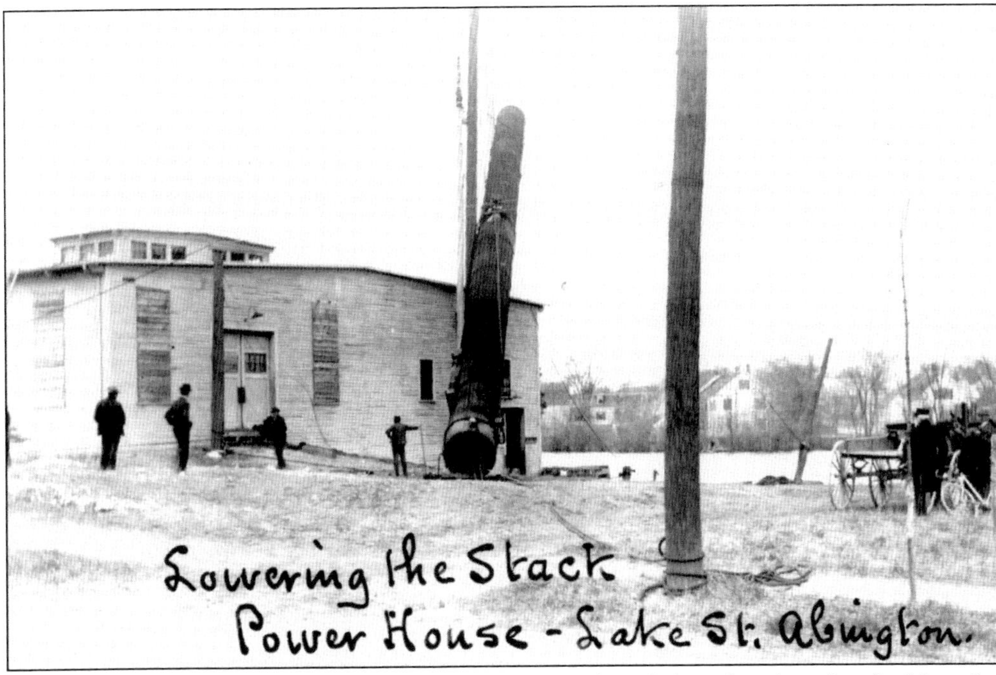

In 1899, the power company's original contract expired, and the substation closed, although a power failure in Braintree once sent it back into emergency operation.

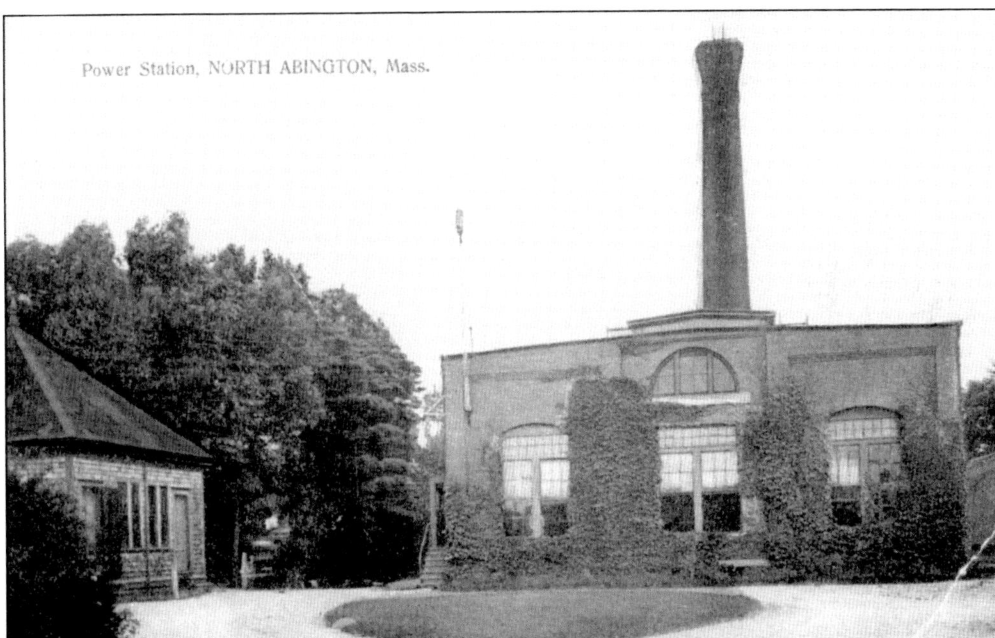

The main station, in North Abington, served several communities for many years. According to its mission, "the policy of this Company is to be frank and honest in all its dealings with all its customers and with the public, and to give the best service possible, at fair and reasonable prices. We do not claim any moral excellence in stating this as our policy, but simply state our attitude as a business policy."

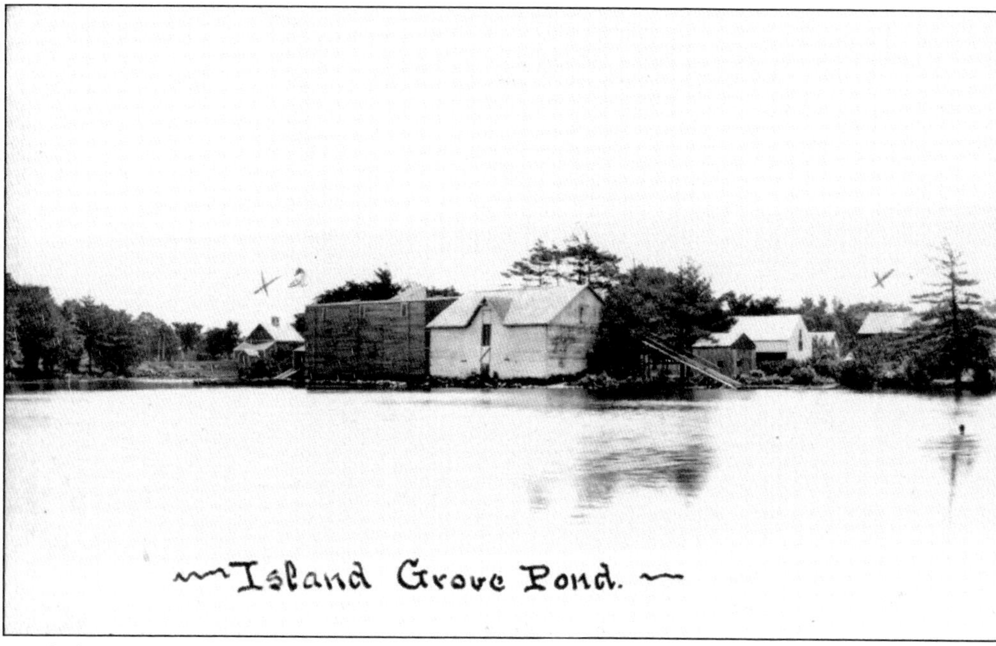

Ice dealers did brisk business in the years before electrical refrigeration. A pond the size of Island Grove Pond was a natural gold mine for businessmen like Charles F. Dudley, manager of the Abington and Whitman Ice Company of 155 Centre Avenue.

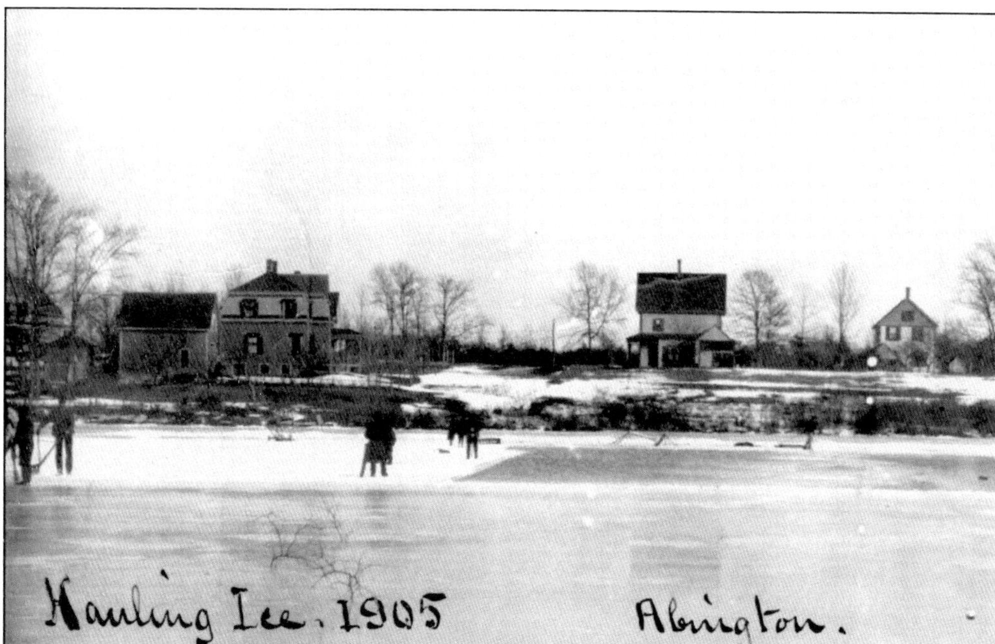

In order to control the cutting process, icemen cut in patterns of similar-sized blocks. Ice, kept cold with sawdust, could be stored throughout the winter for use in spring and summer. Boston's famous "Ice King," Frederick Tudor, found ways to ship ice to places like New Orleans and even India while still making a profit, although some melting naturally occurred.

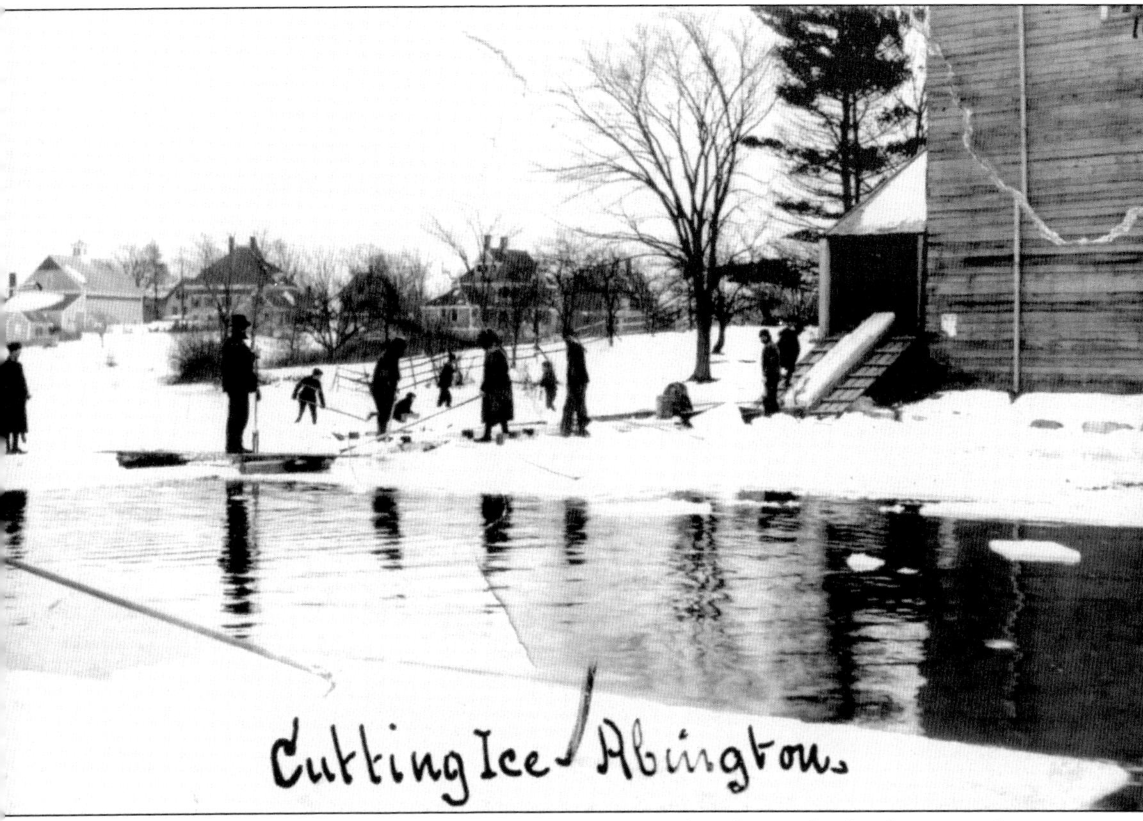

Locally, the ice-cutting game featured the same old routine and no financial risk-taking, or at least nothing along the lines of what the "Ice King" underwrote. Like farming, the industry had its own specialized selection of tools used during the harvest in winter. The blocks of ice passed along a ramp and into the storage facility, where they were kept until they were needed later in the year. In many towns, ice dealers competed with each other for customers. At Wenham, the locals prided themselves on the ice of Wenham Lake. They took a simple mention by Queen Victoria, who stated that she liked it in her drink, and turned it into an advertising campaign calling the ice Pure Wenham. Unfortunately, in some parts of England, where the pronunciation of the letter "w" got mixed with the pronunciation of the letter "v," Wenham ice became known as "pure venom." Charles F. Dudley of the Abington and Whitman Ice Company promised "prices reasonable and satisfaction guaranteed."

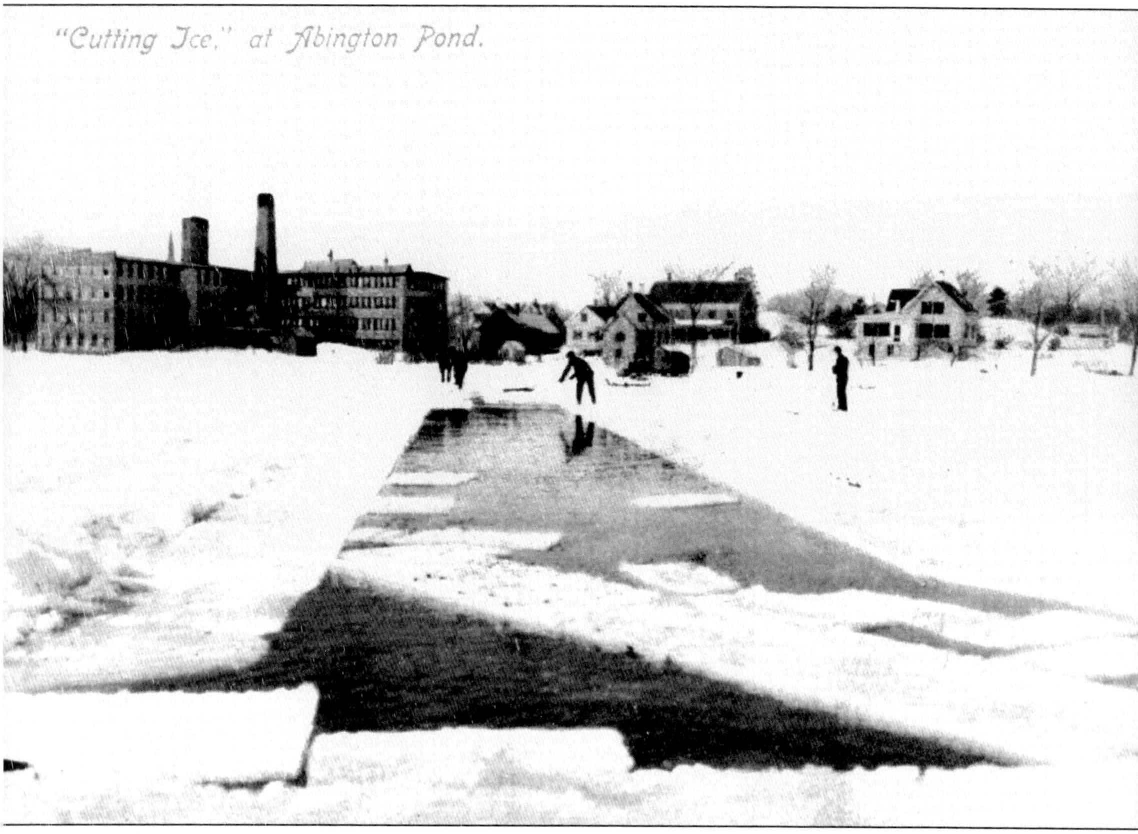

The work of ice cutting was not for the weak or the faint of heart. It involved its share of sweat and aches and pains. Yet, like many of the images captured in Abington postcards over the years, the photographs of ice cutters working at their trade evoke somewhat romantic notions of the past and of sights that are simply never to be seen again.

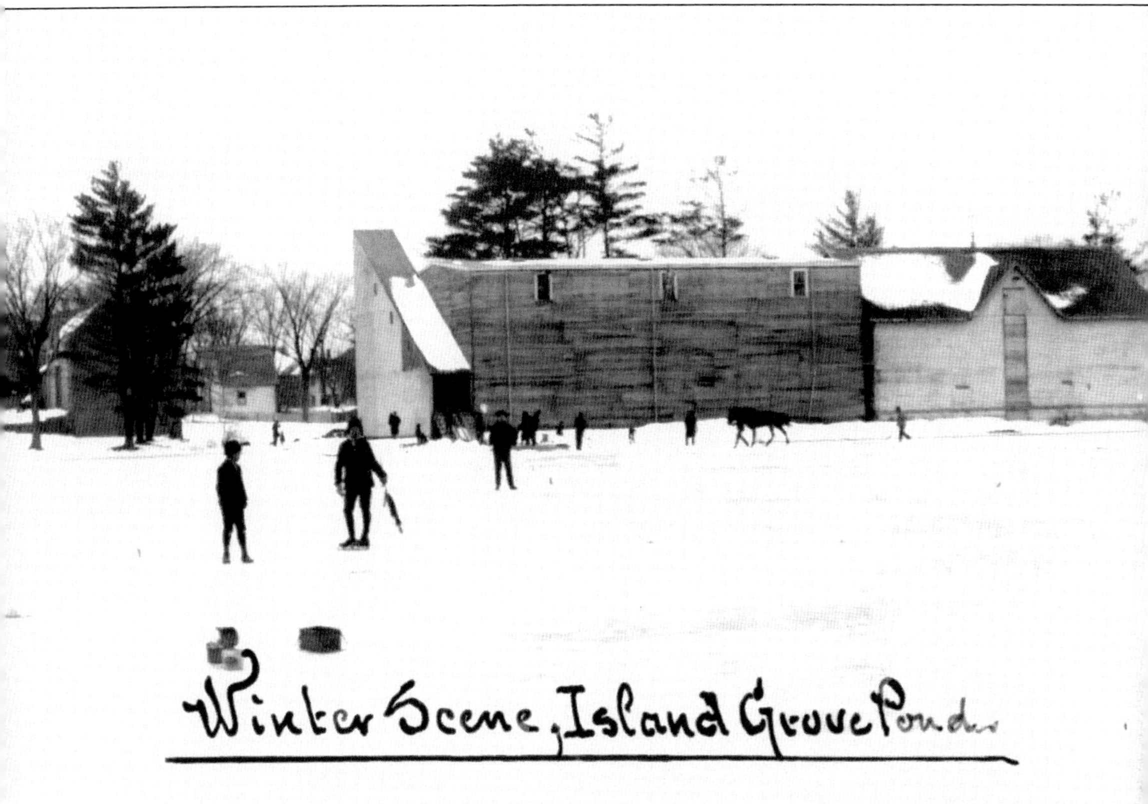

While some men cut the ice for profit, others cut holes in it for fun. Just because the pond froze over did not mean that the fish that lived in it stopped living. Ice fishing and ice-skating were just two of the many joys of winter recreation shared by the people of Abington, especially those who lived near Island Grove Pond.

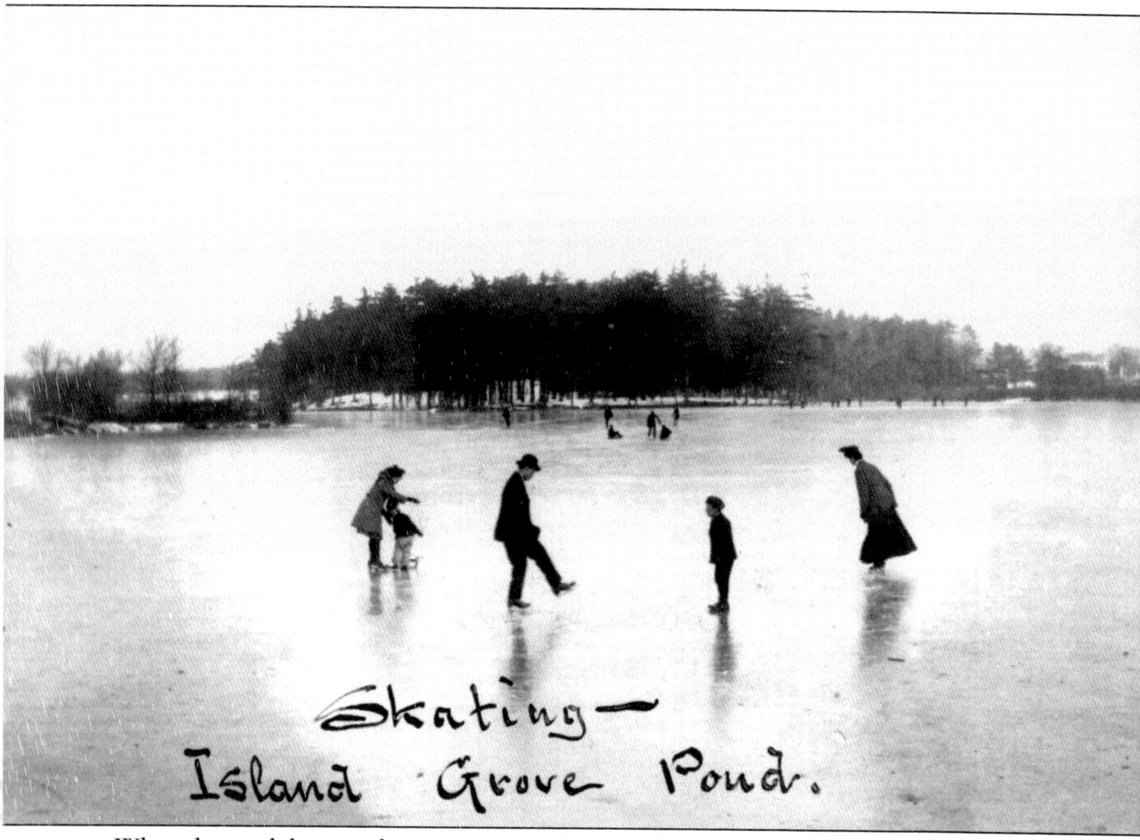

When the workday was done, or even as it was still going on, wintertime revelers took to the pond for fun. Here, Margaret Dexter helps a small child as Frank Dexter practices his figure eights. On the right, Louise Dexter hones her skating skills. Island Grove Pond, like the ground of the grove itself, meant many things to many people.

Eleven

A Place to Rest

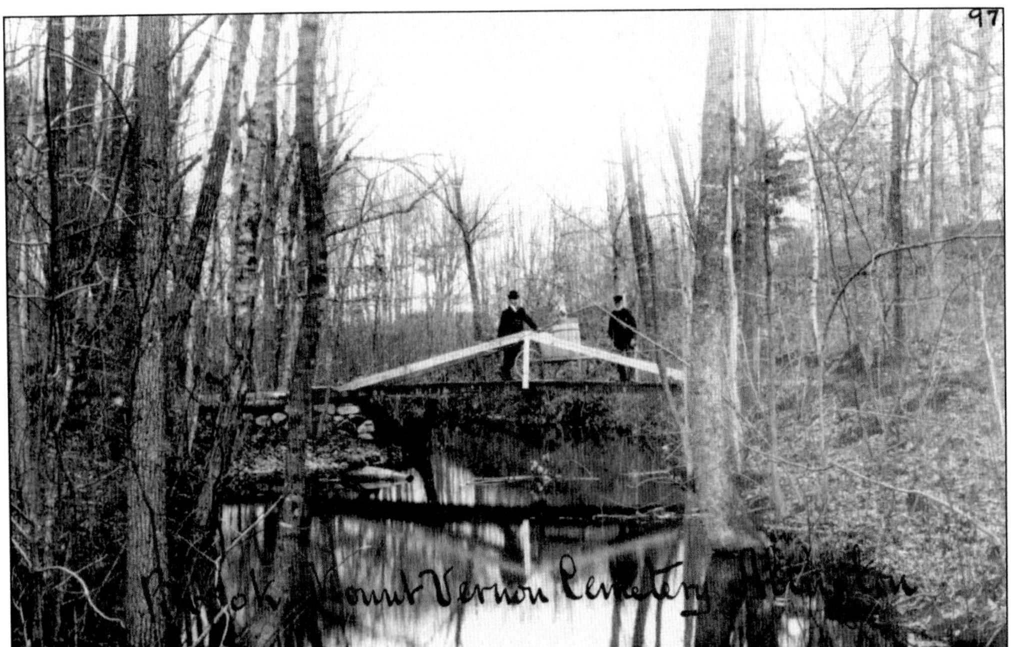

This bridge is at Mount Vernon Cemetery near the Washington Street entrance. The old graveyards, associated with churches or family burial grounds on farms, were either neglected or overcrowded, and in some cases they were a health hazard. In the first quarter of the 19th century, there was a movement to replace cemeteries in the United States. The movement and the design of the new cemeteries were inspired by the Romantic movement of the late 18th and the 19th centuries. The result was the establishment of the garden, or rural, cemetery, the first of which was Mount Auburn in Cambridge in 1831. These cemeteries usually were located outside of the center of the town. In Mount Vernon's case, it is only about a mile from the center of town. The cemeteries were not associated with any particular church and were either owned by the town or by an association, as is Mount Vernon Cemetery in Abington, which was consecrated May 31, 1853.

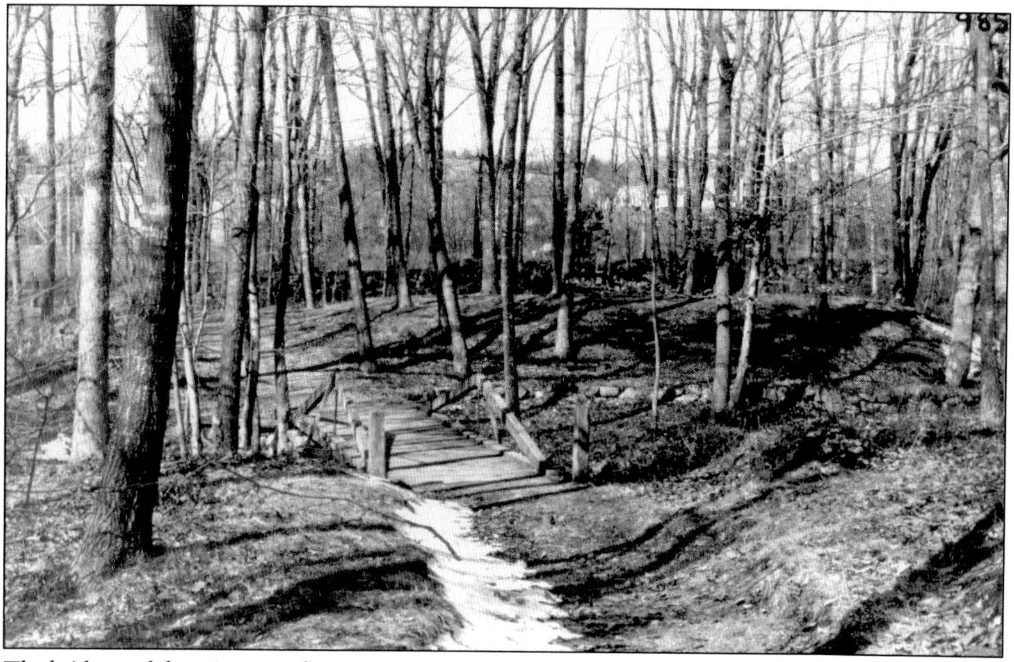

The bridge and the winter are favorite subjects for the postcard photographer. William Wordsworth, a leader of the Romantic movement, may have summed up the love of nature that influenced the landscape design of the garden cemeteries in his lines, "One impulse from a vernal wood / May teach you more of man, / Of moral evil and good / Than all the sages can."

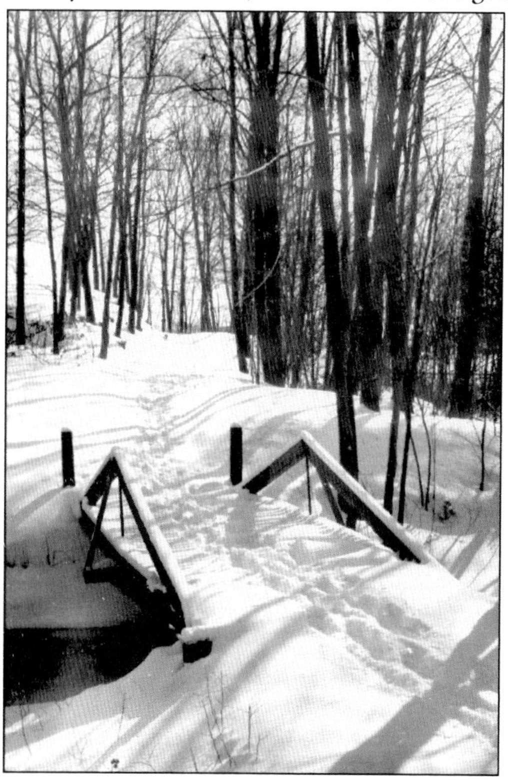

This is the same bridge as seen in the previous card, but the landscape is fully covered in snow. Man's presence is shown by the tracks in the snow.

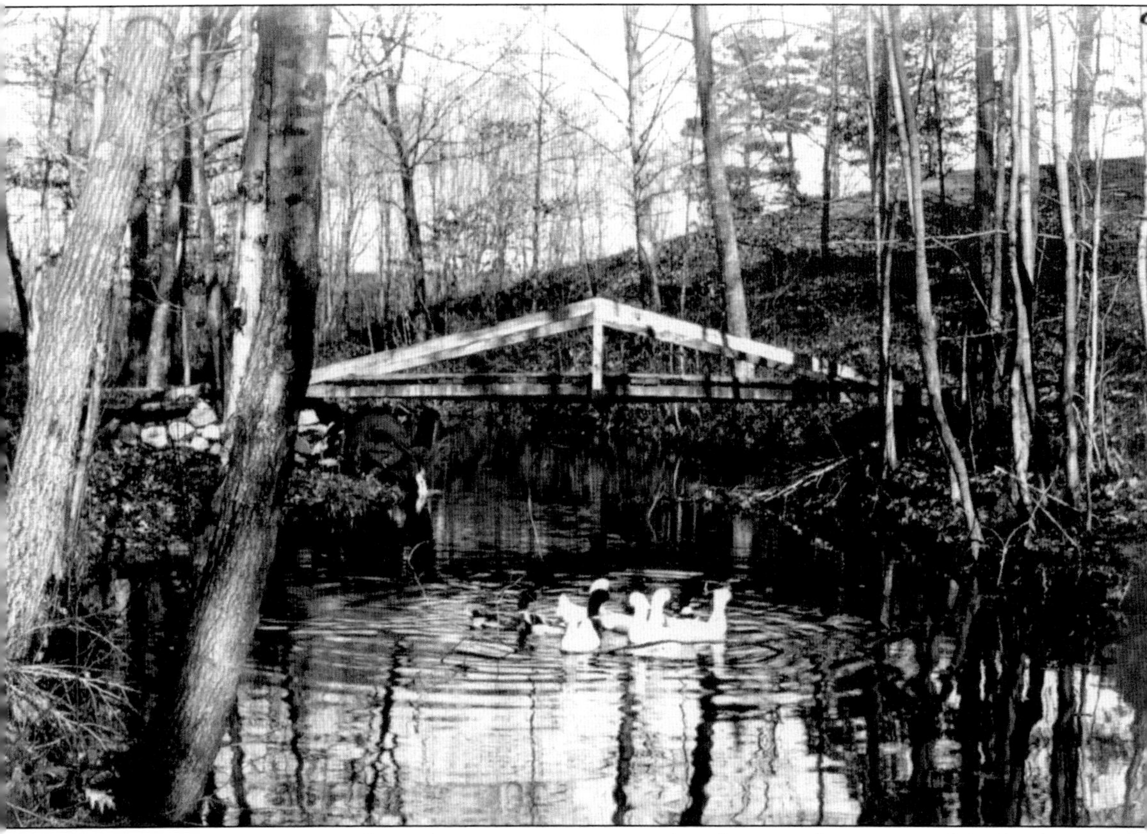

The Romantics' interest in seeking the picturesque meant that the natural contours of the land were preserved. Graves were fitted into those contours. Trees were saved and wildlife was encouraged. Special plantings were added. The first publication of the Mount Vernon Cemetery Corporation notes, "hundreds who have visited the spot during the past season have said . . . that in point of location, variety of scenery, and every other natural advantage, no cemetery in New England surpasses this, not excepting even Mount Auburn." Later cemeteries were designed flat, often solely to ease maintenance.

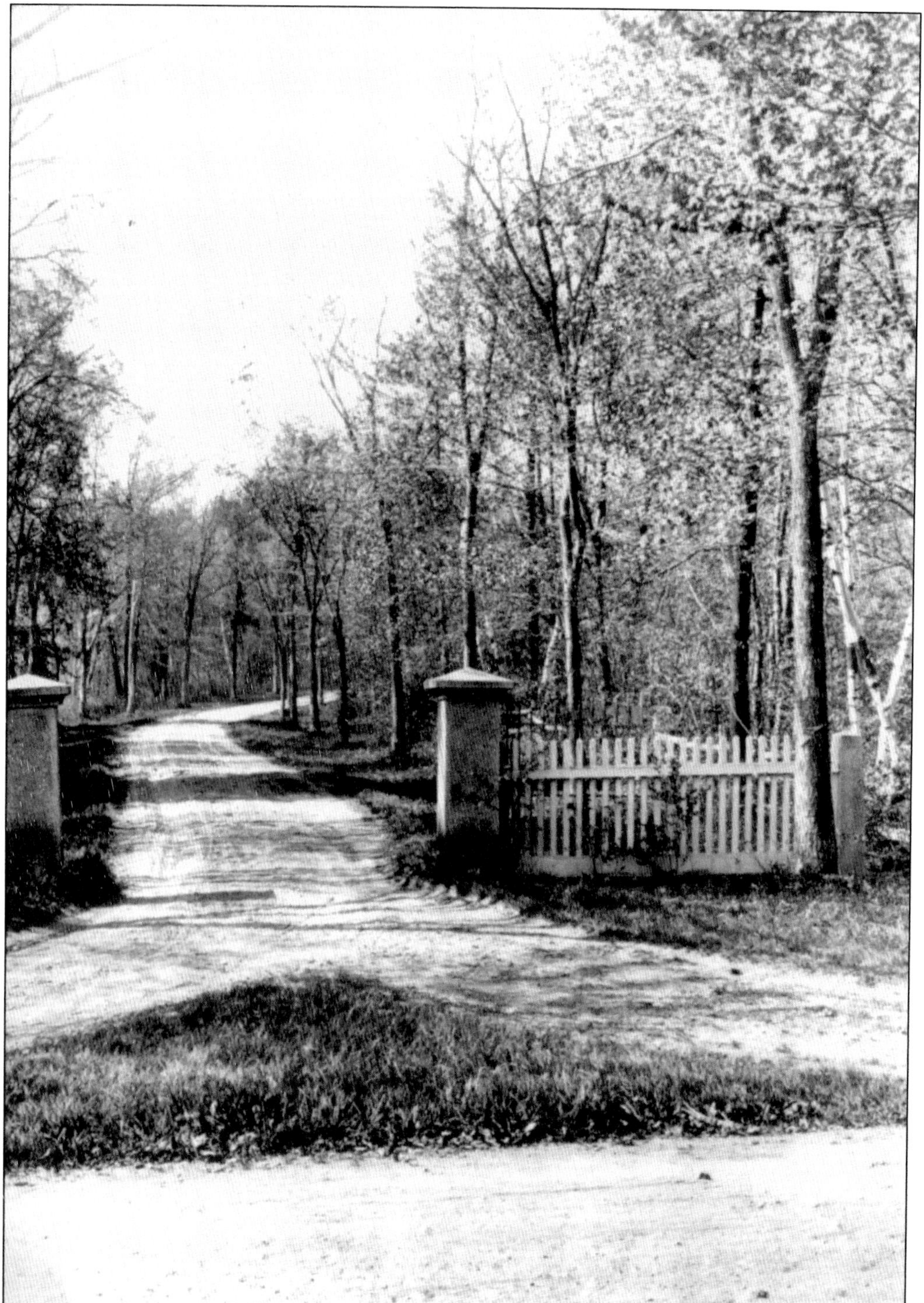

Gates were important parts of the garden cemeteries. Mount Auburn has a large Egyptian Revival gate. Here, the gates are modest and consist of two granite posts with pyramid-like caps. The gate is almost lost in modern times due to development adjacent to the entrance.

Andrew Jackson Downing wrote a book in 1841 called *A Treatise on the Theory and Practice of Landscape Gardening, Adapted to North America with a View to the Improvement of the Country*. This book was popular and influential. Downing advocated public spaces and the picturesque. Frederick Law Olmsted was influenced by the works of Downing, as well as by the garden cemeteries. The result is Olmsted's design of Central Park in New York City in 1857.

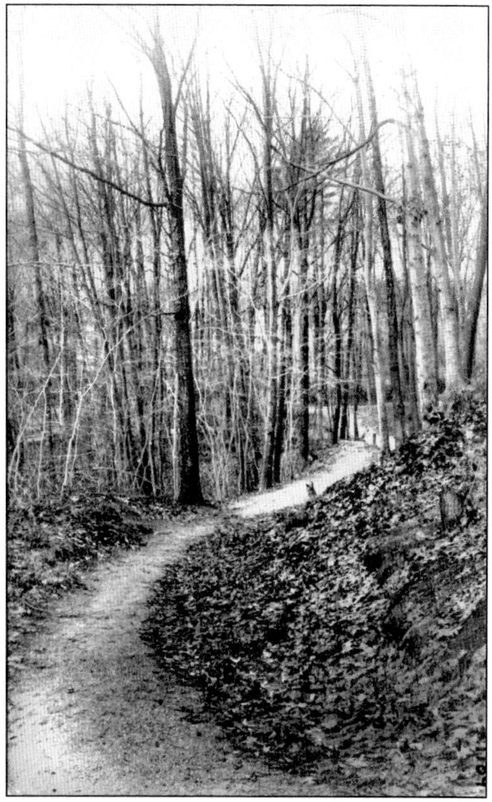

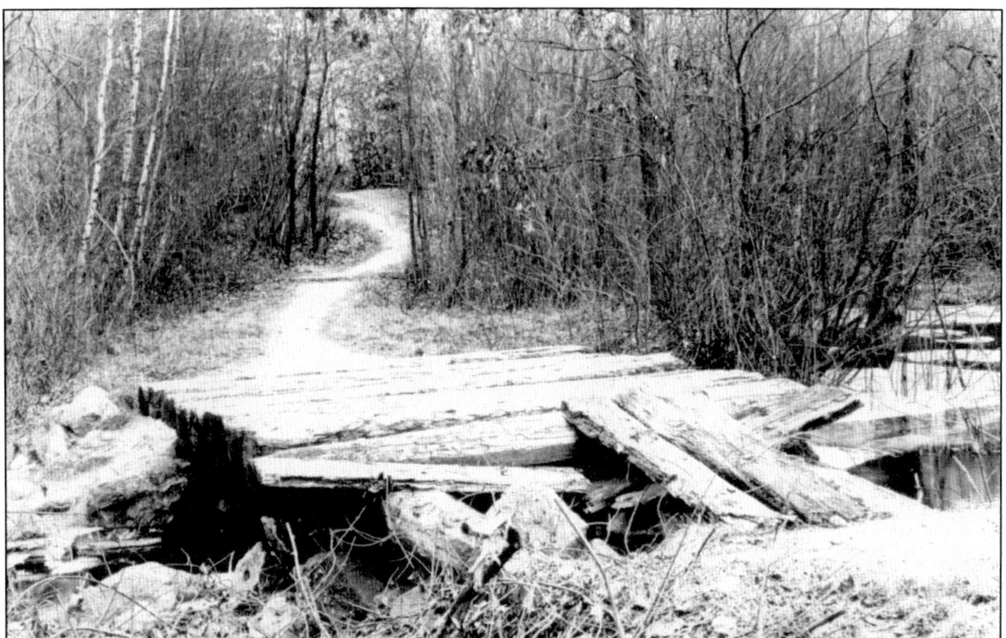

When this photograph was taken, a flood had damaged the bridge (seen previously on page 118). This view looks along a meandering path into the interior of the cemetery.

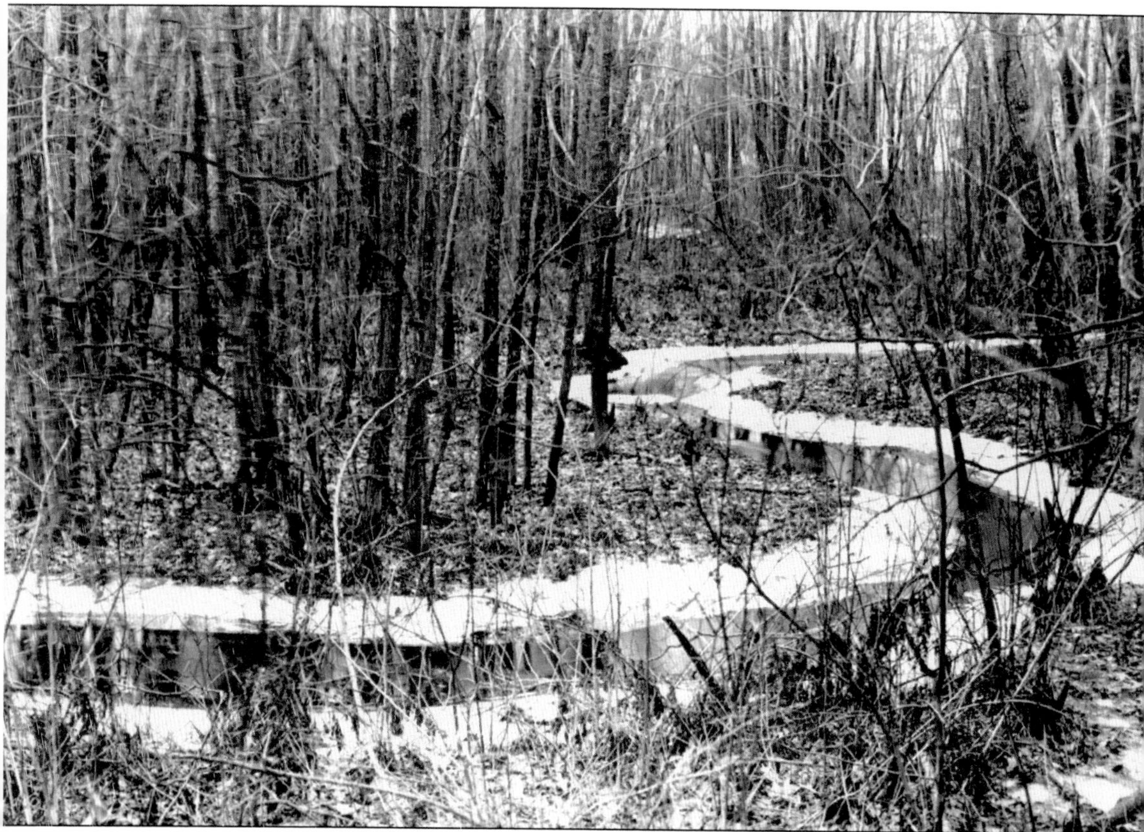

Along with the winding paths, Mount Vernon has a winding brook. At first glance it looks like this scene is well into the woods, but in this winter view you can see a house in the background beyond the trees. As this part of Abington became more urban, Mount Vernon Cemetery became more of a rural oasis.

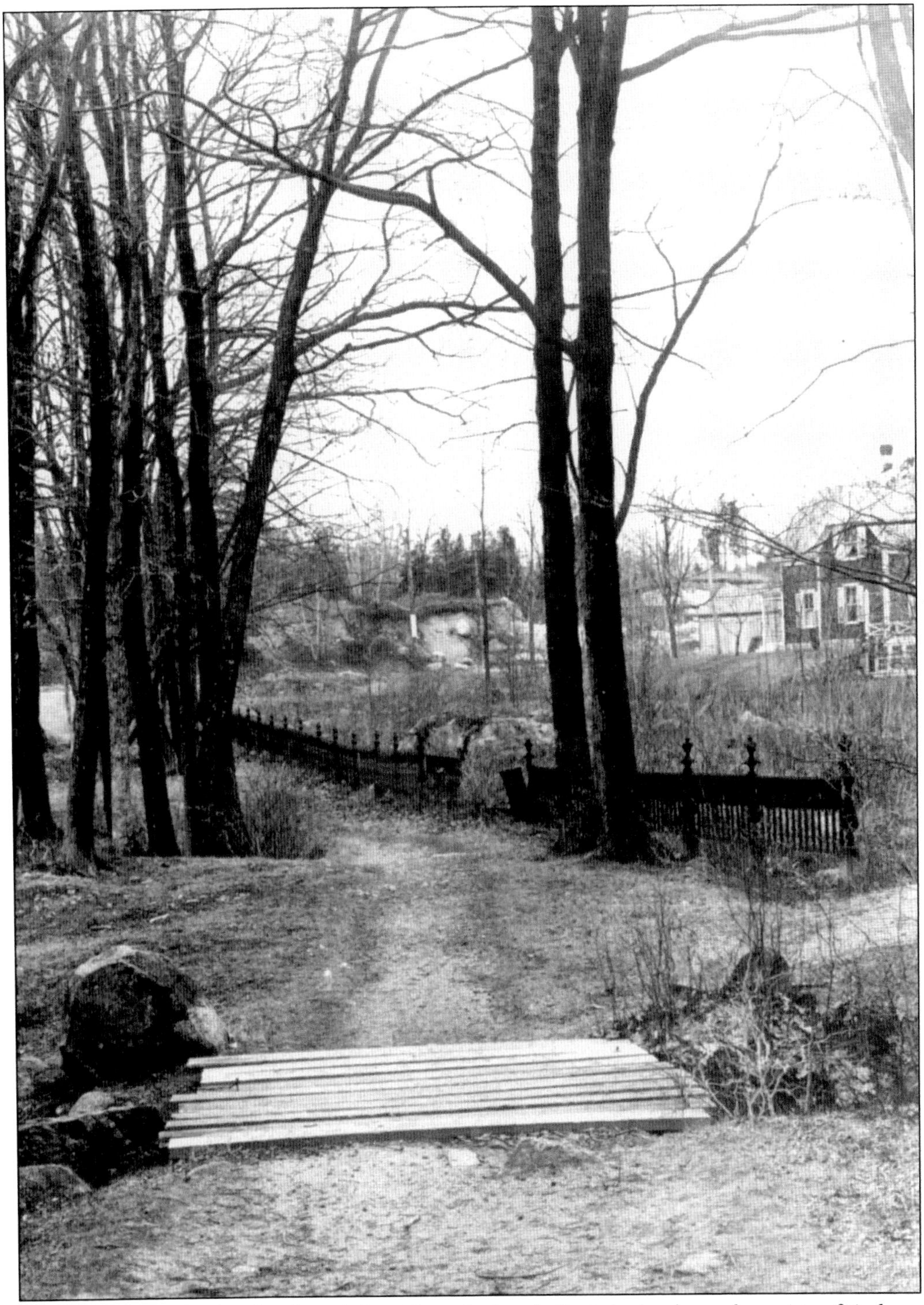

Seen again is the bridge, but here it is without its handrails. It is simpler and consists of timbers, which are not evenly sawed off at the ends. Beyond the bridge is the iron fence that separates the cemetery from the neighborhood. By the time this postcard was made, the fence was badly in need of repair.

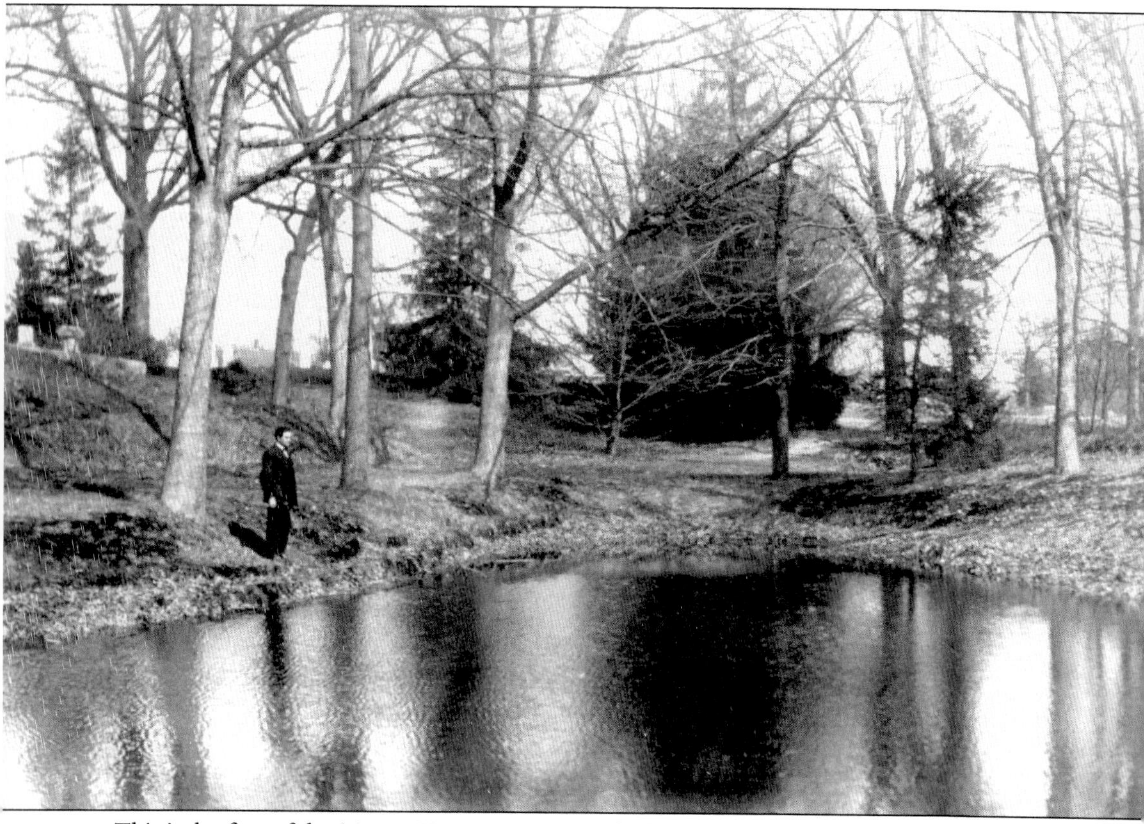

This is the first of the Mount Vernon views in which gravestones are seen. The man seems to be contemplating the still waters of the pond or, perhaps, life and death. This may be a scene staged by the photographer to convey a romantic image. The peace of Mount Vernon Cemetery was shattered by the whistle and roar of the locomotives on the Old Colony Railroad, built adjacent to the cemetery in the 1840s.

Seen is another section of the cemetery's perimeter, the Washington Street side. The path and a section of the iron fence are the subjects of this photograph. This postcard and the others in this chapter have call numbers and no doubt were available for purchase. In the time when people sent them, they may have given comfort to both sender and receiver. They capture a place locals are proud to have in their town, for the Mount Vernon Cemetery is a place that gives people a sense of home.

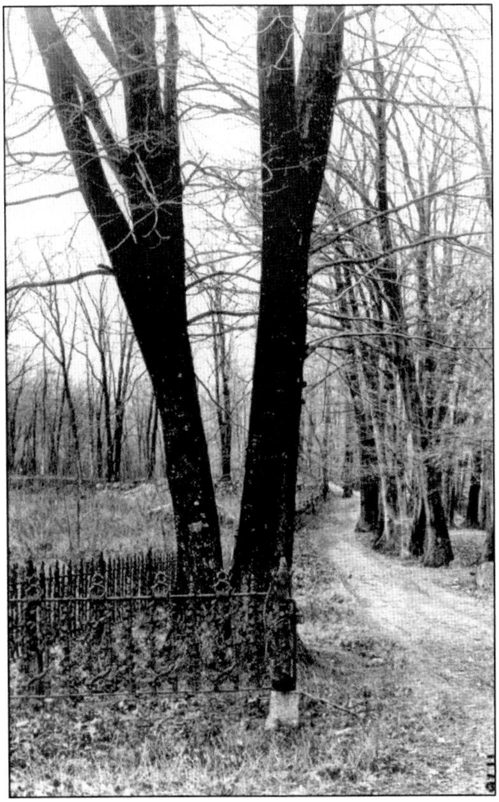

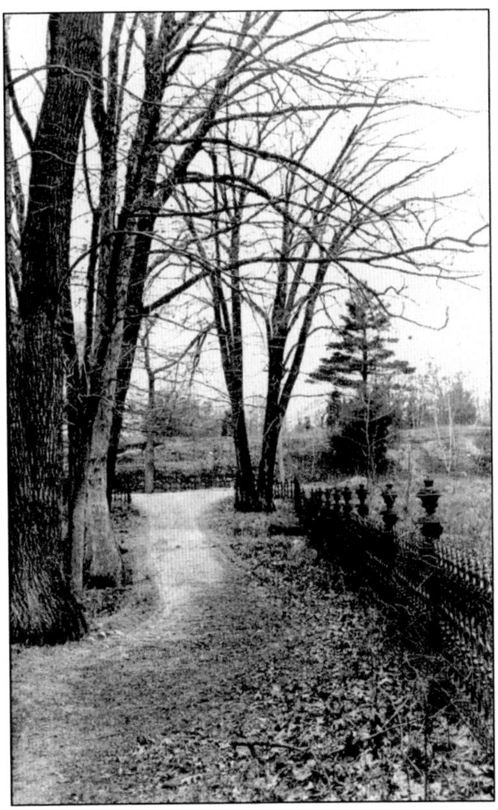

In this view, looking back at the tree seen in the last image, the path is wider than it is in early pictures. This is the carriageway from the Washington Street entrance. One gets a good idea of the quality and design of the iron perimeter fence that marks the bounds of the cemetery.

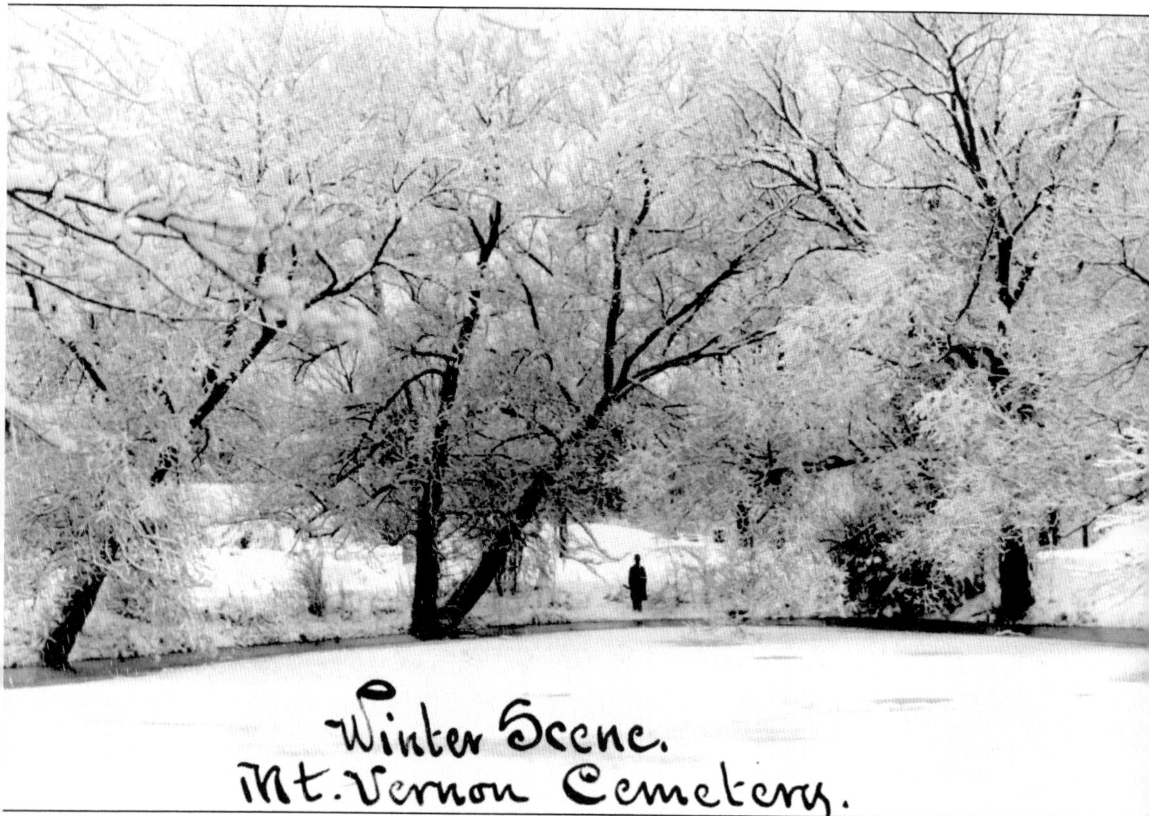

The solitary figure peering over the frozen pond in winter makes for a romantic scene that was the intention of the publisher of this card. This photograph also gives the feeling of pride the community has for this special place. It was not only to give respect to a departed loved one that people visited the new garden cemeteries but also for a pleasant walk or a picnic. Cemeteries became places of physical and emotional escape, even in winter.

Acknowledgments

The authors would like to thank the trustees of the Dyer Memorial Library for once again granting us access to their unrivaled collection of Abington imagery. Also, the book could not have been written without the help of Joice Himawan and Abington history bloodhound Pam Whiting.

A special thanks also goes to the directors of the Historical Society of Old Abington and to president Ken Taylor for both images and information. Kate E. Kelly and Elizabeth K. Shea surprised us when we thought we had found everything we needed, and the history they attached to each postcard they loaned us made our research a lot easier.

Many Abington historians have come before us, most recently and importantly Sharon Orcutt Peters. You cannot write about Abington without finding out that Martha Campbell got to the information first. Important works by Daniel Coughlan and Charles F. Meserve also served us well, as did the reminiscences of many Abington residents stored in the files of the Dyer Memorial Library and the Historical Society of Old Abington.

On a personal note, Donald Cann would like to thank his wife and proofreader, Janet Cann, while John Galluzzo would like to thank David and Kathy Dean, Jay and Leah Kennan, Rich and Felice Eby, Fred Hoth, and Michelle Degni for their constant friendship and support.

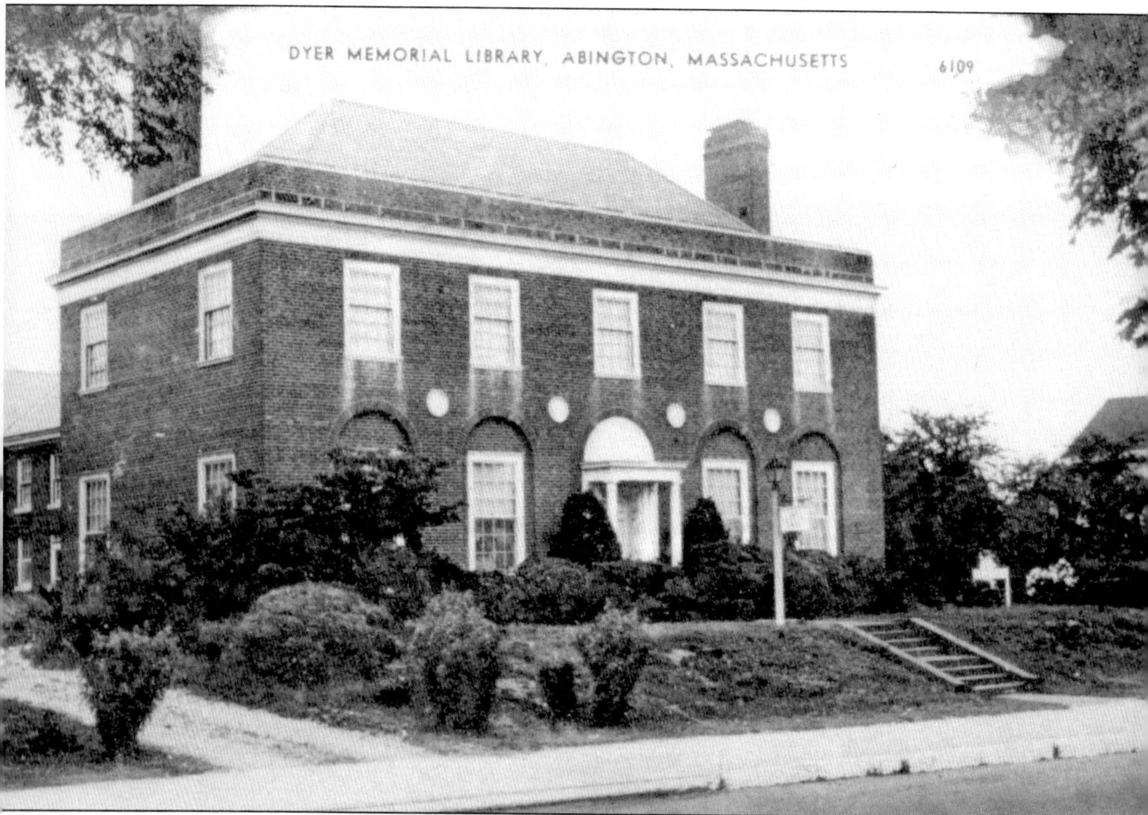

Postcards, a 20th-century phenomenon, have become a wonderful primary source of information for the people of Abington who seek the stories of their town's past. It is our sincere hope that readers of this book will consider donating their postcards and other artifacts to the Dyer Memorial Library or the Historical Society of Old Abington when the time comes for them to pass out of the family's hands. A portion of the proceeds from this book will go directly to both organizations to help with the preservation of the imagery in both collections, so that the collections may be viewable for all future generations of Abington residents.

Dyer Memorial Library
28 Centre Avenue
P.O. Box 2245
Abington, MA 02351
(781) 878-8480